Smart Cities

by Jonathan Reichental

for dummies®

A Wiley Brand

Smart Cities For Dummies®

Published by: **John Wiley & Sons, Inc.,** 111 River Street, Hoboken, NJ 07030-5774, www.wiley.com

Copyright © 2020 by John Wiley & Sons, Inc., Hoboken, New Jersey

Published simultaneously in Canada

For general information on our other products and services, please contact our Customer Care Department within the U.S. at 877-762-2974, outside the U.S. at 317-572-3993, or fax 317-572-4002. For technical support, please visit https://hub.wiley.com/community/support/dummies.

Wiley publishes in a variety of print and electronic formats and by print-on-demand. Some material included with standard print versions of this book may not be included in e-books or in print-on-demand. If this book refers to media such as a CD or DVD that is not included in the version you purchased, you may download this material at http://booksupport.wiley.com. For more information about Wiley products, visit www.wiley.com.

Library of Congress Control Number: 2020939543

ISBN: 978-1-119-67994-3; 978-1-119-67993-6 (ebk); 978-1-119-67996-7 (ebk)

Manufactured in the United States of America

V10019199_061820

Contents at a Glance

Table of Contents

Introduction

Welcome to *Smart Cities For Dummies!*

This is a book about people. At its heart, it's about improving the quality of life for urban communities all over the world. Though the popular term *smart cities* is used, this book focuses on the future of all cities.

To succeed at elevating the human condition for billions of people, cities need to adopt new ideas, new approaches, and new technologies for how they're operated and delivered. That's the definition of a smart city.

Note, however, that this isn't a book primarily about technology, although technology does play a large role. Neither does the book suggest that cities need to create a surveillance society or erode privacy in order to succeed. At their core, smart cities aren't about sensors or algorithms or virtual town halls — they're about a better future for humanity. After all, to quote Shakespeare, "What is the city but the people?" (*Coriolanus*, Act III, Scene 1).

Earth is already a majority urban planet and it's estimated that, by midcentury, 70 percent of all humans will live in an urban area. Put another way, our human future belongs to cities. Most people will spend their days living, working, and playing in a metropolis. If we want to enjoy career opportunities, clean air and water, efficient transportation, low-cost energy, safety, convenient city services, and inclusion while all the time saving the planet from a climate crisis, we have a lot of city work ahead of us.

The city is already the center of the human experience. It is the most complicated and successful of all inventions. Urban areas have lifted billions of people out of extreme poverty, and they continue to shape and define our future.

REMEMBER

The challenges ahead for cities aren't trivial. Cities have come a long way, but they have a long way to go. Building better and smarter cities may be the biggest challenge that humanity now faces.

I wrote this book as the definitive reference guide for anyone who has an interest in creating safer and more prosperous communities. It's also for anyone who wants to understand the opportunities and challenges in the world's cities. When I discovered that cities would be central to our human future, I was compelled to become a part of positive change. I've spent several years helping to build smarter communities and educate city leaders on almost every continent. The realization that, done right, cities were capable of offering the best solutions for a better tomorrow was the moment my passion for cities emerged. This book is my attempt to share the city planning-and-development lessons and ideas I've discovered and executed along the way.

Smart Cities For Dummies is the first comprehensive reference and how-to book that gives you the knowledge and tools to build smarter cities and improve the quality of life for the greatest number of people.

About This Book

This is a practical, action-oriented book about building smarter cities. It doesn't dwell on theory and abstract concepts. The entire text is about how to achieve results, build real solutions, and explore actual examples.

The subject and study of cities is deep, wide, and complex. A comprehensive approach would require multiple books of this size. Few would ever read that much. Who has the time these days? Instead, I have taken the approach to identify and condense only what really matters. This book is thorough, but it has no verbose or unnecessary content. You get everything you need in order to be successful in creating and implementing a smart city strategy.

My hope is that this book inspires and intrigues you about the possibilities ahead for cities. Unlike some topics, the urban world has many dimensions and layers. Everyone can find an area that's compelling to them. Cities involve subjects as diverse as energy, water, climate change, housing, artificial intelligence, digital transformation, policy development, and so much more. This book is focused on people and cities, but it covers hundreds of interrelated and diverse topics.

REMEMBER

Human destiny is tied to cities. If we're going to have a happy and prosperous future, we need new ideas, skilled talent, and informed leaders to build the cities of tomorrow. Everyone deserves a good quality of life. This book can help make that happen.

Whether your job is directly linked to the future of a city or you're a service provider, professor, or teacher — or if you're simply someone who is fascinated by cities — you'll find *Smart Cities For Dummies* a fun, inspiring, and useful guide.

Foolish Assumptions

To get the most from this book, I assume that you

>> Are seeking a comprehensive yet condensed and easy-to-follow guide for planning and implementing a smart city strategy

>> Have little patience for unnecessary jargon and complexity and want to know only the essential knowledge to get stuff done

>> Recognize that the goal of smarter cities is to continuously improve the quality of life for their residents and that the term *smart cities* is far less important than the desired outcomes

>> Recognize that the subject of smart cities is largely still an emerging topic and that the playing field will continue to change in the months and years ahead

>> Keep an open mind to the possibilities and challenges of emerging technologies

>> Know that mitigating the risks of smart city technologies, such as potential impacts to privacy, is a priority for everyone who is passionate about this subject

>> Acknowledge that getting results in government requires strategy and determination and that, for example, simply implementing technology may achieve nothing

>> Understand that this is a book about people and the future of the planet

Icons Used in This Book

Throughout this book, you see these little graphical icons to identify useful paragraphs:

TIP

The Tip icon marks tips and shortcuts that you can take to make a specific task easier.

REMEMBER

The Remember icon marks the information that's especially important to know. To siphon off the most important information in each chapter, just skim these paragraphs.

WARNING

The Warning icon tells you to watch out! It marks important information that may save you headaches. *Warning:* Don't skip over these warnings!

How This Book Is Organized

The book is arranged into six self-contained parts, each composed of several self-contained topics. By *self-contained*, I mean that I do my best to tell you everything you need to know about a single topic inside each chapter, other than when I have to reference other parts of the book to connect parts that are legitimately linked.

Here's an overview:

Part 1: Making Cities Our Home

These early chapters build the context for smart cities. They begin with a short history of cities that takes you from the origins of dense, human settlements right up to the current megacities. Then you'll learn about the role of the industrial revolutions and population growth in shaping the story of cities. You'll recognize what a smart city is and what it is not. Finally, you get a detailed overview of the current needs and challenges of cities that all become the motivation for building smarter communities.

Part 2: Building a Smarter City

In this part, you're quickly introduced to the steps to begin the planning of a smart city. You'll understand the importance of creating a vision and identifying the team to make your goals a reality. After you have agreed on a vision and have the right people in place, you'll want to create a strategy. This is some of the most substantive early work that the smart city team will complete.

This part concludes with guidance on enabling your strategy to succeed. After digesting this section, you'll discover that implementing technology will probably be the easiest part of the journey.

Part 3: Using Smart City Technologies

In these chapters, you dive deep into the innovation processes and technologies that comprise the platform and solutions for your smart city. You'll learn about the different forms of urban innovation that can be implemented.

You'll find a comprehensive list of smart city technologies that includes detailed descriptions of what they are, how they work, and how they can be applied in the real world.

The final chapter in Part 3 explores the essential role of data in cities and how data can be used to solve problems and create solutions.

Part 4: Planning for an Urban Future

Smart cities are secure cities. In this part, you'll find out about cybersecurity and privacy in the age of digital communities. The role of public safety and the ability for cities to bounce back after a crisis is also explored.

Cities continue to evolve as they have throughout history. Local government leaders are now prioritizing for their cities to be greener, more inclusive, and healthier. You'll learn about each of these different focus areas. You'll also discover some of the big ideas that may be part of the cities of tomorrow, such as Hyperloop and flying cars.

This part wraps up with lots of ideas for you to get engaged in your community and become an agent of change. You'll get suggestions for things you can do immediately to make a positive change in your city.

Part 5: The Part of Tens

If you have ever read another book in the *For Dummies* series, this part of the book is like seeing an old friend again — the friend might be wearing a different outfit, but you will recognize the person right away. The Part of Tens is a collection of important advice and suggestions about smart cities, broken into ten easy-to-digest chunks. Part 5 offers guidance on how to avoid some of the most common pitfalls in smart cities. It concludes with a list of ten ways that cities will define our future.

Part 6: Appendixes

This is a practical book. It provides clear guidance on how to develop and implement a vision for a smarter city. Because it's also a relatively new topic, being able to leverage the work of other cities is an important aspect of this subject. In this part, you'll discover lots of examples of work being done in cities all over the world. These examples will support the guidance given throughout the book and will further reinforce what you've learned. Look at what others are doing — you'll be inspired and enlightened by how other cities are implementing their smart city work.

Beyond the Book

Although this book broadly covers the essentials of smart cities, there's only so much that can be covered in a set number of pages! If you reach the end of this book and find yourself thinking, "This was an amazing book — where can I learn more about smart cities and related topics?" head over to www.dummies.com for more resources.

Cheat Sheet: If you're looking for the traditional *For Dummies* Cheat Sheet, visit www.dummies.com and type **Smart Cities For Dummies Cheat Sheet** in the Search box.

The subject of smart cities is quickly evolving. As soon as this book is printed, new items will emerge. I'll include those in later revisions. Updates for this book may also be occasionally available online at the *For Dummies* website.

Fortunately, other books are available that go deep on some of the individual topics in this book. For example, you might want to learn more about solar energy or smart waste management. Experts who specialize in these areas comprehensively cover all the subject details.

If you enjoy my style of writing and presenting knowledge and guidance, I have a lot of complementary material online in written, audio, and video formats. You can find many of my popular video courses on LinkedIn Learning, at www.linkedin.com/learning.

I also speak regularly on the topic of smart cities at events online and in person all over the world. I hope that I'll see you at one of these. Please do come up to me and say hello. I'd love to meet you and hear about your smart city interest and work.

You can keep up with my work and ideas, and contact me, on Twitter (@Reichental), on LinkedIn, or at my personal website: www.reichental.com.

As for you, if you ever end up citing this book or your own smart city experiences on social media, be sure to add the hashtag #smartcitiesfordummies. I'll read them all and will share the ones I like.

Where to Go from Here

You don't need to read this book from cover to cover. You can, if that strategy appeals to you, but it's set up as a reference guide, so you can jump in wherever you need to. Looking for something in particular? Take a peek at the table of contents or index, find the section you need, and then flip to the page to resolve your problem.

1
Making Cities Our Home

IN THIS CHAPTER

» **Examining the origin of cities**

» **Exploring the impacts of the industrial revolutions**

» **Looking at population changes**

» **Introducing megacities**

Chapter **1**

Comprehending the Past, Present, and Future of Cities

For thousands of years, humans were wanderers, existing only in small groups and consumed primarily with daily survival. Then everything changed. The story of why humans went on to eventually build cities is essential for understanding the future of humankind. In this chapter, I briefly describe the origin of cities, including the important impact and role of the industrial revolutions in defining the world today. I also explore how urbanization continues to change the planet, and I introduce the next stop for many major urban areas: megacities.

Discovering the Origin of Cities

The writer and philosopher George Santayana is reported to have said, "Those who cannot remember the past are condemned to repeat it." In other words, ignoring, or being blind to, the lessons of the past puts you at a disadvantage. It makes sense to me: I believe that if you're going to create better and smarter cities, you need to understand a little about their origin. Figuring out why we humans started living in ever-growing urban centers and have now decisively made them our future home helps you understand the present and — even more importantly — what it means for the future of cities.

I don't bore you with an extensive history lesson on the origin of cities, but I do provide you with enough information to give you a sense of the key milestones that have resulted in the urban planet humans now inhabit.

I also help you explore the consequences of urbanization and look at trends that are contributing to today's rapid city growth, and I begin to tease out the impact and challenges to be solved in a future of *megacities* (cities with a population of more than 10 million inhabitants).

What is a city?

But wait — first, what is a *city*? It's a physical location that is permanently settled by a large number of people and has defined boundaries. It has formal systems for supporting areas such as land use, housing, sanitation, energy, and transportation. Most occupants in a city work on nonagricultural activities. A city has some recognized form of governance that facilitates the operations of the area and interactions between the community, businesses, and government.

Charles–Édouard Jeanneret, the internationally influential Swiss architect and city planner, said that cities are "a machine for living in."

Today, most people live in a city. You know, cities are quite popular now. Opportunities that range from employment to entertainment and from education to healthcare all tend to be better in an urban context. For most of human history, as you can read later in this chapter, it wasn't this way at all.

Do you know the origin of the city where you're living now? I'd bet that some people do, but I'm also confident that many don't. After all, for most people, there's little utility in this knowledge.

REMEMBER

If you find yourself in a role today that's directly related to the function and success of your city, historical context is golden. It can inform all manner of future decision-making, by highlighting strengths and challenges, ensuring alignment to culture, and exploring untapped opportunities.

For everyone else, wouldn't it be fascinating to know how your community came to be? I'm a naturally curious person, so this type of detail fascinates me. Learning about your city might surprise you. It may make you happy or perhaps even make you sad. Whatever the emotional response, my guess is that you'll become enlightened and likely curious to go deeper into the areas that spark your curiosity.

Go online and search for your city's website. (Let's assume it has one.) Then find out the answers to these questions about your city:

>> When was it established?

>> Why was it started?

>> What are the current challenges of the community?

>> What are the current priorities of the city?

>> Oh, and does your city have a smart city strategy or something similarly named?

There's no grade for doing this assignment, but isn't it interesting? Talk about it with your family. I'd bet that the discussion is fascinating and enlightening for everyone.

For extra credit, you might repeat this exercise for another city somewhere else in the world that you're curious about.

Okay, let's move on.

Why each of the world's cities came to be is a big part of the broader narrative of the human story. Humans can't change the past, so we're stuck with the current outcome of a myriad of decisions and their consequences — some good and, frankly, many not-so-good. Some of the past humans have been able to control, but there's a fairly good chunk that we haven't been able to. For example, being invaded probably wasn't something the residents of any city welcomed. Natural disasters are acts that humans have no role in creating but must deal with the aftermath of (although the role of human behavior in climate change apparently is making many of these disasters much worse).

On the positive side, getting lucky and establishing a human presence in places that had abundant, in-demand resources like oil or coal created what some could consider unfair advantages, and being strategically located in the supply chain for products that humans fell in love with also helped. The human thirst for coffee and tea, their love of silk, and an addiction to tobacco are all examples of the development of certain urban areas over others. This is because all sorts of inter-mediaries and services were required along the complex global supply-and-trade routes. An exchange of ideas resulted from diverse traders from different geo-graphic areas meeting at the urban centers of these trade routes. This was a cata-lyst for innovation. Cities became engines for a whole new generation of creative solutions.

(Hang on. Writing that last paragraph made me thirsty. I'm going to make a cup of tea.)

The origin of cities, like so much of the human story, is the result of a series of unpredictable and surprising events. Human history certainly didn't progress in a straight line — and any change along the way would have resulted in a world far different from the one we live in today. But this is simply a thought experiment. It doesn't help much to wonder what the world would look like, for example, if there hadn't been colonialism by European nations. What matters is understanding what did happen and what that means for you today and for the future.

Building the first cities

Humans living in cities is a relatively new phenomenon. For most of human history — around 200,000 years of that history, by our best guesses — members of *homo sapiens* lived and wandered together in relatively small groups, tending to their crops and hunting for animals and fish. It was a basic and crude existence. Life span barely ever reached 40 years. Nothing much changed for most of that 200,000 years. The world in which people were born was identical to the world they exited.

A little over 10,000 years ago, the first significant urban areas emerged. Damascus, in Syria, is often cited as the oldest continually inhabited city. Athens in Greece wasn't far behind and, like several other urban centers of that period, was a source of rapidly maturing human development. (Figure 1-1 illustrates Athens' Agora, an important center of developing commerce, political, and artistic life.) A handful of these cities, spanning from the Middle East through Europe and into China and India, were founded in this general period. Though many of these cities were instrumental in defining civilization, they were all modestly sized compared to the massive, industrial megacities of today. Athens, at its peak of enlightenment, was populated by mere thousands of people.

REMEMBER

For most of human history, there really weren't that many people, and most of us lived a rural lifestyle. Until as recently as the early 1800s, the entire world had fewer than a billion people. Compared to today, where over 55 percent of humans live in cities, back in 1800 only 3 percent occupied urban settings.

Cities emerged and grew because they offered a compelling alternative to life in rural areas. For example, rather than hunt, gather, or farm all the materials needed to survive, in a city a person could trade in a specialization to earn money to live. Not to get too technical, but this behavior originates as a consequence of the Neolithic revolution, a time defined as the transition from a rather ad hoc approach to wandering and hunting to settling into permanent areas and formalizing farming. The subsequent agricultural revolution created food abundance, which was highly liberating to humans. No longer tethered to the obligation of acquiring food, humans were free to focus on other tasks (like invent and watch television).

FIGURE 1-1: The Ancient Agora of Athens: An early marketplace and the center of political, artistic, and athletic life.

Once humans started to settle in large numbers in these cities, everything started to change. Needs inspired innovation. Neighborhoods were defined. Law-and-order took shape. Products began to be mass produced. Communities created wealth. Conditions improved, albeit gradually. Cities became bustling centers of commerce, production, social activity, and leisure activities, with increasing varieties of arts and new models for education. Challenges grew in lockstep with prosperity. Crime, poverty, worker exploitation, disease, and other problems all weighed heavily on the emergence of cities and the lives of the new urbanites.

It's an unfortunate fact that early cities were unpleasant places. They had poor sanitation, and deadly diseases ran rampant. Rats thrived. Crime was commonplace because few public safety protocols existed. Before electricity was discovered, lighting was provided by candles and gaslights, and with most buildings made of wood, fires were all too frequent.

The Great Fire of London, in 1666, destroyed the homes of 70,000 of the city's 80,000 inhabitants. Many other cities suffered the same fate.

As a consolation, the vast destruction caused by these fires did force the rebuilding of the cities with improved design. It also resulted in the introduction of building codes, regulations, and fire services — most of which had never existed.

For a small minority of inhabitants, life was good, but for the majority, one set of problems was replaced by another. Chaotic urban planning and rapid population growth all aided in creating issues that, frankly, still haunt humans to this day. In many respects, the phenomenon of smart cities is a late-in-the-game response to these originating circumstances.

Comprehending the Impact of the Industrial Revolutions

For much of the 200,000 years that *homo sapiens* has been around, not a great deal happened. But suddenly, after 199,000 years, a series of significant revolutions occurred that dramatically changed the trajectory of humanity.

Around the year 1300, the Renaissance began in beautiful Florence, Italy. Historians define this time as the transition to the modern era. It was a time of reasoning, scientific discoveries, advances in art, intellectualism, and improved management of knowledge. And more. This period spanned over a few hundred years and set the stage for the age of enlightenment and the scientific revolution. During this time, humans made leaps in their understanding of the world and the universe, but also in mathematics, physics, biology, and chemistry. Today, you might take it all for granted, but if it weren't for these breakthroughs, the world might be quite different. Some argue that humans would be at a better place today had this science emerged considerably earlier in those long, lazy 200,000 years. (It depends on one's perspective, I suppose.)

Though all this may or may not be all that interesting to you, it's all driving me to the punchline: The stage was set for a series of three industrial revolutions that would change the world beginning in the 1700s — and a fourth, which is now under way — that would solidify the path toward the cities people live in today.

The first industrial revolution

The first industrial revolution begins in Britain. The invention of the steam-powered motor is a game-changer. Truly awesome machines could be powered by steam. Until that time, animals, humans, and windmills did much of the pulling and pushing. With the addition of steam, the production of products could be kicked up a notch. Steam also enabled railways to flourish. Britain began producing low-cost iron and steel, and then big machines and bridges could be built. All manner of new production techniques across industries — and particularly in textiles — were introduced.

This industrialization supported the development of mass-production factories, which were typically built in urban areas. These facilities needed increasing numbers of workers. Homes were built around the factories to keep those workers close. Farm workers seeking better economic circumstances flocked to these factories. City populations in these areas began to grow quickly.

New, positive social systems were hatched during this period. This included schools and mandatory education for children, labor unions for workers, and the arrival of the first law enforcers: the police. Healthcare options and sanitary conditions improved. For the first time, the notion of free time and discretionary income meant increased demands for entertainment and other ways to spend nonworking time. In the scheme of things, all this change was happening quite fast. Of course, it wasn't restricted to Britain, either. Similar progress was occurring across Europe and in some of the outposts of the various European empires that spanned the globe at the time.

Still, this period was no utopia. With insufficient safety nets, many people suffered in this new, urban, and industrial landscape. History books are replete with descriptions of undesirable circumstances, including poor housing conditions and air quality, little or no sanitation, long working hours, and rampant, violent crime.

REMEMBER

Sadly, and surprisingly, even in the 21st century, these conditions still exist in many global cities. One in three humans still live in poor urban living circumstances. Come on, let's fix this. Smarter, sustainable, and resilient cities, anyone?

(The United Nations' 2030 sustainable development goals, SDGs, are an earnest global effort to improve these poor conditions. Details can be found in Chapter 2).

The second industrial revolution

Within just 100 years, the second industrial revolution would be under way. It would be defined by the achievement of the wide-scale use of electricity. It's hard to overstate the difference between the world before electricity use and the world after. That truly is the definition of a revolution. Pause for a moment to consider all the items you use that require electricity. Wild, right?

Electricity brought light bulbs to homes and streetlights to cities. It enabled the invention of the telegraph and telephone. Telephones! It powered new levels of manufacturing. Eventually, electricity changed the lives of everyone living in most cities. Today, electricity continues to change lives, though it's fair to say that few people think of it that way. You also need to recognize that 11 percent of the world's population *still* has no access to electricity. There's work to be done.

The third industrial revolution

In the 1940s, a third industrial revolution began. Built on the progress of the previous revolutions, and in particular electricity and telecommunications, the information age began.

In many ways, humans are all now living through this revolution, and it could be argued that we're still only at the beginning of it. It seems like computers, software applications, smartphones, and the Internet have already radically changed the world, but the potential seems only partially met. Just in the past few years, we have moved from static web pages to dynamic websites that support e-commerce to apps that enable people to manage and coordinate many aspects of their lives.

REMEMBER

With still another 45 percent of the world to come online in the years ahead (that's over 3 billion people yet to be connected!) and the potential for the technology to be even more disruptive, this revolution has some ways to go.

The game-changing technology of the information age has been the miniaturization of the transistor. This revolutionary technology uses a special material, called a *semiconductor,* to control the flow of electricity. Like a light switch, a transistor uses electricity to turn a switch on or off. Assigning a value of 1 to the On state and a 0 to the Off state provides the 1s and 0s that are the language of computers. Today, over a billion of these tiny transistors can fit on some of the fastest microchips. My head nearly explodes trying to comprehend the tiny scale of this technology that enables so much of the modern world.

The third industrial revolution has enabled the Internet, the World Wide Web, word processors, spreadsheets, all sorts of cool devices (including everyone's beloved smartphones and their apps), massive automation and artificial intelligence, videoconferencing, online banking, and on and on.

The third industrial revolution is creating new business models such as on-demand taxi services, and slowly destroying others. Consider the fate of the newspaper or the challenge to brick-and-mortar retail coming from the popularity of shopping online.

For most people living in cities, all they have to do is look around to appreciate the vast ways in which computing technology supports their environments.

As this revolution progresses, the cost of computing and storage drops, more devices get connected, software grows smarter, richer data becomes available, and the entry barriers to wild ideas is lowered.

WARNING

Soon it won't be just a question of whether humans *can* create some groundbreaking innovation, but rather a question of whether we *should* create it.

No doubt, this revolution becomes the basis for building smarter cities.

The fourth industrial revolution

Even while the third industrial revolution unfolds, you can now see evidence of yet another revolution. As examples, on the streets of several cities self-driving cars are carrying people to their destinations, drones are delivering packages, experimental flying cars are zooming across the sky, and any number of services, such as surgery and caregiving, that were once the exclusive purview of humans are being augmented by robots and artificial intelligence. The third and fourth revolutions will overlap considerably, just like the first and second industrial revolutions. The fourth industrial revolution will be powered by the convergence of new technologies, new scientific breakthroughs, emerging behaviors, changing demographics, and global economics. It's my view that this revolution is when the vast majority of smart cities will emerge. (I discuss this specific topic in greater detail in Chapter 8.)

In Figure 1-2, I've summarized the timeline and some of the major breakthroughs in each of the four industrial revolutions.

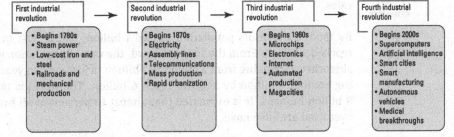

FIGURE 1-2:
The core characteristics of the four industrial revolutions.

First industrial revolution
- Begins 1780s
- Steam power
- Low-cost iron and steel
- Railroads and mechanical production

Second industrial revolution
- Begins 1870s
- Electricity
- Assembly lines
- Telecommunications
- Mass production
- Rapid urbanization

Third industrial revolution
- Begins 1960s
- Microchips
- Electronics
- Internet
- Automated production
- Megacities

Fourth industrial revolution
- Begins 2000s
- Supercomputers
- Artificial intelligence
- Smart cities
- Smart manufacturing
- Autonomous vehicles
- Medical breakthroughs

Responding to population growth

Check out Figure 1-3. The truly striking aspect is that, for most of human history, the population of people on Planet Earth was low. It remained well below a billion for a very long time. *Population growth* is based on the difference between birth and death rates. Poor nutrition and environmental conditions, the absence of healthcare, and other dangers contributed to short life expectancy and high death rates among babies and infants. As a consequence of the eventual positive outcomes of the Renaissance, the scientific revolution, and the subsequent industrial revolutions, birthrates increased and premature deaths decreased.

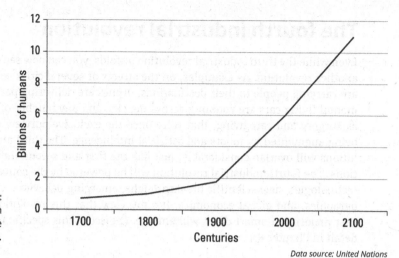

FIGURE 1-3: Population growth since the 1700s.

Data source: United Nations

REMEMBER

Living in cities, despite often terrible conditions in the first and second industrial revolutions, actually made the largest positive contribution to growing population rates.

By 1800, the world's population passed 1 billion, and in just over 100 years, it reached 2 billion. From the 1920s onward, the rate of population growth began to skyrocket, increasing from 2 billion to 3 billion in just over 30 years and then adding another 3 billion by 2000 to reach 6 billion. The world is now approaching 8 billion humans. It is estimated that almost 10 percent of all humans who have ever lived are alive now!

However, this rapid population explosion won't continue. The rate of growth has begun to slow and may, in fact, peak at around 11 billion and then begin to decrease. A primary driver of population decline is the increasing number of women receiving an education in developing nations. As women get more education, they have fewer children.

REMEMBER

Some experts suggest that global population decreases in the future might be humanity's biggest challenge. This is because a declining population cannot sustain economic growth and an aging population has less labor to innovate and support productivity. There's certainly a role for robots here, but that's a discussion for another book. Population decline seems counterintuitive, considering that we spent most of the 20th century worrying about the challenges of a population explosion.

Comprehending and responding to population growth and demographic shifts is vital to planning for the future of the world's cities. Urbanization is clearly a product of rapid population growth. It's probably not lost on you that the smart city movement is partially motivated by unmanaged population increases and the attendant dysfunction that has ensued.

The increase in the number of humans is all happening in cities, powered by better healthcare and living conditions and by the recent unprecedented migration of humans from rural to urban areas. It is estimated that as many as 3 million people now move into cities each week. By midcentury, that number will likely result in an increase of 2 billion people living in an urban setting.

TIP

A smart city strategy for a given city must accommodate population and demographic trends.

Though for many cities this strategy will reflect projected increases in populations (see my discussion on megacities later in this chapter, in the section "Building megacities"), many cities in developed nations could see challenges emerging from population declines. In both scenarios, the use of technology and new approaches to problem-solving will be essential to future community success.

Urbanizing the Planet

I'm hoping that you'll pick up on three essential ideas in this chapter. First, the scientific era is a recent development. For 199,000 of their 200,000 years on this planet, nothing much changed for humans, and life was a miserable experience. Only since the 1300s has the human condition radically shifted in a positive direction. Second, during the first 199,000 years, the population of humans on Earth remained low. The population passed 1 billion in 1800 and added 5 billion in the 1900s — in just 100 years. Finally, until the 1800s, most cities remained relatively small. For example, during the time of the Roman Empire, with the exception of Rome and a handful of other areas, many Italian cities ranged only from 5,000 to 15,000 people.

The conclusion? The nature of cities today is a recent phenomenon. Big, dense urban areas are a product of just the past few decades. (See Figure 1-4.)

China, for example, has undergone a dramatic urban transformation that began in the latter part of the 20th century and continues to this day. Today, over 160 cities in China have a population of over 1 million.

Major global urbanization has occurred over the past 200 years, but at different rates and time periods. Though the regions of Europe, North America, and Australia and others were early to urbanize at a gradual rate, Southeast Asia, China, India, the Middle East, and parts of Africa have progressed later but more rapidly.

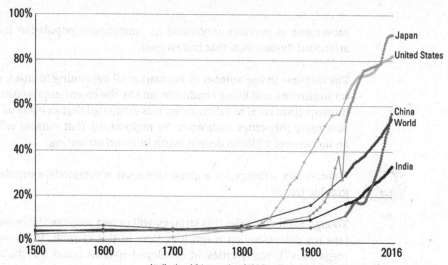

FIGURE 1-4: Share of population living in an urban setting over the past 500 years.

For example, in 1966 Dubai in the United Arab Emirates (UAE) was a cluster of small settlements. Today, it's a glistening modern city with a population of over 3 million.

From 2000 to 2010, Shanghai, China, grew by 7.4 million inhabitants, from 16.4M to 23.8M. This has created a stunning, sprawling, and chaotic megacity. In fact, China's urbanization has been the most notable. In 1960, about 110 million Chinese lived in cities. By 2015, the number was closer to 760 million (about 56 percent of the country).

In Africa, the migration to cities continues at a rapid pace. By the 2040s, it's estimated that African city dwellers will increase by 400 million. Today, cities power 80 percent of the global economy. By 2025, it's projected that just 600 cities around the world will generate 60 percent of the gross domestic product (GDP) of the planet.

In the United States, just ten cities alone are responsible for generating one-third of all GDP.

I am hard-pressed to think of another human achievement that has defined the world more than the urbanization of the past 100 years. With more than half of humans living in cities and billions more joining over the next 50 years, the future belongs to cities.

Changing landscapes resulting from urbanization

Imagine for a moment what Manhattan must have looked like before New York (or what used to be called New Amsterdam). Let's go way back, before there were any buildings and infrastructure. It's a rocky, hilly island covered in chestnut, oak, and hickory trees. There are streams, swamps, salt marshes, and grasslands inhabited by turkeys, elks, and black bears. It's a beautiful, rich ecosystem of life.

Fast-forward to today, and, well, Manhattan looks a just little different.

Urbanization has forever changed the planet. An estimated 3 percent of the world's land has been paved over. Cities are now dense areas of human activity, knitted together with a mix of concrete and asphalt, roads and pathways, wires and pipes, tunnels and bridges, industrial areas and housing, parking lots, apartments, stadiums, warehouses, skyscrapers, and more. They are beautiful and ugly, messy and clean, organized and chaotic, modern and historic.

Humans have built a variety of systems to connect their urban areas — from roads and canals to airports and seaports. Few mountains or other natural obstacles have limited the urban sprawl, as humans have built over them and as they have dug deep tunnels under their feet and through the hills.

Cities have created more opportunities, more prosperity, and a longer life span than any other human invention. But they've also enacted a toll on humanity, from creating bad health conditions to radically altering Earth's climate. Urbanization is accelerating the effects of the *Anthropocene*, the period of Planet Earth's history that continues to this day, when humans became responsible for altering the environment and climate.

Humans are now responsible for the cities we've created, and we could argue that we didn't fully anticipate their massive success and great challenges. Either way, humans now have to deal with the consequences, both good and bad. Many costs were not considered, and now we're faced with the obligation to act.

WARNING

Without a smarter approach to delivering cities, many communities face a daunting future.

Building megacities

In many countries, fire marshals insist on enforcing maximum occupancy regulations for commercial rooms. For example, you'll see placards in hotel meeting spaces or movie theaters that state the limit of how many people are allowed to occupy the space. It's wise, because with too many people in a defined area, the possibilities of problems increase.

However, with a few exceptions, no such limitation exists for cities.

That's right. In most instances, people can move into cities with no consideration of population size, housing availability, job opportunities, healthcare options, or other support systems. It means that, as long as no constraint is imposed, popular cities will continue to see their populations increase and be burdened with the responsibility of responding to the potential crisis this creates.

Curiously enough, though, large, growing cities are often more successful than smaller ones. Increasing populations generate economic and employment activity that benefits everyone. Larger tax yields enable better public services. Diversity creates richer cultural experiences. More people often result in a larger number of social services. Many of them have the resources to prioritize their smart city initiatives.

Today, I'm encouraged that so many of the world's biggest cities are prospering. However, not to get to too far ahead of myself, the challenges of managing a big city are significant and severe. I discuss many in this book.

The future growth of cities, including population and geographic areas, will follow one of these three patterns:

>> **No growth:** Stable and consistent population size with varying economic outcomes

>> **Declining growth:** Shrinking communities and budgets sometimes resulting in almost complete abandonment

>> **Increased growth:** Significant changes as city immigration and natural growth (more new babies than deaths) continues unabated

Though the first two patterns clearly have challenges, the biggest urban phenomenon of the next few decades will be the last one — the rapid growth of many cities. While recognizing the many positives of large urban populations, the demands of cities that exceed a million occupants will continue to challenge the ability of city leaders to deliver. But these cities will begin to pale in comparison to the emergence of an increasing number of cities that exceed 10 million people. These are the megacities! Today, there are almost 50 of them on the planet.

If the 20th century human experience was defined by population growth, the 21st century will be defined by the power and footprint of megacities. These massive urban centers will demand completely new systems of support, green energy options, sustainability strategies, economic diversity, alternative transportation, and much, much more. In the future, it will be successful megacities that ultimately define the notion of smart cities.

Figure 1-5 lists the top ten megacities in the world, as of 2019:

Ranking	City	Country	Population
1	Tokyo	Japan	38,001,000
2	Delhi	India	25,703,168
3	Shanghai	China	23,740,778
4	São Paulo	Brazil	21,066,245
5	Mumbai	India	21,042,538
6	Mexico City	Mexico	20,998,543
7	Beijing	China	20,383,994
8	Osaka	Japan	20,237,645
9	Cairo	Egypt	18,771,769
10	New York	United States	18,593,220

FIGURE 1-5:
The top ten global megacities.

That so many of these cities succeed despite their size and complexity is a testament to human ingenuity.

Chapter **2**

Defining Smart Cities

There's no globally agreed-on definition for the term *smart city* — which is surprising, given the increasing importance and maturity of the topic. Fortunately, some consistent themes can be found in smart city strategies from around the world that are in use by city leaders. This chapter describes common concepts accepted by the smart city community, and it covers misconceptions in order to help you understand what a smart city is not. I help you explore the motivation for building smart cities as well as the different needs of both large and small cities, and then I conclude the chapter by comparing two examples of smart cities.

Identifying Smart Cities

In my view, there's really no such thing as a smart city. Wait — what? That's certainly an odd comment from the author of a book about smart cities. Okay, let me explain. What I really mean is that there's no such thing as a *completed* smart city. I can't think of an example where all the work has been finished and the designers and implementers have, after completing their tasks, washed their hands and said, "We're done. Voilà! Here's your smart city."

Nope. Doesn't exist. After all, is a city *ever* completed?

REMEMBER

With a few rare exceptions, cities are in a constant state of change. Whether they're being updated and improved or expanding upward, downward, and outward (or all of these), our cities are living, evolving entities. Cities are a work in progress. They are shaped by (among many factors) community needs, by societal trends, by crisis, and by better ideas. They shrink and expand, they decline and are reborn, and they are destroyed and rebuilt. They are never finished.

And so I return to the idea that there's no such thing as a smart city. Instead, there are compelling and urgent needs, and a necessary response to demands, for cities that function with greater "smartness" to be smarter in all areas and in every way.

A smart city isn't a city that has merely achieved some level of satisfactory smartness. A smart city is one that identifies with the need to be smarter and then bakes that knowledge into its functioning, action-oriented DNA. It doesn't continue to use obsolete 20th century solutions. A smart city implements 21st century solutions for 21st century problems.

If there's one aspect of smart cities that can be chastised for continuing to cause confusion and excessive debate, it's the absence of agreement on the definition of the term *smart city*. In this chapter, I share the results of my research and perspective on the topic.

What a smart city is

As Sicinius, the bearded protector of the Roman people's interests, states in Shakespeare's play *Coriolanus,* "What is the city but the people?"

Indeed, what *is* the city but the people?

This is the right place to start when discussing the future of cities. After all, cities are defined by the human experience. They exist in support of people, are the invention of people, and deeply reflect a people's culture. In Bangkok and Tokyo, the city landscapes are replete with temples, like Budapest is with hot baths, Amsterdam is with coffee shops, and Vegas is with casinos.

The feel, the look, the behavior, the heartbeat of the city — these are all a reflection of people. Cities communicate the history and life of those who live there. (Some like to say that architecture is the language of the city, which strikes me as a fitting way to look at things.)

Across the planet, cities have emerged for different reasons, and their design has been shaped by various influences. There is no one-size-fits-all solution when it comes to cities. Though they share some common needs, such as energy, transportation, communications, and sanitation, they have as many differences as similarities. Sure, a city can be defined and categorized by such characteristics as its geography, governance, population, and infrastructure, but its purpose, needs, and culture cannot be so easily abstracted and normalized such that you can generalize about their nature. The uniqueness of each city must be viewed through this lens.

Many cities suffer the same challenges. Finding a parking space, for example, is a universal pain. But the way problems are solved is often specific to each community. For every challenge that is similar, others are often unique.

It's this backdrop that is essential for an understanding of how to think about smart cities. To be able to confidently say that Barcelona and Dublin are smart cities (or are becoming smarter) means that there would need to be a globally agreed-on definition and an agreed-on set of extensive standards and measurements.

These don't exist, and they may never exist.

Okay, to be fair, there are a small number of proposed and voluntary standards for smart cities. Two strong examples are:

>> International Organization for Standardization (ISO), sustainable cities and communities; indicators for smart cities found here: https://www.iso.org/standard/69050.html

>> British Standards Institute, smart city standards found here: https://www.bsigroup.com/en-GB/smart-cities/Smart-Cities-Standards-and-Publication/

The term *smart city* is much less important than the purpose of the work and the outcomes. In fact, to clear up confusion, many other terms are used that are all simply synonyms. They include connected city, hyperconnected city, intelligent city, digital city, smart community, and others. Smart city (or smart cities) is the term that has stuck. I use that term throughout this book.

REMEMBER

A smart city is defined by its people, not by some outside arbiter. If Helsinki believes that it's creating a better quality of life for its people in its innovative use of technology, it has the right to call itself a smart city.

John Harlow, a smart city research specialist at the Emerson College Engagement Lab, states that "smartness in cities comes from people understanding what's important to them and what problems they are experiencing."

The most basic definition of a smart city is one that responds to its citizens' needs in new and improved ways.

I expand on this definition shortly, but first, some additional contextual basics.

The future of humanity is firmly rooted in cities. For better or worse, as rural communities rapidly decline, immigration to cities is booming. By the end of the 21st century, all things being equal, most humans will live in urban settings. This remarkable shift will define the future more than just about anything else humans do (other than perhaps populating other planets).

Despite our many misgivings, on balance, cities are largely a success story. More than anything else, they have lifted billions of people out of poverty, providing jobs, shelter, accessible healthcare, and other support systems and regulations to assist in life's needs. Edward Glaeser, the American economist and author of *Triumph of the City*, makes a compelling case that cities are humanity's greatest invention.

But it's been a tough, ugly journey. The world's early cities weren't pleasant places for most people, and suffering was common. Fortunately, cities are now in much better shape, and an urban migrant should find options and opportunities to at least have the choice of a better life.

However, though conditions in general are better than they've ever been, the challenges presented by cities today are more complex in many ways and are vastly more difficult and expensive to solve.

Here's a list of just a few of the city challenges awaiting solutions:

>> Overburdened and inefficient social support systems

>> Transportation congestion and poor public-transport options

>> Inequality

>> Poverty

>> Crime

>> Homelessness

>> Environmental damage

>> Poor air quality

>> Aging and broken infrastructure

>> Lack of jobs

>> Weak civic engagement

>> Food insecurity

>> Inclusiveness

This list is only a small reflection of the massive number of unique challenges that cities on every continent have to address. But it should be suggestive to you of the type of work that lies ahead.

An obvious question right now is this: Why haven't humans solved these types of problems?

Though a comprehensive answer to this question goes beyond the scope of this book, some of the answer lies in leadership priorities and insufficient budgets as well as in the scale and complexity of the problems involved. Clearly, if these problems were cheaply and easily solved, they'd have been addressed by now. They are neither.

However, the history of innovation is a reminder that humans have the capacity to solve big, intractable issues. Improved sanitation changed the trajectory of healthcare, for example, and fertilizer made food abundant. Might innovation also help with the current challenges of the world's cities? I would argue yes, and technology powered innovation might offer some of the best opportunities.

This kind of thinking may draw you closer to a definition of what a smart city is.

The Smart Cities Council (see Appendix B), a network of companies advised by universities, laboratories, and standards bodies, maintains that smart cities embody three core values: livability, workability, and sustainability. Specifically, the council states that using technology to achieve improvements in these three areas is the definition of what a smart city needs to be. (I like that.)

So, considering everything I've discussed so far in this chapter, including researching the literature on the topic, what might a definition look like? Here's my proposal:

> A *smart city* is an approach to urbanization that uses innovative technologies to enhance community services and economic opportunities, improves city infrastructure, reduces costs and resource consumption, and increases civic engagement.

Fair?

Many smart city definitions include references to specific technologies — I think this is a mistake. The definition should be about outcomes, and it should outlive technologies that come and go. There will always be better tools in the future. Limiting a definition to tools that exist now will make any definition quickly outdated.

Finally, don't lose sight of these two important qualities:

>> **Technology use:** There are many ways to address city issues, but when technologies are used as the primary tools, this helps to make the city smarter. A smart city is a system of systems that optimizes for humans.

>> **People first:** Don't become too enamored by the use of technology. When deployed correctly, technology is largely invisible, or at least non-intrusive. What matters are the outcomes for people. A smart city is ultimately a human-centric endeavor.

After all, what is the city but the people?

What a smart city is not

Establishing the definition of a smart city is vital because it helps you comprehend the scope of the topic. But recognizing what a smart city is *not* also has value.

Here are five things that a smart city is *not:*

>> **An upgrade from a dumb city:** I attend many smart cities events each year, and inevitably a speaker or panelist makes a joke about cities being dumb before they were smart. The joke usually draws a chuckle. Fair enough — the notion of "smart" isn't precise enough for what it is, but as I've said many times, it's the title that has stuck. All cities are complex, amazing feats of human creativity. They aren't dumb and have never been — quite the opposite. Becoming a smart city is more about becoming smarter in the use of technology to make what the city does better and to provide solutions to problems that traditionally have been difficult to solve.

Let me make one last, related point on this topic. One point of view is that a smart city can exist only with smart people (I'm assuming this to mean people with a higher education, but it's not clear to me). I don't think this perspective is fair or inclusive. Communities are made up of all types of people, and everyone, if they choose, has something to contribute.

TIP

When building smart cities, ensure that all your efforts and experiences embrace the majesty of all people. You should, in fact, add this as a goal in your strategy.

Note: The irony of the title of this book isn't lost on me. . . .

>> **A surveillance city:** Implementing a smart city should not mean the end of privacy for its residents, businesses, and visitors. It's true that smart cities deploy sensors in support of their efforts — possibly for monitoring air and water quality, improved traffic management, noise detection, energy management, and much more. (I discuss sensors in Chapter 8.) It's important to

acknowledge privacy concerns where they arise, and city leaders need to listen carefully and respond with assurances. However, you should recognize that these efforts are made to improve services, not to impinge on privacy or create a surveillance city where everyone is being monitored. In developing and executing on a smart city strategy, stakeholders must ensure that privacy is upheld, data is anonymized, and the community is engaged in the process to provide transparency and build confidence.

TIP

Deploying smart city technology that includes sensors should be specifically and carefully regulated by rules — even legislation — in order to protect the community. Make that a priority.

>> **A strategy about gadgets and apps:** Yes, technology is definitely at the center of developing a smart city, but if you look at many of the vendors in this emerging space, you can easily believe that the subject is really all about cool new toys and apps. Sure, plenty of those are available. However, transforming a city, solving complex challenges, and creating a higher quality of life for the greatest number of people are goals that require comprehensive changes in processes, rules, technologies, and the talent and skills to plan and implement it. Don't be distracted by novel, piecemeal solutions. Sure, consider those factors in the mix, but recognize that creating a smart city is an undertaking that requires a significant focus on technology strategy, extensive solutions architecture, and systems integration.

TIP

Remind yourself (and others) often that smart cities are about people, not technology.

>> **A temporary technology trend:** You might believe that the smart city movement is a recent development, perhaps just two or three years old. In reality, applying technology to make cities operate better has been under way for several decades. It isn't possible to determine the first-ever use of the term *smart city,* but it certainly has references at least to the early 1990s. Even with a reasonably long history already, the real action of smart cities is happening now, and the most significant results will be seen in the years ahead. More than some sort of temporary trend, for cities to function well and bring a high quality of life to as many people as necessary, the smart city movement will last for multiple decades. Though the smart city concept may change over time, the goal doesn't really have an expiration date. For many skeptical city leaders, it's time to shrug off the belief that it's a passing fad and get onboard to embrace the benefits of urban innovation.

>> **A concept that matters only to big cities:** If you review the literature on smart cities, it certainly would appear that only big cities can be smart cities. The same names pop up all the time: London, Paris, Moscow, Melbourne, Dublin, Vienna, Barcelona, San Francisco, and others. Sure, these incredible cities have impressive smart city initiatives, but any city can pursue the goal of becoming smarter. After all, most cities in the world today are small. The big ones are the outliers. (I discuss this point a little later in this chapter.)

Working with digital infrastructures

It's impossible to define the notion of a smart city without introducing the concept of a digital infrastructure.

A digital infrastructure (DI) is a prerequisite for a smart city.

Okay, so what is it? A DI is foundational capability — such as communication networks, computer processing, or computer storage — to enable the operations of information technology in a city (and most other organizations as well). It typically refers to physical assets and software. A DI provides the systems needed to support, automate, and control the availability and movement of data, information, and services between people, between people and machines, and between machines. Figure 2-1 illustrates the basic components of digital infrastructure.

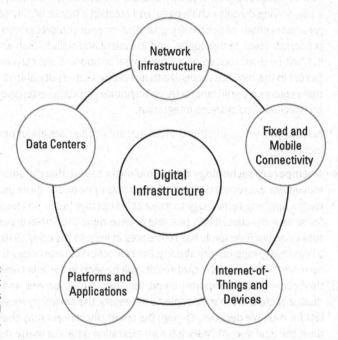

FIGURE 2-1:
The basic components of digital infrastructure.

Today, the DI is expected to be reliable, fast, and intelligent. It's meant to support wireless and fixed access to the Internet from a variety of devices, including smartphones and personal computers. In addition, it should enable traffic signal operations, support data centers, connect sensors, manage emergency systems, provision city applications delivered from the cloud, support Wi-Fi, and much more.

Smart cities leverage DI to add *digital intelligence* to communities. Whereas emotional intelligence is about relationships between humans, digital intelligence is the relationship between people and technology. Through the underlying DI and what it enables, city employees and residents can learn to take advantage of the benefits of technology. As examples, businesses can run more efficiently with fast Internet access and more city services can be provided conveniently online and via smartphone apps. Digital intelligence enables those tasked with delivering smarter services to have the skills and tools to achieve better outcomes.

REMEMBER

Societies with mature digital infrastructures often benefit economically as they boost productivity and innovation, attract businesses, and enable their cities to operate more efficiently.

In a city, the basic DI consists of these components:

>> **Fixed broadband:** A citywide wired network that provides homes and businesses with connectivity and access to the Internet

>> **Mobile connectivity:** A variety of citywide wireless network technologies that provide Internet and communications access to devices like mobile phones

>> **Network infrastructure:** Equipment for efficiently moving data across a variety of networks, such as Wi-Fi, and connecting both people and things

>> **Data centers:** Facilities that manage networks, storage, and computing; may be physically local or provided online via cloud computing

>> **Platforms:** Systems and software for developing, deploying, and supporting service solutions

>> **Internet of Things (IoT):** A variety of devices, ranging from sensors to smart devices and from robots to vehicles, that are all connected to the Internet and exchange data and instructions between systems

Building the Case for Smarter Cities

In June 2015, the Indian prime minister Narendra Modi announced the Smart Cities Mission, an urban renewal-and-retrofitting program to develop 109 cities all over India to make them citizen-friendly and sustainable. The mission recognized that considerable investment and a deliberate strategy are required to address the large number of significant challenges facing these communities. Without action, old, broken, and insufficient systems would continue to dominate the landscape and completely miss the mark in meeting expectations and improving the lives of millions of people.

In many communities around the world, some services are still delivered the way they have been for decades. A walk-in service that was designed for, say, 100 people per day 30 years ago remains the same, even though it now has to serve 1,000 people per day. The result? No one is happy. Crowding, errors, and insufficient processes cause frustration for both the service provider and the customer.

The challenges of old, broken, and inefficient solutions can be observed and experienced across the urban landscape. This list describes some problem areas:

» **Traffic congestion:** Despite the addition of more lanes, congestion grows worse. Parking spaces are scarce, and traffic becomes snarled as drivers meander the streets, desperately looking for spots. This frustration, by the way, causes up to 30 percent of traffic in urban centers.

» **Flooding:** After rainstorms, water floods the streets and freshwater flows out to the ocean instead of being captured for productive use.

» **Public transport:** The lack of options restricts employment choices for people who can't travel to available jobs.

» **Internet access:** Unevenly distributed access to the Internet creates a life-limiting digital divide. Even where access is provided, Internet speed can vary considerably.

» **Environmental damage:** A dependency on carbon-based energy results in continued and potentially irreversible damage to the environment.

You know your own city's issues because you know your city best. These aren't hidden problems. Everyone experiences them in their respective communities every single day. The need for better solutions isn't an abstract concept. Cities are our lives. More than many problems in the world, all city dwellers experience the challenges of urban life firsthand. Ask anyone to specify what problems exist in their community and you'll get a detailed answer. Residents know what their cities do well, but they know *really* well what their cities don't do well. (That sentence is a tongue twister.)

REMEMBER

Who would argue against the suggestions that cities need to function better and that more people deserve to have a better quality of life? Of course, no one would. To apply solutions, supported by new and existing technologies, to make cities function in a smarter way — that's the case for building smart cities.

Small cities versus large cities

It may surprise you to read that most people around the world live in small cities — the ones with fewer than 500,000 inhabitants. Based on how cities are covered in the media, this statistic is surprising even to me. You might think that most people live in the world's megacities, or in the many cities in China with well over a million people. The big, glamorous cities of the world garner all the attention while most of the people live in the smaller, lesser known cities.

This is an important point relative to smart cities: Large cities need innovation, and their challenges are definitely big and complex. Attention to these cities and their successes is welcomed because it does motivate further innovation and provides best practices for others. They also create benchmarks and indices that help frame and understand progress being made worldwide to improve cities. However, you must recognize that the smart city movement is applicable to all cities, large and small.

The problems experienced by cities large and small certainly have some overlap, but many are also distinct. I can usually win a bet if I suggest that traffic congestion is an issue in any urban setting (there are certainly exceptions, but cities without back-to-back traffic at some point in the day are sadly too rare). Where cities large and small greatly vary is in their ability to solve their challenges and the way they approach them. Smaller communities have more modest budgets, less access to specific talent, and not as much capacity available. However, on the positive side, they can also make decisions more quickly and get things done in less time.

REMEMBER

If you live in or work for a small city, the smart city movement is as applicable to you as it is to the mayor of New York City. It's vital to have better-operating communities and a higher quality of life for everyone in every city.

Smart nations and other smart things

Like me, you've probably noticed that the term *smart* has become quite popular. Who hasn't heard of a smart home or a smart device? (Okay, Siri. Hey, Google. Hi, Alexa.) Many people own smartphones and buy products made with smart manufacturing at a smart factory. Apparently, people like the term. Marketers apparently do, too. It seems we're using it liberally to suggest something that is innovative, connected, and technology-centric. That certainly fits for some of the aspirations of a smart city.

Though this book focuses on smart cities, much of the guidance I provide can be applied to other domains that exist within the realm of cities as well. Let's look at a few other relevant smart items:

>> **Smart island:** Eleven percent of the world's population lives on an island. Island communities are eager to become self-sufficient and reduce their carbon footprints. The nature of island life means that residents have always had to be quite innovative to sustain their communities. Islands are also

experiencing the effects of climate change in advance of others. The need to innovate in this area is pressing. Energy costs have historically been high due to a reliance on imports, so a focus on renewables and smart grid technology (discussed in Chapter 8) has become a priority. Island communities around the world are collaborating to share their lessons with each other. You can consider a smart island a microcosm of a smart city. Figure 2-2 lists some islands that are pursuing a smart island strategy.

Aruba
Isles of Scilly
Balearic Islands
Texel
New Caledonia
Outer Hebrides
Greek Islands
Belle-île-en-Mer

FIGURE 2-2:
Eight examples of islands with smart island initiatives.

>> **Smart nation:** This term is most associated with the efforts of Singapore. (Learn more about this aspect of Singapore at www.smartnation.sg.) However, it's being adopted by other countries to reflect a whole-of-nation effort to become more connected and more efficient, and to improve the lives of all people in a country. In Singapore, much effort is placed on digital services. Objectives include services that are digital end-to-end, score high in community satisfaction, and make use of artificial intelligence, data, and data analytics to improve government decision-making and reduce the time to deliver services.

>> **Smart stadium:** The purpose of a smart stadium is to improve the experience of fans. New stadiums are being built with technology deeply integrated, and many older, world-class stadiums are being retrofitted. These stadiums have fast Internet connectivity, provide additional real-time insights to the audience via big screens and smartphones, and use data to provide information on available parking spaces and the length of bathroom lines.

>> **Smart factory:** This type of highly connected manufacturing facility uses artificial intelligence, robotics, analytics, data, and the Internet of Things to largely run autonomously. Production lines can self-correct and learn in order to become more efficient and flexible. Data from a smart factory can improve the supply chain and the design process, resulting in increased production optimization and higher-quality products.

>> **Smart hospital:** The concept and implementation of a smart hospital is beginning to gain traction, although most of the goals are still aspirational. Using data, artificial intelligence, and connected devices, hospitals can become more efficient and increase positive outcomes for patients. In addition, robots can deliver routine services 24 hours a day with predictability and at a lower cost than their human equivalents.

Other smart domains include smart regions, smart villages, smart airports, and smart campuses. (I discuss a subset of a smart city, called an *innovation district*, in Chapter 7.)

United Nations' Sustainable Development Goals (SDGs)

In 2015, after several decades in the making, 193 countries signed the United Nations (UN) 2030 Agenda for Sustainable Development. The agenda is made up of 17 sustainable development goals (SDGs) that contain 169 targets. These include ending poverty and hunger, improving health and education, making cities more sustainable, combating climate change, and protecting oceans and forests. The goals are focused on these five broad areas:

>> People

>> Planet

>> Prosperity

>> Peace

>> Partnership

The participating countries committed to meeting these goals in 15 years by 2030.

At the signing ceremony in 2015, UN Secretary General Mr. Ban Ki-moon said, "It is a roadmap to ending global poverty, building a life of dignity for all and leaving no one behind. It is also a clarion call to work in partnership and intensify efforts to share prosperity, empower people's livelihoods, ensure peace and heal our planet for the benefit of this and future generations."

In short, the 17 SDGs are the world's plan to build a better world for people and the planet by 2030.

Here's a listing of all 17 SDGs; see Figure 2-3 for a graphical representation:

>> End poverty in all its forms everywhere.

>> End hunger, achieve food security and improved nutrition, and promote sustainable agriculture.

>> Ensure healthy lives and promote well-being for all at all ages.

>> Ensure inclusive and equitable quality education and promote lifelong learning opportunities for all.

>> Achieve gender equality and empower all women and girls.

>> Ensure availability and sustainable management of water and sanitation for all.

>> Ensure access to affordable, reliable, sustainable, and modern energy for all.

>> Promote sustained, inclusive, and sustainable economic growth, full and productive employment, and decent work for all.

>> Build resilient infrastructure, promote inclusive and sustainable industrialization, and foster innovation.

>> Reduce inequality within and among countries.

>> Make cities and human settlements inclusive, safe, resilient, and sustainable.

>> Ensure sustainable consumption and production patterns.

>> Take urgent action to combat climate change and its impacts.

>> Conserve and sustainably use the oceans, seas, and marine resources for sustainable development.

>> Protect, restore, and promote sustainable use of terrestrial ecosystems, sustainably manage forests, combat desertification, and halt and reverse land degradation and halt biodiversity loss.

>> Promote peaceful and inclusive societies for sustainable development, provide access to justice for all, and build effective, accountable, and inclusive institutions at all levels.

>> Strengthen the means of implementation and revitalize the global partnership for sustainable development.

There's a clear intersection between the SDGs and cities. With over half the planet living in cities already — and up to 70 percent by 2050 — if countries are going to make good on their commitments, a lot of the work will require efforts within cities.

SUSTAINABLE DEVELOPMENT GOALS

FIGURE 2-3:
The 17 United
Nations
Sustainable
Development
Goals.

Take a moment to review each of the 17 SDGs again, and consider them through the lens of urban efforts. It becomes glaringly obvious that action must happen at the local city level to achieve these macro outcomes. They're not all city-based, but many of them are. Out of 17 goals, numbers 6–16 clearly have a direct or indirect city alignment, and goal 11 is a central city challenge.

The intent of smart cities and all 17 goals overlap in important ways. Many of the themes — such as inclusion, the environment, resilience, sustainability, innovation, and health — are areas that this book covers in detail.

If you needed more justification for your sustainable smart city strategy, beyond the specific requirements of your community, you don't need to look much further than the SDGs. It seems well aligned and supportable that if your goals are to improve the quality of life for your community, you're likely directly contributing toward the intent of the SDGs. The topic can help with your project planning and with shaping the dialogue around your smart city strategy.

REMEMBER

Integrating aspects of the SDGs into your smart city strategy can add credibility and increased value to your efforts. Introduce the SDGs early in the process, and determine what areas are good complements and targets.

TIP

Elevate your knowledge of your city's smart city work to your national SDG leadership so that the contributing efforts can be captured and recognized.

Finally, the ambitious targets of the SDGs can't be achieved by cities working in silos. Exploring regional efforts will not only increase the chance of better results but also may provide opportunities for smart city strategy and urban innovation knowledge and cost sharing.

You can find additional details and all 169 SDG targets and current progress at www.un.org/sustainabledevelopment.

Finally, my lawyer says I have to include the following sentence: The content of this publication has not been approved by the United Nations and does not reflect the views of the United Nations or its officials or Member States.

Examining Examples of Smart Cities

The smart city movement is truly global. In almost every part of the world, cities have declared smart city initiatives. Even cities that don't overtly align with the smart city nomenclature are doing work that has all the hallmarks of smart initiatives. In addition to existing communities, new cities are being built, or are in the process of being built, that are designed with urban innovation at their core. These include Yachay in Ecuador, Masdar in the United Arab Emirates (UAE), Songdo in South Korea, Konza in Kenya, Neom in Saudi Arabia, and a new capital in Egypt. This list alone demonstrates the global nature of the smart city movement.

Let's take a look at two cities from two perspectives: an existing built environment and a completely new city. First, I focus on Amsterdam, a beautiful, world-class European city, the capital of The Netherlands, that began as a fishing village in 1275. Second, I describe Konza Technopolis, a new, in-progress smart city located 60 kilometers south of Nairobi, the capital of Kenya on the central east coast of Africa.

Amsterdam, The Netherlands

The smart city efforts of Amsterdam, which began in 2009, are focused on these six themes:

>> **Infrastructure and technology:** Adopting new technologies, such as drones, a smart grid, and the Internet of Things

>> **Energy, water, and waste:** Improving the performance of three essential areas that are relevant to every city

>> **Mobility:** Reducing traffic congestion and pollution and increasing safety

>> **Circular city:** Minimizing waste and pollution by recycling, reducing, and reusing

- **≫ Governance and education:** Ensuring that decision-makers have the tools to make the right decisions and that Amsterdam attracts and retains skilled talent
- **≫ Citizens and living:** Ensuring that citizens are engaged and have a way to contribute and participate in new ideas for the city

Konza Technopolis, Kenya

In 2008, the Government of Kenya approved the creation of Konza Technopolis (formerly Konza Technology City) as a flagship Kenya Vision 2030 project. Vision 2030 aims to create a globally competitive, prosperous Kenya with a high quality of life by 2030. To that end, its smart city goals are highly focused on economic opportunities.

The smart city efforts of this new city are focused on these four types of services:

- **≫ Infrastructure:** These include technologies in support of transportation, utilities, public safety, and the environment.
- **≫ Citizen:** Within this area, the focus is on easy access to services and for citizen engagement in the city.
- **≫ City:** These technologies support efficient and effective planning and development.
- **≫ Business:** This area includes a range of services to support enterprises and local commerce such as rapid business registration and training.

In both initiatives, a large number of projects accompany each of the goals. In Amsterdam, these projects must be integrated with legacy challenges, including existing infrastructure and technology, to ensure that no existing systems are impacted in their daily operations. Konza has the benefit of not having to consider legacy limitations, because everything is new. If you've ever managed a big project, you'll recognize how much easier the latter is.

These two examples are reminders of the global nature of smart cities and the variety of focus areas that reflect local needs and priorities. Both instances have recorded successes, but they've also faced significant challenges. In particular, Konza has had many setbacks related to financing and competing national priorities.

There's no sugarcoating it, building smart cities is hard. However, for the upside, it's definitely worth it.

TIP

In Appendix A, you find the smart city strategies for a long list of cities from around the world. Spend time reviewing these strategies for guidance and inspiration for your smart city efforts.

Chapter 3

Responding to the Needs and Challenges of Cities

Cities are in a constant state of change — some more than others. This change is being driven by a number of factors, including new challenges and needs, population changes, and the introduction of novel innovations. In the 21st century, communities also have higher expectations of their cities. In this chapter, I explore some drivers of change and explain how they provide the motivation to create smarter responses and solutions.

Mapping the Evolving Needs and Challenges of Cities

In the late 1800s, horse manure was a problem in many large cities. In those days, thousands of horses provided transport for people and goods. (Figure 3-1 shows an example of a horse-drawn carriage called a hansom cab.) In London, for example, horse-drawn buses required 12 horses per day, which resulted in a demand for at least 50,000 horses for the bus system alone. As you can imagine, the scale of the manure problem was significant. In addition to the smell and the mess it created, manure attracted flies, which spread typhoid fever and other diseases. The streets of London were poisoning its people.

FIGURE 3-1:
A hansom cab:
London, 1877.

In 1894, *The Times* (London's major daily newspaper) published this headline: "In 50 years, every street in London will be buried under nine feet of manure."

Of course, it didn't happen. Why? Things changed. The automobile was invented.

I know it's a cliché, but it has never been truer than it is today: The only constant is change. Humans are living in a time where everything they take for granted appears to be evolving. This is a period of opportunity and of enormous challenges, both of which are characteristics of the fourth industrial revolution. (For more on the nature of this revolution, see Chapter 8.)

I've worked in various innovation roles in my career, and I've formed a hypothesis for why innovation is often so difficult. Here it is: With innovation, you're typically creating a new solution for a world that doesn't yet exist. Think about that statement for a moment. If you assume that society is in a constant state of rapid change, you have to be able to build today for a world that will be different in the not-too-distant future. If you get it right, you strike gold. Get it wrong and you need to pack up and go home. What you create today must have application in the future. It's not easy, but it's reality. Based on my own experiences and observations, this hypothesis has yet to be unproven.

Like everything else, cities are evolving at a more rapid pace than before. They are changing to meet the needs of communities. Similarly, communities are responding to the changes around them. Over time, we design cities and cities design us. The rest of this chapter looks at how that process may play out.

Economic shifts

One fundamental change in society over the past couple of hundred years has been the migration, not just of people, but of economic power from rural areas to urban areas. For much of human history, trade within and between groups and small villages was the main engine of economic activity. As each empire emerged, its governing centers (Athens, Rome, Istanbul, Paris, London) prospered and grew as money flowed back from new markets. But they were the exceptions. Much of the world remained rural.

In time, empires collapsed and wars wrought destruction that ultimately resulted in new states and centers of power being formed. The industrial revolutions ushered in increasing rates of urban migration. Many industrializing cities across Europe, North America, and Japan in particular began to see strong productivity and economic growth. After World War II, the rebuilding of cities in Europe and Asia and the attendant economic activity resulted in strong financial positions for many developed regions throughout the 1950s and 1960s.

In the last quarter of the 20th century, many developed cities that competed in areas such as coal mining, electronics, automobile assembly, steel production, and manufacturing in general were battered by recessions and lost economic value from globalization.

The rapid emergence of a developing Southeast Asia further expanded urban growth and wealth distribution. In the 21st century, this trend is continuing. For example, in the next decade, India will contain the top ten fastest-growing cities in the world in terms of gross domestic product (GDP).

Despite many ups and down, the trajectory of many cities — always with exceptions — has continued upward. Today, cities are the dominant economic force on the planet, generating 80 percent of all GDP.

REMEMBER

Globalization is forcing cities to redefine themselves as their legacy industries decline because of irrelevancy or competition from lower-cost regions. Service industries are beginning to dominate in many places.

In the 21st century, cities paradoxically find themselves positioned for economic success but nevertheless face significant challenges imposed by global competition, endangered relevancy, and increasing operating costs.

Increasingly complex city requirements

Operating a city efficiently in the 21st century is complicated. The services, as well as the channels that are served, have grown considerably over the past 50 years.

In addition to the *built environment* (all the physical aspects, such as buildings and roads), there's an expectation that cities must support the entire stack of digital services. Take, for example, the need to attain a permit for constructing a home extension. In many cities, this is a hands-on experience that requires multiple visits by a requestor to a physical permit center. Many years ago, this whole experience would have been exclusively a person-to-person interaction. Today, all or parts of the permitting process can be delivered online. Now a city has to integrate both the analog and digital worlds of permits. Both the requestor and the provider gain great advantages but also higher complexity in ensuring that everything works smoothly, including, for example, that data is secure and available when needed.

In the years ahead, you'll see a greater use of technology — such as digitalization, robotic process automation (RPA), real robots, and artificial intelligence — used in city services. Paradoxically, the same innovative technologies that will be used to streamline processes and create efficiencies will enable less complexity on the front-end but likely increase the complexity on the back-end.

To ensure consistent quality, keep costs down, reduce errors, and support the needs and expectations of all constituents, complexity is headed higher.

TIP

Prepare for complexity because it will define the world's urban future.

Interdependencies between systems

When I started my career as a technologist in the 1990s, not many systems were connected. In 1990, the Internet wasn't yet available to the general population. Only the geekiest people had dialup modems that used their home landlines to connect them with remote systems.

When I say "the geekiest people," I mean me.

Today, everyone's devices are connected, and millions more devices are coming online every few days. The need to send and receive data between computer systems is now a requirement. People connect to internal networks that can span one building or hundreds of facilities, and people are connecting to many public networks as well. Most business requirements necessitate sophisticated architectures — digital infrastructure (which I discuss in Chapter 2) — to function and cybersecurity solutions to protect them.

Imagine something as straightforward today as a cloud-based-payroll-and-expense-reimbursement solution. Yes, cities need them too. A system like this one must support data entry from staff, using their computers and apps on their smartphones. The system must connect to numerous banks. It may connect to credit card companies to automatically pull in credit card purchase information. All of this must be done securely, ensuring that only the appropriate people have access to the right capabilities. Folks are only concerned that they get paid and reimbursed, and any deviation from that expectation can spell trouble. Many interdependent systems need to play nicely with one another for it all to work smoothly.

REMEMBER

The interdependencies of systems isn't limited to technology systems. Cities comprise a system of systems. Complex networks of connected city resources include first responders, transportation, buildings, energy supply and demand, waste management, public works, street festivals, governance, water distribution, sustainability initiatives, safety, and much more.

The more the complexity of cities increases, the greater the number of system interdependencies. Additionally, when an increasing number of systems interact with each other, their connections — also known as *nexus points* — increase the risk of cybersecurity breaches. In security parlance it is said that the attack surface has increased. Increased complexity is commensurate with greater cybersecurity risks.

Smarter cities must use intelligent digital and physical infrastructures that are capable of carrying out a variety of tasks, including

» Sharing and acting on data

» Utilizing sustainable materials

» Optimizing water and energy use

» Efficiently using and connecting transportation options

» Connecting people and things by using high-speed telecommunications

If a city continues to be poorly architected or underinvested in, interdependencies can break down and create significant, frustrating inefficiencies — inefficiencies that can even result in outright havoc.

REMEMBER

Smart cities optimize for complexity and the interdependency of systems.

Population changes

It's intuitive that population and demography are core defining dimensions of a city. After all, a city is about people. Understanding these dimensions will help you better make sense of the direction of a community. For example, a city where the majority of people are younger than 35 years old will function differently than one where most people are older than 40. It will influence areas such as health needs, purchasing patterns, job opportunities, and tax income for the city. Let's take a look at urban population and demography in more detail.

Urbanization

The United Nations states that as many as 3 million people per week are migrating into cities. It's a staggering number, and it will continue for several more decades. The primary reason for this movement is that people are seeking a better quality of life. For example, in the United States, a city worker earns, on average, 30 percent more than a worker in a rural area.

WARNING

In the years ahead, the world will likely also see city migrants because of climate change. Deteriorating agricultural opportunities and extreme weather events will be contributors. This will create an increasing class of displaced people called *climate refugees*.

However, not every city is impacted by migration. People are moving into a small number of large cities in just a few regions of the world. (Remember that most cities in the world are small.) In Figure 3-2, you can see the top 10 cities with the highest rate of migrant population growth. Delhi ranks as number one, and several other Indian cities are in the top 20. To help you gain a sense of the rate of change, an estimated 30 people per minute move from a rural area to an urban area in India. By 2030, 600 million Indians will live in a city. Other dominant areas are China and several African nations.

FIGURE 3-2:
The top ten fastest-growing city populations, by inbound migrants.

Rank	City	Country
1	Delhi	India
2	Shanghai	China
3	Dhaka	Bangladesh
4	Kinshasa	Congo
5	Chongqing	China
6	Lahore	Pakistan
7	Bangalore	India
8	Lagos	Nigeria
9	Cairo	Egypt
10	Beijing	China

Deurbanization

It's easy to focus on population growth. But what about cities where the population is declining? This is called *deurbanization*. Though growing populations can drive economic growth, larger tax revenue, and greater prosperity, shrinking cities can result in the opposite. Cities where no immigration exists, birthrates are low, and people are leaving will struggle and may eventually fail. The years of decline can be exceptionally difficult for those remaining as city services get cut, infrastructure decays, jobs disappear, and a sense of hopelessness sets in.

This isn't some rare occurrence. Globalization, aging populations, declining birthrates, and people migrations to larger, more prosperous urban areas are major factors that are precipitating cities in decline. The example of Japan, a highly urbanized country, is striking. Without immigration, a fertility rate of 2.1 (the number of children per woman) is required in order to have a stable population. Currently, Japan isn't hitting this rate. If nothing changes, Japan's population will decline from around 126 million currently to 88 million in 2065. By the year 3000, the population will be zero. (Okay, I'm kidding about that last part, but you get my point.)

As with everything else, there are exceptions to the rule. Some cities are prospering as a result of getting smaller. Others are managing declining populations — called *smart shrinkage* — as a matter of strategy.

The significance of population age

The average medium age of a population is another factor to consider. *Medium age* is the point at which half the population is older than that age and half is younger. Although over the past 50 years it has only increased upward globally by a few years, this doesn't give a clear picture. Medium age varies wildly across the world and tells an important story about the future of cities. The vast majority of African countries have a medium age of under 20. Life expectancy is still below that of western developed nations, but is improving quickly. By contrast, in Germany and Japan, the medium age is around 47 years. Both countries also have a high life expectancy, at more than 80 years.

REMEMBER

Age distribution matters in a city. An insufficient working-age population may indicate low productivity and dwindling tax revenues available for social support. (On the other hand, low numbers of workers and an aging population can prove to be a catalyst for greater automation.) A large, nonworking elderly population places significant stress on already stretched systems. Too many unqualified young people trying to enter the labor force may result in high unemployment, which can lead to frustration, tension, and even high rates of crime.

It's anticipated that in the next few years, Africa will have over 700 million people in the 15-to-39 age group. African cities have an opportunity to prosper in the years ahead through this large consumer market and high availability of labor. However, education and skill-building will be essential for this situation to succeed. The dynamic of many western nation cities will be substantially different, with their populations aging into large numbers of retirees.

Aging infrastructure

Potholes! It's probably the factor most often cited when people complain about their city's infrastructure. It's those holes in the pavement, typically caused by overuse and weather damage. The complex network of roads in every city means there's no shortage of these nasty bumps when you hit them with a car or bike.

If the only problem cities needed to worry about were fixing potholes, the world probably wouldn't have a pothole problem. However, a pothole is symbolic of the challenge of every city to maintain its aging infrastructure. I'm talking about the myriad of assets in the built environment, such as these and more:

>> Public buildings

>> Bridges

>> Parks

>> Paths and sidewalks

>> Water systems

>> Power lines

>> Tunnels

>> Walls

>> Dams

If you live in a new, glistening city in China or the Middle East, this probably isn't a top-of-mind issue. (Eventually, it will be.) But for the vast majority of modern cities built over the course of the past 150 years, stuff is either breaking outright or not being well-maintained. After all, upkeep is expensive, budgets are limited, and city leaders are forced to navigate competing priorities demanded by their constituents. Communities also want to build new facilities and infrastructure. Only the most affluent, smaller cities have a good handle on keeping their infrastructure in order.

WARNING

In the years ahead, infrastructure maintenance projects will no longer be able to be delayed or ignored. Infrastructure is already a crisis, and the dangers of ignoring it are real. Just in the past few years, several bridges have collapsed while people and cars have been crossing. In August 2018, the Ponte Morandi motorway bridge in Genoa, Italy, collapsed and killed 43 people. Sadly, I could name plenty of other examples of these types of tragedies.

Though there are many reasons that aging infrastructure is difficult to address, costs dominate — how will cities afford the significant price tag of upgrading their aging infrastructure? (I discuss the important topic of funding in Chapter 6.)

SMART CITIES AND THE SUPPLY CHAIN

Few people ever ponder the source and journey of the products they purchase. At the grocery store, you buy meat, fish, and vegetables, typically without a moment's consideration for how they got there. They're just there, fresh and delicious, simply waiting for you. The same applies to products like televisions, smartphones, and computers. These types of items are available to you in beautiful packaging and at a price you can afford as a result of a massively complex chain of events. These events include the harvesting of natural resources, the sourcing of raw materials, the transformation of these ingredients into products, and then their delivery from factory to distributor to retailer and then to your home or office. It's a miracle of the modern world. It's called the global supply chain and it works because of sophisticated supply chain management (SCM).

You only realize the significance of SCM when products are delayed or are unavailable for a period of time. Global events such as conflicts, pandemics, trade disputes, and natural disasters are often the culprits. When the global supply chain works, it's a remarkable human achievement. When it fails, it causes considerable concern. Smart cities have the capacity to build upon the success of the supply chain and make it more resilient. In addition, cities will need to be smarter in how they manage the anticipated 40 percent growth in urban freight by 2050.

One of the core ways in which smart city efforts can improve the supply chain is in improvements in logistics infrastructure. This can include areas such as sea and airports, road systems, parking, and support for the last mile — the final part of the journey to your delivery location. The last mile infrastructure is the geographic area of the city and it is the most congested. At this level, the supply chain has typically been reduced from huge containers and other large storage solutions to small packages that must make their way through choked urban zones.

Improving logistics means engaging stakeholders of the supply chain in the relevant areas of the smart city strategy. These professionals need to provide guidance and suggestions to help shape the infrastructure components of the plan.

Smart cities can improve SCM with the following:

- Providing geographic information systems and other real-time data for improved trip optimization

- Supporting regulations for new methods of delivery such as ground and air-based drones

- Issuing permits to repurpose locations such as malls as distribution centers

(continued)

(continued)

- Implementing more electric vehicle charging stations for electric-powered delivery vehicles

- Creating improved parking options for trucks loading and unloading, including real-time information on space availability

- Deploying dynamic traffic signaling systems that enable traffic signals to give priority to certain traffic at specific times of the day

- Supporting the experimentation of autonomous delivery vehicles in real urban environment

As one SCM leader put it, "smart cities will never be smart if they can't improve upon the rapidly declining urban challenges of the last mile of delivery."

To learn more about this topic, check out *Supply Chain Management For Dummies*, by Daniel Stanton (Wiley).

Lifestyle choices

People no longer think of cities as being just convenient places to live and work — they now expect them to offer a wide range of choices of things to do in their free time. Among many options, great cities are full of exciting and exotic places to eat, to be entertained, to watch and play sports, to learn, and to escape. People want choices in their housing — perhaps an apartment, a small house, a canal boat (for the adventurous), or, if you can afford it, a much grander residence.

What we know is that the choices people make in their lifestyles continue to evolve. We've come a long way from working to exhaustion during the day and then spending the evening telling stories around the fire or gathering in front of the radio to listen to the latest sci-fi serial.

Cities understand that lifestyle choices continue to evolve and that communities are increasingly demanding more options. For some communities, offering desirable amenities is necessary to attract the talent required for the industries of the future. A city without good Internet access and a range of connectivity choices can immediately be a turn-off to a prospective employee who is considering moving there.

REMEMBER

Newer generations are demanding some basic requirements from their cities, including clean environments, streets with parks and quiet areas, places to walk a pet or allow a pet to run around with others, activities for all age groups, diversity in employment, quality schools, and safe and well-lit areas. It's a tall order to fill, but expectations have certainly risen over the past few decades.

The most successful and attractive cities in the world are playgrounds for all manner of activities.

Environment

It's possible that no other topic will be as important or as defining in the next few decades as the health of the planet. It's potentially an existential issue. Sure, the planet will survive in the long run, but will we humans? More pointedly, how humans behave in cities will ultimately determine the trajectory of the current climate emergency.

In other words, the future of humanity depends on the environment of cities.

As megacities grow, more resources are consumed and more energy is required. Cities now consume over two-thirds of the world's energy.

REMEMBER

Although large cities are the biggest contributors of carbon emissions, every person is an independent and responsible participant. In other words, a smaller city where carbon use is high per person, can elevate that city's impact beyond its size.

People are managing waste better, but cities can't help it: They create massive volumes of it every day. Powering and processing complex city operations produces a catastrophic level of carbon exhaust — over 70 percent of global carbon emissions, to be precise. Transportation is a big chunk of that number. (Figure 3-3 illustrates the carbon producing congestion from cars in cities.)

The countries and their respective cities with the highest carbon footprint include these:

>> **China:** Hong Kong, Guangzhou, and Shanghai

>> **United States:** New York, Los Angeles, and Chicago

>> **South Korea:** Seoul, Busan, and Taegu

>> **Russia:** Moscow, St. Petersburg, and Novosibirsk

Surprisingly, there's research that suggests that large urbanization has a positive impact on the environment. Based on condensed living space, reduced energy-use per capita, and the preservation of the countryside and nature, these factors can contribute to a more environmentally friendly organization of human settlement.

Can people's behaviors, models, and approaches to contemporary living evolve in time to save the environment? Changes appear to be underway, but the scientific consensus is that we're not yet doing enough. City dwellers, the future of the planet is up to you.

FIGURE 3-3: Transportation accounts for 15 percent of global carbon emissions.

Health

There's one topic that every person in the world cares about: their health. It turns out, perhaps unsurprisingly, that the relationship between city life and health is inextricably linked. It wasn't always a good relationship. The first big cities were breeding grounds for disease. The vast numbers of rodents, the lack of sanitation, and the close proximity of humans provided some of the context for the most devastating epidemics the world has ever seen. Plague, for example, is said to have killed one in four Athenians in 430 B.C. This disease became a regular in Europe and decimated communities periodically up until the 18th century. With plague largely vanquished, it was replaced by cholera and yellow fever. Cholera was particularly catastrophic in cities, until it was determined that dirty water was to blame.

One motivation for the design of the grid system in Manhattan was to provide better air flow around the city. (This was because some diseases were thought to be caused by still air!) The real reasons for disease, such as bad bacteria entering water and food and mosquito bites, had yet to be discovered. Thank goodness for modern medicine.

Though humans have generally avoided major epidemics in cities over the past few decades (SARS, in the early 2000s, was an exception), cities are still major determinants of human health.

Unfortunately, after I wrote the first draft of this chapter, the world was hit with a pandemic. A new virus, named Covid-19, turned out to be highly contagious and was spreading from person-to-person. Where there was density of people — cities! — the virus was infecting the most amount of humans. Cities lend themselves to close human proximity, including public transportation, sports stadiums, offices, and theaters, which were all contexts for rapid spread. Major cities began imposing stay-at-home orders and requiring people to stand six feet apart from each other when out and about. While the rate of infection eventually began to decline, this story remains open. There will be a lot to be learned from it, as it's certain that nobody wants to be faced with such a disaster again. While the solution appears to lie in the discovery of therapeutics and a vaccine, there's little doubt that other changes in how people live, work, and play, and in the design of cities will soon be underway as well.

Here are just a few of the ways city life can negatively impact health:

>> Poor air and water quality

>> Noise and inability to escape to quiet areas

>> Lack of access to healthcare options

>> High cost of healthcare

>> Mental health problems caused by the stresses of urban life

>> Loneliness

>> A sedentary office lifestyle

>> Lack of safe and beautiful areas in which to walk alone

Today, city dwellers want a great city experience and good health. It's driving city leaders to explore the important ways that the urban environment can become healthier. The movement even has a name: healthy cities. The World Health Organization (WHO) specifies the following elements as the objectives of a healthy city:

>> Creating a health-supportive environment where, for example, health factors are a priority in relevant city decisions

>> Achieving a good quality of life

>> Providing for basic sanitation and hygiene needs

>> Supplying access to healthcare

More than anything, it will be a new generation of community members who will demand that health becomes one of the essential drivers of positive urban change. (For more on the healthy cities movement, see Chapter 11.)

Water management

The earth, the air, the land, and the water are not an inheritance from our forefathers but on loan from our children. So, we have to hand over to them at least as it was handed over to us.

—MAHATMA GANDHI

In 2018, the beautiful, modern city of Cape Town in South Africa suffered a water crisis. With a dry climate, rapid urbanization, high per capita water consumption, and three years of little rainfall, the city was in trouble. If drastic action weren't taken, the city would run out of water.

The most important step was to reduce demand. The city implemented a wide range of water-saving initiatives. People were instructed to take only 2-minute showers. A campaign slogan was created — "If it's yellow, let it mellow" — to promote the reduction of toilet flushing. Residents were restricted to a maximum of 50 liters a day. To put that amount in context, a shower typically uses 15 liters per minute. Filling swimming pools, washing cars, and running fountains were all banned. Failure to observe the long list of water limitations was punished with a large fine. Enforcement included the deployment of water management devices that could record and limit the water supply to properties. Social media was widely used to communicate with residents and for people to offer advice and support.

Fortunately, with these strict rules in place and an effective use of technology — in addition to some welcome rain — the city of Cape Town averted the worst-case scenario of running out of water. It came perilously close, though. As the city continues to grow and water demand increases, the risk of future shortages remain.

Unfortunately, Cape Town's situation isn't unique in the world. Today, *water stress* — defined as a situation where the water resources available are insufficient for needs — affects almost 2 billion people. More than 1.2 billion people lack access to clean drinking water. It's anticipated that by 2030, 700 million people could be displaced by intense water scarcity. Water scarcity is being driven by two converging phenomena: growing freshwater use and depletion of usable freshwater resources.

The sixth goal of the United Nations Sustainable Development Goals (SDGs, see Chapter 2 for more) is, "Ensure availability and sustainable management of water and sanitation for all."

I discuss a smart city technology solution for improved water management in Chapter 8 in a section called "Smart water."

REMEMBER

Water is life. It's necessary for the survival of all living things on Planet Earth.

Housing crisis

The number of buildings in the world is going to double by 2060. We're going to build the equivalent of a new New York City every month for the next 40 years."

BILL GATES, *cofounder of Microsoft and co-chair and cofounder of the Bill & Melinda Gates Foundation*

As city populations continue to grow in the years ahead, so too does the need for more housing. However, though the demands for new housing will be substantial in the future, the world is already in the midst of a housing crisis — a crisis that's largely about housing availability, affordability, and acceptable conditions. *Affordable housing,* a central challenge, is defined in this context as the ability to afford a home (rent or mortgage) with 30 percent or less of your income.

Despite the common misconception, this housing crisis isn't restricted to big cities such as New York, London, and Sydney. All types of cities, big and small, are impacted. The worst is being experienced in rapidly urbanizing cities of the developing world. Continued high levels of poverty, government debt, and weak economies results in many residents of these cities being forced to live in substandard housing lacking electricity, running water, and basic sanitation.

In the developed world, there are many reasons for this housing crisis. At the most basic level, cities simply haven't built enough homes. Over several administrations, many leaders have poorly estimated capacity needs. In addition to this poor planning, however, there are also restrictive land use issues, geographic limitations, and a not-in-my-backyard (NIMBY) sentiment.

Housing has also been turned into a popular investment mechanism, which has resulted in an oversupply of luxury housing and an undersupply of affordable housing. Though difficult for cities to manage and regulate in a free market, local governments can develop plans that accommodate the appetite for housing investment with the need to incentivize lower-cost homes.

REMEMBER

Those individuals who are part of what are now known as the knowledge, professional, and creative classes may be able to afford expensive homes and have some money left over, but members of the working-and-service classes are being pushed out to the periphery of cities.

The housing crisis may be largely defined by affordability and availability, but these issues contain subtle complexities that are reflected in the lifestyles of today's society. For example, young knowledge workers may be happy to share rental properties in convenient locations, whereas other demographics, including older adults, may prioritize homes near schools and parks. More people in cities are living alone. In many cities, households without children outnumber those with children. Because urban living is more expensive, home ownership is decreasing while renting is increasing. Renting is also becoming more of a popular choice for those who enjoy the freedom it provides. The common types of available housing — apartments, row houses, and single-family homes, for example — have all been resistant to change. Innovation in housing has been slow.

REMEMBER

A city's housing crisis has no simple set of answers. The dynamics of each city — its unique economic situation and politics, for example — play a role. (See Figure 3-4.) Solutions require multiple approaches, including rethinking and redefining the standard notion of housing.

Despite the enormity of the problem, you can use some proven methods to at least address some aspects of your city's housing problems. I recommend considering the ones described in this list:

>> **Build for density.** This one includes lifting restrictions on the heights of buildings and the proximity of properties to each other. It can include constructing smaller homes.

>> **Relax zoning laws.** Look at other restrictions that limit housing projects and lessen or remove the rules.

>> **Reduce red tape.** Low-income housing builders will benefit from simpler development processes and legal requirements.

>> **Revitalize neighborhoods.** Take action to make less attractive areas more compelling for developers. Clean the streets, plant trees, convert buildings (for example, a school or industrial building transformed into apartments), and put in place tax incentives to attract amenities and businesses.

FIGURE 3-4:
In Tokyo, Japan, housing and offices occupy dense areas of the city.

>> **Institute rent caps.** Enforce a limit on what a landlord can charge for certain types of properties by area.

>> **Provide more public and nonprofit housing.** Despite more homes, many still can't afford those available. Government can have a role in owning or subsidizing homes for low-income residents.

>> **Encourage housing innovation.** The blueprint for homes needs to evolve, as in these examples:

- *Tiny house movement:* Also known as the small house movement, participants advocate for simple living in small homes that are 400 square feet or smaller. A subset of tiny houses is called microhomes. These small homes fit between buildings, under bridges, and on rooftops.

- *Co-housing:* This is when homes are clustered around a shared space that includes a common house, large kitchen and dining areas, and gardens. Residents also share parking spaces and resources such as handy household items.

- *Partial home rental:* A homeowner rents a garage, a basement, or an outside unit as living quarters.

- *Conversion of shipping containers:* Done either as do-it-yourself (DIY) or by purchase, shipping containers are being used for homes. They can be stand-alone or even stacked to enable a larger home or multiple homes.

- *Sky cities:* These proposed skyscrapers house thousands of people but also include stores, indoor farms, hospitals, gyms, and police stations.

- **3D-printed homes:** Custom-designed and -produced homes with additive manufacturing, the process of building by successively adding material layer by layer. These can use a variety of materials and have the potential to be low-cost.

- **Mixed-use buildings:** Rather than restrict a tall office building to just commercial use, a mixed-use building combines multiple uses into one structure, such as residential, hotel, retail, parking, cultural, and entertainment.

Expecting Different Results

It's all too easy to forget the progress of the past 40 years. Humans still live in a time with considerable challenges, and it often feels like they take three steps forward and two steps back. But, in many essential areas, conditions have significantly improved — including major reductions in extreme poverty. (*Extreme poverty* has been defined by the World Bank as those living on $1.90 or less per day.) It's now less than 10 percent — still too high, but a significant drop from over 30 percent when I was a child. Other notable improvements include extended longevity and greater access to education. The team at Human Progress (https://humanprogress.org) does a great job of researching and presenting the facts about our improving world.

Humans by their very nature are never completely satisfied. Each goal that is reached becomes the floor for a new set of goals. What was good yesterday is no longer enough today. In this new century, everyone's expectations have risen. People's level of tolerance for things that don't measure up has gone way down. Poor products head right back to the store. Refunds are quickly demanded for bad products and service.

As the world enters the third decade of the 21st century, everyone is raising the bar on expectations for how city experiences are delivered and for the quality of services provided. City dwellers want their local governments to behave at the same level of performance as they expect from providers in the private sector. They want their city services to be as seamless as booking a table at a restaurant on their favorite smartphone app. For the generations who have grown up on digital, the city is just another app — one with options that can deliver at the speed of a swipe. (Okay, so maybe that's taking the metaphor just a little too far, but you get the point.)

Delivering the services of a city experience today isn't business as usual. Just ask any city manager or mayor. Expectations are completely different from just a few years ago. A connected and empowered community, with elevated and ever-increasing standards, will make its voice heard. It's a driving force, and the message has reached a new generation of elected and appointed city leaders. Choose any city in any region and it's becoming clear that communities are expecting different results. Better results.

Changing community behaviors and expectations

In the early days of the Internet — you know, back in the old days of the late 1990s, when it became clear that this new platform would allow anyone to be a publisher — the belief of many was that, though they would have many options when it came to writing, there would not be enough topics to write about. This sentiment seems so quaint now. Now it seems that everyone is writing about anything possible. The Internet has enabled everyone to become a publisher so that they can spin up some thought and beam it unhindered across the globe to anyone who's prepared to listen. It has been empowering while also presenting people with a range of new challenges.

New digital tools and the power they give to people and groups are representative of a world that is changing in terms of who has a voice and how that voice is heard. Coupled with new expectations, people can hear more points of view loudly and clearly, for better or for worse.

The new community activist is armed with a digital megaphone and data.

It's a whole new day, and many would argue that, for the most part, it's been a positive development for democracy.

Digital has opened up a new world of options for constituents. It has made it easier to communicate (assuming that it's possible to rise above the noise) and to connect with those in power. (In Chapter 8, I discuss many of these new communications tools in detail.) It means being able to build solutions when others don't or can't build them, or having access to data to defend an argument or build a case. These tools are quickly changing behaviors and raising expectations.

But it's not just about tools. It's worth making the point over and over: Smart cities don't happen because humans throw technology at them. They happen because of the choices people make, the behaviors they assume, and, yes, the manner in which technologies are deployed to enable new outcomes.

REMEMBER

A smarter city is enabled by the collective decisions that people make to change how they choose to live.

From building safer cities to fostering sustainable communities to tackling climate change and more, community groups are partnering with city officials to lead positive change. Increasingly, too, when they don't find available partners at city hall, they're taking matters into their own hands. To magnify the potential impact, the levers of digitalization provide many more tools to enable change.

TIP

You'll never succeed in building a smart city if you don't account for changing community behaviors and expectations. To do this means understanding your community. It means having an open, two-way dialogue. It's about listening. Then it's about delivering.

Expanding community engagement

It is said that democracy isn't a spectator sport. Participation means being part of decision-making, holding others and yourself accountable, and being an agent of change. Voting is the most obvious tool of engagement, but its infrequency and the choices it enables are limited.

Town hall meetings — despite being neither restricted to towns nor necessarily held in town halls —are a favorite of cities the world over. They are an essential part of how cities function and how individuals can participate in their city's operations.

Typically held in person, a town hall meeting has these main functions:

>> Providing a meeting place for elected officials and community

>> Acting as a forum for community members to raise and discuss issues

>> Serving as a space where legislation, regulations, projects, and budgets are discussed, considered, and acted on

>> Offering a place to share information of relevance to elected officials and community

REMEMBER

Though town hall meetings are still mostly held at physical locations, increasingly it's possible to attend remotely. Meetings are often available to watch on a television channel and streamed over the Internet. More sophisticated cities enable remote participants to talk or interact electronically with the meeting.

Historically, voting, town hall meetings, and committees have been the dominant mechanisms of community engagement. But times have changed and in the digital age a much broader set of channels and forums is available.

Here are a few new ways that technology is supporting increased community engagement:

>> Social media channels (see Chapter 8)

>> Online discussion platforms (see Chapter 8)

>> Civic apps

>> Open data portals (see Chapter 9)

>> Events such as a hackathon or urban challenge (see Chapter 7)

>> Texting

>> Survey and polling tools

Though traditional analog forum methods are able to capture the participation of those who are prepared to show up in person (a diminishing number), they provide a narrow option for broader engagement. Digital tools, though not typically *synchronous* — they don't necessary support decision-making in progress — have the ability to cast a much larger net. In addition to convenience, these tools have become a 21st century expectation of city democracy. That expectation must be met by city leaders who embrace these channels, provide support for them, ensure that posted content is shared with the right people, and educate the community on options and use.

REMEMBER

To be considered an inclusive city, all residents need to have a channel open to them.

Expanded community engagement is a good news story. More voices mean a stronger, more informed, more engaged, and more vibrant democracy. A smart city demands increasing community engagement.

Engaging in participatory design

An increasingly popular form of community engagement is the process of *participatory design,* an approach to urban design that involves engaging a broad range of stakeholders in the design process, including members of the community. Its goal is to ensure that the results of a design effort reflect participant needs and preferences. Popular applications include public art projects, new housing, bridges, park improvements, public spaces, and even smart city initiatives.

At the outset of an effort, stakeholders are invited to work with the core project team of experts. Together, everyone helps to define the problem to be solved, explores solutions, and then assists with making the decisions about what direction to take. Evidence indicates that engaging many perspectives in the design process results in more innovative outcomes than when a designer creates alone. Participatory design also empowers residents and increases democratization.

A related concept, *participatory budgeting,* invites members of the community to a democratic process of deciding how to spend part of a public budget.

Transforming Urbanization

Urbanization appears to behave like a biological system. It's born and then it consumes, produces waste, grows, keeps growing, shrinks (possibly), and (sometimes) dies.

Cities seldom remain the same, continually evolving and being shaped by people and the environment. They are impacted by a broad set of internal and external forces, including economic conditions, cultural aspects, or the arrival of a new innovation, like the gas-powered automobile or an invading army.

Urban centers can look different from one decade to the next. Over time, they can grow outward, upward, downward, and even inward.

Cities reflect the trends of the time. This concept is best illustrated via the architectural choices each person can observe as they traverse the urban landscapes. Buildings are pulled down, and new shapes and designs emerge from the rubble. New materials are used that change the light and color in a neighborhood. Taller projects create shadows that didn't exist before.

Urban worlds create joy, and they create sadness. They can be both nightmares and makers of dreams. To help understand who humans are, you only have to go outside and look around.

To understand the future of cities means that you need to accept that they're constantly evolving and being transformed. If humans are to prosper in that transformation, they need to understand some of the biggest influences that are changing the urban landscape in the next few years. In this section, I explore some of these forces of change.

Transportation

Moving people and goods in, out, and around a city is a vital and complicated function. It's an area that has seen dramatic change over the past 100 years, and it continues to evolve. In fact, the next 50 years may see more change in this area than at any time in history, and it will dramatically shape the planning and design of cities.

In addition to new innovation opening up new possibilities for transportation options, new community demands and behaviors are shaping this future as well. For example, early data evidence shows a declining interest in car ownership and increasing demand for more non-carbon-based and accessible public transportation options. This serves the public, but also the local government. City leaders are particularly keen on less car usage as it solves a number of large challenges, from meeting climate change goals to reducing congestion. For example, in a game-changing decision made back in March 2020, Luxembourg made all public transport — trains, trams, and buses — free.

Recognizing that our transportation networks are a horrific source of fatal accidents and injuries is motivating smart city programs to set ambitious safety goals. For example, one particular program, Vision Zero, is a strategy to eliminate all traffic fatalities and severe injuries. You can learn more about it at https://visionzeronetwork.org/.

The world is entering an urban transportation revolution. Drivers of change (see what I did there?) for this revolution include the elements described in this list:

>> **Vehicle electrification:** Many countries have already set deadlines for when the last gasoline-powered vehicle will be sold. Norway, ahead of the pack where 52 percent of new car sales were electric in 2017, has set the ambitious goal of 2025. Other examples include India and China, sometime around the 2030s, and France, which is targeting 2040. Better battery technology is extending trips and making electric vehicles more attractive to more people. The transition to electric vehicles and the end of the gasoline-powered engine seems possible, but despite human ambition, it doesn't seem like it will be quick or easy. Producing electric vehicles means significant investment in new infrastructure for charging stations, although the promise of fully solar-powered vehicles seems possible at some point. (Check out https://lightyear.one for more info on solar-powered cars.)

>> **Autonomous vehicles:** Perhaps the most game-changing of all transportation shifts will be the transition to cars that drive themselves. In this future world, humans truly can change some of the fundamentals of city design. As examples, will people still need traditional grid systems, traffic signals, lanes, and parking spaces? In addition, in the best-case scenario, autonomous

vehicles (AV) could significantly reduce accidents, eliminate car ownership, and radically lessen congestion. (It's a big topic, and I discuss it in more detail in Chapter 8.)

>> **On-demand transport:** Requesting a ride via an app, sometimes called *e-hailing,* and part of the *sharing or gig economy,* has become popular across the world. Some cities have embraced it while others have struggled, particularly with managing the concerns of incumbent services. Though providing a popular service, e-hailing has put more cars on the road, and it still remains expensive relative to other options. The likely arrival of autonomous on-demand vehicles in the medium term may change the economics and accelerate the decline of car ownership.

>> **Increased use of bicycles:** Perhaps no city better exemplifies the embrace of bicycles as a popular form of urban transportation than Amsterdam. This city has more bikes than people, and cycling is used in around 30 percent of all journeys. Its popularity is a mix of the investment made in cycling infrastructure, convenience, low cost, positive environmental impact, and flat terrain. Cycling is gaining popularity in cities across the world. Upgrades are required in order to support large numbers of users, including bike lanes and storage facilities.

REMEMBER

The safety of cyclists and all road users must be a priority in any city cycling strategy.

>> **New forms of personal transport, including e-bikes and scooters:** A new generation of city dwellers is seeking the convenience and low cost of innovative personal transportation options called *micromobility.* With prolific smartphone use and cloud-based payment systems, users can easily find and pay for bikes, scooters, e-bikes, electric mopeds, per-hour rental cars, and other transporters. The long-term sustainability of the business model for many of these options is still to be determined. Cities also need to determine their comfort level and the rules for placement of the vehicles across the city.

>> **Light rail systems:** These systems were popular from the late 1880s through the 1900s. In many cities they continued to thrive, but in others their demise was the result of the introduction of the automobile. Entire rail systems were shut down and paved over. However, the benefits of their low-carbon footprint, lower costs, and the demand in recent years for more public transport has resulted in a light rail system renaissance. (See Figure 3-5.) The initial costs are high, but the long-term operating costs are relatively low. Installing a new system may require significant city disruption and street redesign.

>> **Ground- and air-based delivery drones:** In Redwood City, California, a small, autonomous, ground-based drone that looks a little like R2-D2 from *Star Wars* delivers a meal to a home in a neighborhood. In Africa, an experimental

air-based drone delivers essential medical supplies to a remote location. Transportation and delivery drones aren't yet part of the urban landscape, but they appear to be coming. From rapid delivery times to lower-cost operations for the package delivery companies, the benefits seem clear. Passenger drones, too, could be on their way. (I discuss flying cars in Chapter 11). In a few years from now, the skies and streets of cities may be replete with a myriad of drones. Safety and noise issues are just two of the many issues to be worked out. (I discuss drones in greater detail in Chapter 8.)

FIGURE 3-5:
Light rail offers a convenient, low-carbon, public transport option in cities.

» **Transportation innovations, such as Mobility as a Service (MaaS) and Hyperloop:** The pressing issues of urban transportation are creating an intense focus on innovation. Barely a month passes without a new idea making the news. Mayors and other city leaders desperately want new solutions, and they are willing to invest. Mobility as a Service (MaaS) and Hyperloop best illustrate the diversity of emergent ideas. The MaaS Alliance (https://maas-alliance.eu) describes MaaS as the integration of various forms of transport services into a single mobility service that is accessible on demand. It facilitates a diverse menu of transport options, whether they're public transport; ride-, car- or bike-sharing; taxi or car rental/lease; or a combination thereof. Data produced by MaaS solutions can help cities and transportation agencies look for opportunities to optimize the interconnectedness of different transport modalities. MaaS is being used in a few cities — Berlin's Jelbi service is just one example — but the solution remains in its infancy with many considerations yet to be determined, such as governance, regulations, and the viable economics of the vendor ecosystem.

Hyperloop, still in the concept stage but gaining traction, is a passenger vehicle that moves through a tube (underground and aboveground) via electric propulsion. The vehicle floats above the track using magnetic levitation and moves at airline speed for long distances. The infrastructure additions and changes needed to support Hyperloop and similar transport innovations are significant. (For more on Hyperloop, see Chapter 11.)

Energy

Beginning with the first industrial revolution, the introduction of mechanically produced energy began a global transformation that continues to this day. The introduction of electricity in the second industrial revolution further accelerated societal progress, ushering in mass production, telecommunications, and rapid urbanization. Electricity transformed cities by lighting up the streets, office buildings, sports arenas, and homes at night, powering the telephone and television and keeping food fresh in refrigerators and ice cream frozen in freezers.

Complex electrical grids and their attendant poles and wires began to paint a new urban tapestry from street to street, and industry hummed and innovated through its seemingly magical powers. In the mid-20th century, a third industrial revolution ushered in the computer, a device born out of the science of electricity.

Electrical energy now powers the world economic system. Of all of humankind's achievements, leveraging this electricity stands among the greatest.

Surprisingly, the project to electrify the world, which began in the 1800s, isn't yet complete — some 1 billion people still have no access. (A billion!) Cities have been the biggest benefactor, so the remaining areas are almost all rural.

REMEMBER

Cities continue to have an unquenchable thirst for power. Today, they consume over two-thirds of all the world's energy. Megacities, in particular, are continuing to demand more as they prosper and grow.

Where does city power come from? Here are the ten main sources:

>> **Fossil fuels:** Created by burning coal, natural gas, and oil

>> **Nuclear:** The result of a nuclear reaction that creates heat

>> **Solar:** Harvesting the energy of the sun

>> **Wind:** Using the wind to turn large turbines

>> **Biomass:** Involves burning crops, plants, and trees

>> **Hydroelectric:** Typically uses water passing through a dam to turn turbines

>> **Waves:** Produced by the motion of waves in the ocean

>> **Tidal:** Utilizes the rise and fall of the daily tides

>> **Hydrogen:** An abundant element that can be used to produce energy

>> **Geothermal:** Tapping into the heat deep beneath the ground

The mix of sources that each city uses is varied. For much of their history, cities have used fossil fuels. However, in the past few years, there has been a notable shift toward the renewables in this list. Already, over 100 major cities worldwide obtain 70 percent of their energy from non-carbon sources — hydroelectric being the most common, followed by wind and solar. Though renewable energy innovation over the last 10 years has made it increasingly viable, a mix of sources, including fossil fuel, is still required to power most of our cities. Rapid progress in research and development suggests a fully renewable future may be closer than we think. There's an urgency to transition as much energy to renewables as possible because the damage from burning fossil fuels has already caused the world's temperature to rise, on average, by more than 1 degree in the past 100 years, and this has created a climate crisis. One degree may not sound like much, but it may take only a 1- or 2-degree additional change to destabilize the living ecosystem on the planet.

REMEMBER

The race is on to change the energy sources of cities. An energy revolution is under way. From solar rooftops, wind turbines, microgrids, and smart grids (see Chapter 8) to homes and buildings relying less on the electrical grid, urban landscapes are evolving in response to everyone's changing energy profiles.

Buildings

Buildings often define the skyline and brand of a city. Some are so iconic that their silhouette alone is enough to identify the city. The Empire State Building in New York City, Burj Khalifa in Dubai, Petronas Towers in Kuala Lumpur, and the CN Tower in Toronto are just some that come to mind.

Skyscrapers have come to represent the dense, urban centers of many modern cities. Today, mixed-use towering buildings combine offices with housing and shopping areas. They are the pride of many communities and are often a symbol of economic success.

Tall buildings are the result of one important innovation: the elevator and its safety brake. Before the availability of an elevator that could reliably travel many floors and protect its occupants in the event that the cable snapped, buildings could be built up to only a few stories. This single building innovation changed the urban landscape across the planet.

Building innovation continues to shape cities.

City buildings have an impact on the health and well-being of communities. These buildings use resources and produce waste and are expensive to maintain and operate. Buildings consume 70 percent of the electricity within cities and produce 30 percent of greenhouse gas emissions. Better energy management can help stabilize and reduce their carbon footprints.

Architects and city planners are now increasingly focused on what are known as *green buildings*, which are built to improve the health of occupants and to lower operating costs and reduce their negative environmental impact. Given the positive urban outcomes of constructing or retrofitting buildings to be environmentally responsible, green buildings can be considered a substantial sustainability baseline and an important incremental step toward a smarter city.

One global standard to drive the adoption of green buildings is LEED — Leadership in Energy and Environment Design. This globally recognized certification for building sustainability achievement focuses on nine areas of green buildings:

>> Integrative processes

>> Location and transportation

>> Sustainable sites

>> Water efficiency

>> Energy and atmosphere

>> Materials and resources

>> Indoor environmental quality

>> Regional priority

>> Innovation

More information on LEED can be found at www.usgbc.org/leed.

Buildings, much like the areas of transportation, energy, sustainability, and other dimensions of the urban environment, must be considered as part of an interconnected and interdependent infrastructure. Smart planning and design of these dependent components is essential for the greatest positive impact. For example, a green building should offer charging stations to support and incentivize occupants who park their electric cars there. Waste management behaviors and systems must work together across city functions to enable the highest level of recycling and lower levels of resource consumption. Transportation networks must be designed to seamlessly connect people to their work and home areas in a sustainable manner.

Telecommunications

The first telephone call was placed by its inventor, Alexander Graham Bell, on March 10, 1876, to his assistant, Thomas Watson. With his first words, "Mr. Watson, come here, I want to see you," the world was changed forever.

Imagine the world before the telegraph and telephone. The only way to get a message to someone was to have it brought to them by a person. Depending on the distance, this could take days or weeks. Sure, carrier pigeons were an option, but as you can imagine, they weren't commonly available. There was no quick way to communicate between parties in battles or long journeys or between towns and cities or to tell a date that you'd be late. A world where it was impossible to quickly contact and communicate with someone was quite a different world, indeed.

Fast-forward to today, where most people are overwhelmed by ways to communicate. The popularity of mobile phones (4.7 billion users in 2020) means that every human who has one is technically contactable, assuming it's within reach and powered on. Even then, you can leave a message to be accessed later.

Innovation has squeezed the cost of calls and data communications to make it low-cost or, in some instances, effectively free. Today, everyone and everything is being quickly connected in the pursuit of a hyperconnected planet.

Telecommunications are typically a visible part of the urban infrastructure. The wires that carry calls and data hang between poles and buildings — often, in an unsightly fashion. (See Figure 3-6.) The towers that send and receive wireless data are dotted all over the landscape. Even more is hidden in subterranean cavities and tunnels.

In the past few years, the high rate of adoption of wireless devices has increased the number of towers and other supporting technology being deployed. With the number of additional wireless devices, including sensors and the Internet of Things (see Chapter 8), anticipated to skyrocket in the years ahead, and with the deployment of new wireless technologies such as 5G (again, see Chapter 8), telecommunications infrastructure will further shape the urban canvas.

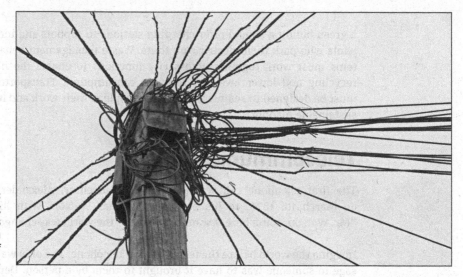

FIGURE 3-6:
Messy-looking telephone poles have become a visible part of almost every city.

TIP

A smarter city with intelligent physical and digital infrastructure requires a reliable and sophisticated telecommunications network of providers and options. Significant investment will be required by cities and the vendor community in cities all over the planet. (For more on digital infrastructures, see Chapter 2).

Sustainability

By midcentury, 70 percent of all humans will live in an urban environment. If trends continue, the percentage will be even greater by the end of the century.

I've said it before, but it's worth repeating: The future belongs to cities.

Human behavior in these urban environments is determining their present and their future. It is also determining the fate of all life on the pale blue dot.

REMEMBER

Sustainability is about meeting the needs of the present while preserving the ability of future generations to meet their needs.

Humans have hopelessly failed in the goal of achieving sustainability ever since the onset of the first industrial revolution. For much of the past 200 years, it was barely a consideration. Instead, humans have recklessly overconsumed and hurt the planet, leaving the forests, oceans, air, water, food supply, climate, and more all in damaged and diminished states. Today, for example, 70 percent of all carbon emissions are the operating exhaust of cities.

Recovery is possible but not guaranteed. People have been living better by permanently borrowing from the future, living as though they have multiple copies of Planet Earth's beautiful and limited resources. Today, despite humans' progress and prosperity, they have created what appears to be an intractable set of sustainability challenges. If humans are going to solve them at all, most of the work will have to take place within cities.

Sustainability is typically characterized by these three pillars:

>> Economic sustainability

>> Social sustainability

>> Environmental sustainability

Making cities sustainable will require long-term structural changes to economic models, social systems, and daily behaviors. These changes will be required in order to reduce environmental damage and excessive resource consumption.

REMEMBER

Cities have broken the planet, and cities are the only hope to fix the planet.

2

Building a Smarter City

IN THIS PART . . .

Create a smart city vision and team.

Understand the steps needed to create a smart city strategy.

Explore essential areas to enable the execution of your strategy.

Chapter 4

Starting from Zero

It may appear that the smart city movement is well under way and that thousands of cities around the world are in the process of getting "smarter." The reality is that cities are at the beginning of the transition that many of them will eventually undergo to utilize new technologies, data, and reengineered processes to improve the quality of life for their constituents. Most communities that make the decision to embark on the smart city journey are starting from zero. At that point, the pressing question for any city leader is, "How do we start?"

This chapter suggests that the right starting point (assuming that the motivation is there and there's agreement on pursuing a smart city strategy by city leaders and members of the community) is to establish a vision for the effort ahead. The vision should be created by participants who are empowered to move forward and make the magic of smarter communities happen. I propose here the types of leaders and teams who should be put in place to increase the likelihood of success. All these steps set the stage for creating a successful smart city strategy.

Establishing a Vision

So you, your colleagues, and members of the community have decided that increasing the quality of life and solving complex challenges by using technology — coupled with data, new processes, and a progressive disposition toward innovation — is the right path for your city. You want to take a smarter city approach going forward.

Well done!

No, seriously. The decision to act on something, to take a particular path relative to the action itself, can be the hardest part. It's always possible to become entrenched in debate, to fail to find common ground, or to reach an impasse. But once some form of agreement is reached, even if just marginally directional, you should celebrate.

REMEMBER

Anyone who has worked on a project of some significance knows the difference between the big decisions and the many small decisions that happen. Without those big decisions, the project team might struggle. But it's a great relief when direction is given. The project team can then move ahead with their work.

One of the most important big decisions that has to be made at the beginning of a smart city effort is the establishment of a vision or vision statement. This vision is a top-level guide for almost all decisions to come.

TIP

Singularity University has a term for efforts with a bold vision that motivates meaningful change. It's called *massive transformative purpose* (MTP). An MTP is aspirational and focused on creating a different future. Realizing an MTP requires a mindset and work environment that leans into complex problems and strives to think big. MTP needs talented and dedicated teams working smartly with a huge amount of motivation. They have successes and sometimes failures. Creating a smart city may not be the equivalent of finding cures for all types of cancer, but the outcomes of smart city efforts are significant and can impact a lot of people. I suggest you consider your vision exercise as your MTP.

WARNING

The smart city movement remains largely in its infancy. The vast majority of cities in the world have yet to embark on this journey (assuming that it's the right direction for many of them). They are starting from zero. As with any initiative, it's easy to jump directly into the tactics after receiving direction to pursue smart city goals. But I think that would be a mistake. The first step on any smart city journey needs to be the establishment of an agreed-on vision. That vision guides strategy, and strategy directs the work.

I help you explore this topic in the next couple of sections.

Identifying the role of city leadership

Leadership and management are terms that are often used interchangeably. That's a mistake. Although there are some underlying similarities, they are different. Each requires and utilizes a specific approach and mindset.

Management is doing things right.

Leadership is doing the right things.

It's an essential distinction attributed to the management guru Peter Drucker. It's one of the reasons that management can be learned, but leadership has qualities that some fortunate people possess from birth and can't be easily acquired by training — such as charisma.

Sure, many aspects of leadership can be learned, but it's obvious that remarkable leaders don't necessarily acquire their skills from books. It's a little frustrating for those trying to be great leaders when they realize that they can learn and practice most skills but will always have a deficit relative to those unique leadership qualities that require something special.

That said, the body of knowledge today on leadership is enough to help most leaders acquire the essential skills. Any given leadership team will have some with learned skills and some with natural abilities. That's the case on city leadership teams, too.

Smart city work suffers without great leadership. After all, research from across all industries suggests that projects generally succeed or fail depending on the availability of consistent high quality leadership support.

Who are these city leadership teams, and what might their responsibilities be relative to smart city work? To answer these questions, I've divided city leadership into these four basic parts:

>> **Elected leaders:** Assuming some form of democratic process, these leaders, which can include the popular role of mayor, are chosen by the city's constituents via voting and serve for a predetermined period. This is by far the most common process. In some jurisdictions around the world, city leaders are appointed by other bodies. In either case, these leaders typically have the primary function of setting policy, approving budgets, and passing legislation. They may originate an issue to debate, or an issue may be brought to them by any number of stakeholders, from community members to city staff. For example, if city staff proposes the smart city effort, elected officials are responsible for suggesting modifications, requesting more information, and approving or declining the request. Elected leaders absolutely must sign off on the smart city effort — particularly the vision, goals, and, ultimately, budget. A healthy public debate by elected leaders on the merits of the smart city work is valuable, as is eliciting public comment.

>> **Appointed leaders:** Running a city on a day-to-day basis requires a set of hired leaders. The city inevitably has some form of overall leader — the public agency equivalent of a chief executive officer (CEO), such as a city manager or

city administrator. This leader has assistants, deputies, and an executive team that manage the various areas of the city. These areas may include transportation, public works, planning, energy, libraries, healthcare, technology, and many more. Big cities have a large number of managed areas. The city leader and the team have the primary responsibility to implement and maintain policies. They make daily decisions and ensure that the city is operational and responsive to community needs. These leaders also propose initiatives to elected officials. A smart city effort may originate this way. It's also possible, for example, that a strong mayor will ask for staff to develop a smart city plan and propose it to the elected leaders for approval. Appointed leaders are accountable to elected leaders and, by extension, to the community.

» **Leadership support and oversight:** In this category, a small leadership team is tasked with originating a draft policy, recommendations, or other decision-making instruments on behalf of either the elected or appointed leaders. These teams, which have a guiding function, aren't decision-making bodies. However, they are essential contributors toward city leadership. These teams can be permanent or temporary, depending on their function. For example, the elected leaders may opt to create a committee to oversee and make recommendations and provide reporting oversight on the efforts of a smart city initiative. The team may exist only as long as the smart city initiative continues. Alternatively, a city may have a permanent transportation committee whose role is to make recommendations on matters related to transportation. Because this area is often included in smart city work, it may be the body that's approached for leadership input. These teams are typically made up of suitably qualified members of the community.

» **Regulatory leadership:** This category is a broad one, in order to capture a range of other leaders who may have input in a city's decision-making process. The most obvious groups include those who make regulations at a regional or national level. For example, a national set of rules on how drones can be deployed in cities may be made by a leadership group outside of a particular city, but that city would be required to adhere to the rules. This can make sense so that all cities in a region or country follow the same set of rules.

REMEMBER

People often debate how much power a city should have over its operations relative to the power of those at the regional or national level. Cities clearly want as much autonomy as possible, but the benefits of standards at a national and even global level have important merit as well. An example of an area where a city can benefit from national decision-making in the smart city domain is telecommunications. A national commitment to supporting infrastructure standards, and also financial assistance, benefits everyone. An example of global leadership is managing the climate crisis. Even though cities and nations have to sign on, the leadership and guidance may come from a global entity.

Creating a vision

Your city has decided to embark on a smart city journey. Great! Now it's time to create a vision or vision statement. What is a vision, and how is it created?

REMEMBER

I use *vision* and *vision statement* interchangeably in this section. There's little difference between them, other than the number of words. A vision generally takes a few paragraphs to describe. A vision statement is typically only a few words long. The intent is identical.

A *vision* is a statement of what you desire the future to be. It's not tactics or operations. It's not projects or deliverables. It's simply a statement that guides the development of a strategic plan — called the *envisioning* process — and the decisions made throughout the journey.

I discuss how to create a smart city strategy in Chapter 5, but to help you better understand the role of a vision in the strategic plan, let's take a quick look at how I define strategic planning:

> *Strategic planning* is the systematic process of envisioning a desired future and translating this vision into broadly defined goals or objectives and a sequence of steps to achieve them.

Put another way, the *strategic plan* is the translation of a strategic vision into outcomes.

REMEMBER

A vision written correctly and agreed on by relevant stakeholders holds the initiative accountable and provides essential guidance in times of uncertainty. Though it's easy to overlook or omit this step, its value can't be overstated. Do it. You'll be happy you did.

A vision isn't the same as a mission. An organization's *mission* is what it does and how it does it, and it includes its shorter-term objectives. Your vision is none of those things. It's long-term and future-oriented, and it describes a big-picture future state. It has clarity and passion.

Here are ten tips for creating an outstanding vision statement:

>> Think long-term.

>> Brainstorm what a big future outcome would look like. Choose the one that gains consensus.

>> Use simple words. Don't use jargon.

>> Make the statement inspiring.

» Ensure that the entire vision statement is easy to understand.

» Eliminate ambiguity. Anyone should be able to have a common understanding of what's actually involved.

» Consider making the statement time-bound. For example, use language such as "By 2030 . . ."

» Allude to organizational values and culture.

» Make the statement sufficiently challenging that it conveys a sense of ambition and boldness.

» Involve many stakeholders.

Here are some brief vision statement examples:

Ben & Jerry's: "Making the best ice cream in the nicest possible way."

Habitat for Humanity: "A world where everyone has a decent place to live."

Caterpillar: "Our vision is a world in which all people's basic needs — such as shelter, clean water, sanitation, food and reliable power — are fulfilled in an environmentally sustainable way, and a company that improves the quality of the environment and the communities where we live and work."

Hilton Hotels & Resorts: "To fill the earth with the light and warmth of hospitality."

Samsung: "Inspire the world, create the future."

Smart Dubai: "To be the happiest city on earth."

TIP

Though vision statements are typically short, no rule prohibits a more elaborate vision, as long as it adheres to many of the tips I offer earlier in this section. As an example, here are the five goals of the San Jose, California, smart city vision:

» **Safe city:** Leverage technology to make San José the safest big city in America.

» **Inclusive city:** Ensure that all residents, businesses, and organizations can participate in and benefit from the prosperity and culture of innovation in Silicon Valley.

» **User-friendly city:** Create digital platforms to improve transparency, empower residents to actively engage in the governance of their city, and make the city more responsive to the complex and growing demands of the community.

» **Sustainable city:** Use technology to address energy, water, and climate challenges to enable sustainable growth.

» **Demonstration city:** Reimagine the city as a laboratory and platform for the most impactful, transformative technologies that will shape how people live and work in the future.

More details of San Jose's smart city work can be found here:

```
https://moti.sanjosemayor.org/smart-city-vision
```

Building a Smart City Team

To succeed in moving forward with a commitment to design and to build a smarter city requires the assembly of one or more smart city teams. In fact, it's probably the first step for the executive tasked with sponsoring the effort, a person appropriately called the *executive sponsor*. This person is ultimately accountable for the outcomes of the strategy. The role is usually appointed to an existing senior leader in the organization. Above all, this person must have the authority to approve or decline significant strategic recommendations. It wouldn't be unusual for the city manager or city administrator to be the executive sponsor.

REMEMBER

Choose your team carefully. Your team, or a subset of a team, should participate in the creation of the vision; that means this team needs to be in place from the outset so that they have input into all phases of the work. This strategy helps with commitment and buy-in. You're only as good, and as successful, as the teams you put in place.

Building one or more teams requires a set of answers to some important questions, which might include these:

>> What type of governance should be considered? (For more on governance types, see Chapter 6.)

>> What skills will be required?

>> Is this a full-time or part-time commitment for team members?

>> Will existing staff be used, or will people be hired?

>> Will the team be made up of only city staff, or will other stakeholders be engaged?

Identifying team members

Let me tell you right off the bat: The teams I refer to in this section are those with responsibility for the design and build of smart city initiatives. In this section, I don't consider the talent you need in order to maintain the work after it's deployed. Operations, support, and maintenance of completed solutions should be determined in the project scoping phase of each smart city solution.

REMEMBER

Don't let the unknowns of scope derail the first pass at identifying the teams. Regardless of the city and scope, I would pull a few key players — as suggested in the tiers described in the following list — into the first round of appointments. Assuming a medium-size governance structure, you may have three tiers, with a senior executive sponsor having overall accountability and oversight:

>> **Strategy/steering committee:** This team has overall responsibility for the success of the initiative. It's at the executive level, and it includes only those with significant decision-making authority, including, most importantly, all funding decisions. A director-level job classification is typically appropriate. These teams are sometimes referred to as a steering committee because, well, they *steer* the work.

The types of candidates in this group might include

- City managers or their appointees
- Elected leadership representatives
- Qualified members of the community
- Executives from a management consulting organization
- City department leaders from these areas:

  Technology

  Public works

  Transportation

  Information security

  Communications

  Telecommunications

  Finance

  Legal

  Planning

This may be a good opportunity to include senior executives from the community who have appropriate experience. The strategy team can determine the smart city vision or wait to include the operations team as well. This choice is one that the team can make. After the scope has been determined, this group will likely add members.

TIP

Meeting frequency is determined on a case-by-case basis, but I recommend no less than once every three months. As a bonus, this steering committee forces disparate departments to work together. Though cross-department work does happen between a handful of teams, it's seldom frequent, and it doesn't happen that often between a large number of departments.

>> **Operations/program management:** This team concerns itself with the day-to-day running of the smart city initiative. They are hands-on, they have an appropriate level of decision-making authority, and they are experts in their respective areas. Members develop work plans, assign responsibilities, monitor and review progress, provide regular and timely guidance, and solve operational challenges.

A smart city initiative made up of many projects may be called a *program*. In this case, the operations team can be said to be responsible for program management. The candidates for this group are appointed by, and then accountable to, the strategy team. Eliciting nominations can be a great way to get more participation from across the organization. Members of this team are typically made up of only city staff. This team should include members of city staff who are passionate about the topic of smart cities — you'll find these people in every organization. Tap into their passion.

TIP

Determine the meeting frequency for the operations/program management team on a case-by-case basis. I suggest no less than once every month.

>> **Project management office (PMO):** Each solution that's designed and built in the smart city initiative is likely to have a project team. This is the least mysterious part of team governance because project teams exist as a product of most organizational efforts. After all, that's how complex work with a defined beginning, middle, and end typically gets developed and deployed. Project teams can be made up of city staff only or city staff and vendors. Sometimes, a vendor does all day-to-day work under the guidance of a single city project manager. Project teams are accountable to the operations team.

Depending on the scale of activities involved, you can consider establishing a project management office (PMO) specifically for the smart city work.

Here are the typical core functions of a PMO:

- Prioritizing projects based on strategy and resources
- Managing resource capacity and skills
- Enforcing project standards, methods, and processes
- Producing project and program reports
- Monitoring progress, resources, budgets, and schedules
- Providing administrative and operational support

>> **Working group:** This team, which is typically temporary, is tasked with a specific set of goals. Experts in a particular area, they have a defined period in which to research, develop insights, and report back on a given assignment. Given the scale and complexity of smart city efforts, working groups (plural because you typically see several in the life of a program) are highly valuable teams that can bring important knowledge and recommendations to the

steering committee and operations team. Here are some types of work a working group typically performs:

- *Developing a recommendations document*

- *Creating a standard, such as a naming convention, or technology implementation*

- *Resolving complex problems that need independence from other teams*

- *Suggesting improvements*

- *Identifying possible issues now and in the future*

- *Conducting research*

To help you conceptualize the reporting relationships of the tiers, I've created a visual of a high-level organizational structure in Figure 4-1.

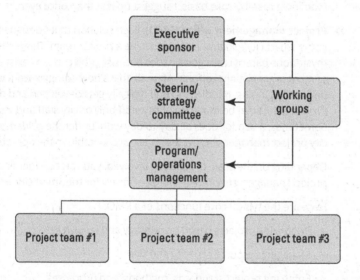

FIGURE 4-1:
Basic smart city team organizational structure.

Consider having a backup staff member for each primary designee on each team. The backup person attends meetings whenever the primary person cannot.

TIP

Creating a RACI chart

Without a doubt, developing and implementing a smart city strategy is large, complex, and messy work. There are going to be a lot of teams, participants, and responsibilities. Despite your best efforts, some team members are going to get confused about what their roles are in each step of the work. What you'll want is a tool that everyone can use to quickly achieve clarity on roles and responsibilities. What you need to create is a RACI chart.

A RACI chart is a simple matrix used to assign roles and responsibilities for each task, milestone, or decision on a project. RACI stands for Responsible, Accountable, Consulted, and Informed. By documenting which roles and responsibilities are involved in each task, you can eliminate confusion. RACI charts answer the frequent project question: Who's doing what?

With a RACI chart, expectations can be set for everyone on the team. It should also help to avoid multiple people working on the same task or in conflict with each other because responsibilities weren't clearly defined or understood at the beginning of the work.

The four role responsibilities are described here:

>> **Responsible (R):** Performs the work to complete the task

>> **Accountable (A):** Determines if the work has been completed satisfactorily

>> **Consulted (C):** Provides input through expertise and experience

>> **Informed (I):** Kept in the loop on progress with the task

A RACI chart doesn't require any fancy software, although plenty exists. I use a basic spreadsheet. See Figure 4-2 for a simple example.

FIGURE 4-2:
A simple
RACI chart.

Tasks	Project Manager	Business Analyst	Developer	Tester
Gather requirements	A, C, I	R	I	I
Write code	A, I	I	R	I
Test code	A, I, C	C	C, I	R

Getting the team on the same page

I would bet that many people believe that a smart city strategy is another technology initiative. For this reason, city leaders and staff often assume that the smart city strategy will be managed and executed by the technology team. As I discuss in Chapter 2, in the sections that spell out what a smart city is and what it is not, it's not simply a technology-centric endeavor. Sure, technology plays a big role, but it should be considered an enabler, not the definition of the outcome.

REMEMBER

Designing and building a smarter city is, first and foremost, all about improving the quality of life for the community. This means it requires the input and actions of leaders from almost all city disciplines, which is reflected in the suggested types of leaders I describe in the steering committee overview, in the earlier section "Identifying team members."

When the executive sponsor kicks off that first meeting of the steering committee, it's essential to get the team on the same page. A common understanding of the nature of the initiative is important to establish from the outset.

Here are some suggested topics to discuss (possibly over more than one meeting):

>> What is the motivation for the smart city initiative?

>> Is there a notion of the scope of the endeavor at the highest level?

>> What might success look like along the way?

>> How will progress and outcomes be measured?

>> How will the effort be communicated, and to whom?

>> Who might be involved?

>> How much might the initiative cost? (This item is particularly complex. For example, it might be the job of the steering committee to provide estimates only after the scoping effort is completed. However, an estimated range is valuable in order to give the team a sense of the magnitude of the work ahead.)

Of course, many more topics can be discussed, which should be determined on a case-by-case basis dependent on your city.

Here are some additional techniques for getting new teams on the same page and having them remain there:

>> Using icebreaker exercises that are relevant to the topic.

>> Involving team members in as many aspects of planning as possible.

>> The creation of, and agreement on, initiative values (which should be displayed in meetings and included in meeting minutes and in any online platforms).

>> Sponsoring one or more education events that may help to level the knowledge playing field when it comes to the smart city domain. You'll never go wrong by offering training in business analysis, project management, communication skills, and facilitation techniques.

>> Communicating often and mixing communication methods between electronic and in-person modalities.

>> Prioritizing transparency.

>> Taking advantage of collaboration tools.

>> Centralizing information.

Chapter 5

Creating a Smart City Strategy

This chapter is all about getting down to brass tacks — more specifically, it focuses on how you go about creating a smart city. As with any major enterprise, your first step is to come up with a strategic plan, including the major steps and milestones needed to get you from where you are today to some future state. Given the time and investment that are required, spend some quality time upfront discussing and finding consensus with stakeholders on the broad details of the Why, What, How, and When. There's no doubt this process is tough and takes some time to complete, but it pays dividends as the work unfolds in the months and years ahead. When the work begins, keep everyone apprised of progress as well as the challenges that may arise. Engaging with stakeholders throughout the smart city journey helps to maintain support. There's plenty on the line here, but the effort is worth it, and the results may positively impact the lives of the people in your community, businesses and organizations, and those who visit your city.

Building the Plan

You've decided that a smart city initiative is right for your community. You now have a bold and ambitious vision. It's time to get started so that you can actually realize this vision. You must initiate a process of translation to move from your vision to a set of actions. For this, you need a plan.

Do not let the enthusiasm for progress and results curtail the essential and sometimes tedious upfront work of strategic planning.

This popular adage is a favorite of mine: Failing to plan is planning to fail. (I'd give credit, but the source is disputed.) You always increase the chances of success in an effort if you have a plan. (Having a Plan B is a good idea, too.) As smart as you and I are, we probably always have some sort of plan in place when we embark on a major work project. But is it a viable and flexible plan? Is it a plan that can actually absorb the pummeling a long-term effort will experience and still succeed in its goals? What I'm driving at here is that there's a big difference between having a plan and having a great plan.

What you need in order to get started is a process to define the strategy of how your smart city vision will be realized. You need a systematic process of envisioning and executing the steps to a desired future. Urban planning and development are typically deliberate and detailed activities. A smart city initiative is fundamentally an urban plan and therefore requires much of the same rigor.

You'll make complex decisions that include trade-offs and compromises, and you'll do all this with many other stakeholders. The art and science of strategic planning is a repetitive, inclusive, often exhaustive exercise, which is a characteristic of much of the work in the public sector. You really do produce better results when you include as many people (those who can add value) as possible in almost any process. People want to be involved, and they want to have a voice in decision-making. After all, decisions that are made that affect the nature of a city have the potential to impact *a lot* of people.

REMEMBER

Everyone is better served when input is derived from the broadest set of participants. I suspect that by the time you finish reading this book you'll think that I sound like a broken record on this point. That may well be true, but it's just such an important point that it's worth repeating again and again.

REMEMBER

A strategic plan is a living document. That is, it is never locked down. It must be open to revisiting and to making course corrections as circumstances dictate. The plan must also be an artifact that's referenced often, and progress must be measured against it.

The worst strategic plan is the one that's developed and agreed on and then never consulted. It's the one that sits on the shelf, gathering dust. It's pointless, and even soul-destroying.

A strategic plan must be shared widely. It becomes a communication tool that helps stakeholders know what's happening and when events will take place. The plan must be posted for easy access and made available in both electronic and physical forms. Your smart city initiative should have a dedicated website, or at least a dedicated section of your city's website. A large number of people — ranging from community members to city staff and from other cities to the vendor community and more — will be interested in what's coming their way.

REMEMBER

It's worth spending the time to create a well-developed strategic plan. From better outcomes to clear directions for all who are involved and impacted, the benefits are numerous. But let me be sober about this point: Creating a well-developed strategic plan is difficult, and the plan can be contentious. Be ready for the work ahead. Sure, it's hard, but it's well worth it. Perhaps I can suggest a new adage: Preparing a well-developed plan is planning to succeed.

Developing a strategic plan

Though business books might use different terminology, critiquing several of them reveals a consistent set of logical steps to move from an idea or need to a result. Whether it's creating an art piece, developing a project, or planning a strategy, the following four steps typically spell out what needs to happen (I call them the four D's):

1. Define.

2. Design.

3. Develop.

4. Deploy.

Some form of measurement should be baked in, too, to hold everyone accountable.

Using these basic four steps, I've created a version that can be applied to the process of developing a smart city. (See Figure 5-1.) Keep in mind that the work of urban planning and development is never done, so by extension, it's a little misleading to think in terms of completing a smart city. It's a topic of considerable debate. (Another, similar debate involves determining which city in the world is "the smartest." I don't think it's a fair question — each city is smart to the degree that it reflects the needs, culture, and aspirations of its citizens.)

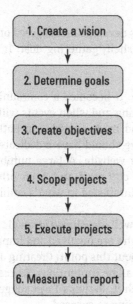

1. Create a vision

2. Determine goals

3. Create objectives

4. Scope projects

5. Execute projects

6. Measure and report

FIGURE 5-1:
The basic steps in creating and executing a smart city strategy.

Returning to the idea of the process of creating a smart city (assuming my assertion that, by definition, this process can never be completed), it should be clear by now that this may be an iterative process. Thought of another way, smart city efforts may have phases, and they may be redefined as time passes.

I'm dwelling on this topic because it directly relates to how you might think of scoping the smart city strategy exercise. Specifically, what are you including in the scope of the process to define, design, develop, and deploy?

The answer is that you and your teams must decide what to include.

Having a vision that may take a decade or more to accomplish is reasonable, but, realistically speaking, it's likely a series of shorter actionable and consecutive strategic plans rather than a single big plan. I therefore suggest that you focus on the activities that are doable, relative to the larger vision, with the understanding that you're dealing with a shorter time horizon.

Take another look at Figure 5-1. Strategic planning involves Steps 1–4. The first step is to create your smart city vision. (I cover this topic in detail in Chapter 4.) The next step is to define your *goals* —the desired results of the vision broken into specific, measurable areas. Moving from vision to goals, which is an exercise that is fun and critical, requires what is called the envisioning process. For more on that process, check out the next section.

Envisioning the envisioning process

At its core, *envisioning* is an interactive process for engaging stakeholders in imagining a desired future and identifying the activities in support of realizing it. It can be thought of as a more rigorous brainstorming process. Envisioning takes many forms: It's performed at the beginning of an initiative but can also be used at various other times during the course of an initiative if it's deemed valuable.

Done well, envisioning can bring with it many of the following advantages. It

>> Gets everyone on the same page

>> Identifies creative ideas

>> Builds cohesiveness in a group

>> Enables all voices to be heard

>> Supports achieving consensus

>> Reduces the risk of pursuing ideas that may not be practical

BE SMART

Before you review the steps for creating your goals and objectives, remember this old trick in defining each of them — make the steps SMART:

- **Specific:** Avoid generalizations, focus on the result, and phrase your goals and objectives so that everyone can have a common understanding of them.

- **Measurable:** The result should be assessable by the use of a meaningful qualitative or quantitative metric.

- **Achievable:** You must be able to achieve your goals using attainable resources, an existing budget, and a desired time frame.

- **Realistic:** This one is simple. Can your goals actually be achieved? (Sometimes, the *r* stands for relevant. In that case, ensure that the goal or objective is aligned with the vision.)

- **Timebound:** Ensure that you've defined a delivery time frame. Avoid anything without a reasonable deadline. (The original source for the SMART approach apparently dates back to a paper written in 1981 by George T. Doran.)

To help guide you through the envisioning process that forms the basis of your strategic plan and goals, follow these steps:

1. **Define the scope of your smart city vision.**

   Using the smart city vision that has been already determined, identify and debate (using the tools of your choice) the major city areas within the scope. Though it's tempting to use only existing challenges to lead the process, I suggest turning those challenges into what you want the city to become. For example, instead of saying "Fix transportation congestion," perhaps consider saying "Implement innovative and efficient transportation options that provide more options and shorter trips." The details of how you go about achieving these in-scope items come next.

2. **Create a short list of goals.**

   Step 1 will likely result in a large number of scope areas. Be sure to validate them carefully against the agreed-on smart city vision. A scope item not aligned with that vision might need to be tabled, or it might mean that the vision needs expanding.

   Next, group together common scoping areas and consider new language to cover the range of these areas in a single goal statement. For example, many ideas might be related to transportation, but they should roll up to a master goal. Later, you will create objectives for these goals that will define specifics. Here's an example of a transportation goal: "Create a transportation environment that is friendly to the environment, is efficient, and reduces parking needs by 60 percent."

   There's no hard-and-fast rule on how many goals you should have, but you should be guided by what's possible. If you have 50 goals for your small city, well, you're probably kidding yourselves. Each goal generates many objectives, which in turn generate even more projects. Be realistic about what's achievable at least from the perspectives of capacity and budgeting.

3. **Consider a time frame.**

   By definition, executing on a vision takes a long time. You're certainly looking at several years, but not so long that it becomes impractical. Agreeing on a general time frame around the defined goals in Step 2 creates an important boundary and helps to sharpen everyone's focus. Though recognizing that a smart city strategy is never finished, you must articulate a time frame for this round of visionary goals.

4. **Identify your city's strengths.**

   This step requires some careful and honest introspection. Articulate your city's qualities that lend themselves to the work ahead. Recognizing these strengths helps you focus everyone's efforts, understand potential risks, optimize for strengths, and assist in prioritizing objectives.

5. Create a first draft of Steps 1–4.

Combine Steps 1–4 into a cohesive narrative. This isn't an essay. It should begin with the agreed-on vision. Additional support for the vision can be considered — notes on how the vision was derived, including some background and motivation, for example. This is followed by each of the goals, listed in sequence. Under each goal, provide additional supporting details and desired outcomes, and specify how they align with the vision. Include a statement on how city strengths support each goal, give approximate timelines, and provide a proposal on how the goal may be measured. (Later in this chapter, I provide more details on measurements, also known as *metrics*.)

REMEMBER

Don't make the strategic plan document a massive tome. If it is, you've done something wrong. Make it succinct enough that most stakeholders are comfortable reviewing it and can recall many of its highlights.

6. Circulate the draft to your stakeholders.

The next few steps are what I like to call rinse-and-repeat. The draft strategic plan for the future of your smart city must be circulated among a broad and diverse community. Create a mechanism to make it easy to elicit feedback and track changes.

7. Review, redraft, and recirculate.

The first round of feedback will likely elicit a high volume of comments. In subsequent circulations, you should expect reduced volume.

8. Finalize and socialize.

With several iterations completed, it's time to lock down the document. It's clear at this point which topics have resonated with your stakeholders. I suggest that you engage the right talent to create the final strategy document. Make this document easy to consume — one that everyone is proud to reference and share. Make the document version-controlled because, I assure you, you'll create many versions. Be comfortable having the document undergo regular reviews and updates. If changes are requested, follow a similar rinse-and-repeat process.

You've reached the end of a major milestone in the strategic planning process. Now share it widely and often. With so many channels available for both analog and digital sharing, use them all. For the core online presence — possibly, a stand alone website, or separate section of your city's main website — consider a way for people to provide comments and information on how to reach members of the team.

Converting your vision to action

Now that you've completed a high-level strategy document and it's been endorsed by all the right stakeholders, you're ready to move on to how the strategy will be put into action. The document so far includes your city's vision for what it wants to become, and it lists the major goals that manifest the vision. Each goal is a specific area that articulates a desired future result within some defined period.

A goal typically doesn't provide the level of detail necessary to follow a set of steps. What you need are supporting objectives for each goal. These objectives then tie directly to projects, which is how the work gets done. (Figure 5-2 should help you visualize the relationship between a vision, goals, and objectives.)

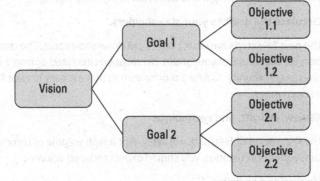

FIGURE 5-2:
The relationship between vision, goals, and objectives.

What is an *objective?* It's a specific action that supports a result in a defined time frame. It's short-term with a clear definition and is a necessary building block in a strategic plan.

I use the example of transportation to explain how you take a goal and create objectives. In my smart city, Goal 1 is to implement innovative and efficient transportation options.

The smart city steering committee or the operations team may designate a group of people who will work on determining the supporting objectives for this goal. In a smaller city, assigning a new group may be impractical, so perhaps the operations team is appropriate to do this work. At minimum, people with the proper expertise should be part of the team. In this area, you definitely want experts in the transportation and planning areas, with input from public safety team members also potentially quite valuable. The team who is assigned should be fully aware of the purpose of the goal, the way it supports the vision, the desired timeline, and the manner it is being proposed to be measured. This content lies in the approved strategy document as it stands. Conducting interviews with relevant stakeholders is a good approach as well — it might mean reaching out to people who haven't yet been engaged in the process.

REMEMBER

Stakeholders are both internal and external to the organization.

Once the team is comfortable with scope, it's time to think about objectives. You can follow any number of models, including brainstorming and design thinking. For more on the latter, check out *Design Thinking For Dummies*, by Christian Müller-Roterberg (Wiley).

The team must always be conscious of available capacity and funding and the timeline. Deviating from this guidance may result in objectives that, when reviewed, are quickly discarded and considered a poor use of everyone's time.

To return to the transportation goal I mention in Step 2 of the earlier section "Envisioning the envisioning process," here's what the objectives associated with that goal might look like:

Goal: Implement innovative and efficient transportation options.

Supporting objective 1.1: Support migration to electric vehicles by providing electric charging stations at 60 percent of city-provided parking spaces by 2025.

Supporting objective 1.2: Upgrade all traffic signals to enable dynamic signaling based on real-time data by 2024.

REMEMBER

I've made my examples here deliberately lightweight for the purposes of simplicity and clarity. Your actual goals and objectives may be more detailed. Let your teams determine what's appropriate for your agency and for the purpose of increasing understanding. It's a good idea to include clear details on any mentioned technologies and unfamiliar terms. You want all stakeholders to understand what is being proposed.

After all the goals have their associated objectives identified, you enter into a cycle of *rinse-and-repeat*, when the document is sent out for review and comment and then updated and reviewed again. This process repeats until general agreement is reached. The steering committee then needs to sign off on the approved objectives.

TIP

Integrate the new objectives document into the strategic plan, or simply add it as an appendix — it's your choice.

Finally, the completed strategic plan should be brought to your elected officials, or the equivalent, for sign-off.

Codifying the Plan

Strategic planning is a stepwise process. Each step is deliberate and builds on the preceding step. Skip a step, say, by defining projects before goals and you'll have a problem. A well-developed strategy enables any stakeholder to trace the origin of a downstream activity, such as a project, to its original genesis. This tracing quality is called *traceability,* and it's essential for ensuring the integrity of any approved plan. I can assure you that, at some point during the smart city effort, someone will start to ask questions that require airtight responses derived from traceability of the effort. You'll be glad that you followed a stepwise process.

The strategic plan now includes background information, the vision, goals, objectives, timelines, strengths, and metrics. It has substance to it. It's been codified. However, the document probably shouldn't reach 300 pages, if you can avoid it. This task is a challenge, for sure. Typically, successful plans are relatively short, living documents that have all the essential information and nothing more. I know: It isn't the clearest guidance in the world, but it's at least a suggestion of the notion of brevity and focus.

Your strategic plan will generate projects for each objective — and perhaps even more than one, for some of them. These projects identify the technologies that may be implemented. (I discuss many popular smart city technologies in Chapter 8.) These projects and the attendant documentation are managed outside the plan, but must reference the plan. Remember traceability.

TIP

Completing a ratified first version of your smart city strategic plan is an accomplishment worth celebrating. It's a big deal. A codified strategy is an agreed-on roadmap to move your city forward in addressing challenges, preparing for the future, and, ultimately, increasing the quality of life for your community. Don't celebrate too long, though: The work must begin. In preparation for that, you have a few other steps to take, which I discuss next.

Identifying metrics

William Edwards Deming, the notable American engineer and professor, said, "What gets measured gets done."

TIP

When you embark on an effort of any type, having some forms of measurement for progress and completion is a healthy way to keep yourself and others accountable.

Simply comparing your progress relative to a deadline gives you enough data to know whether you're behind schedule, on schedule, or ahead of schedule. Of course, everyone wants to be on schedule. Sometimes, it's useful to be ahead of schedule. (At other times, it can be problematic. If the project has dependencies, for example, you might find that it has to pause.) Generally, it's a good idea not to fall behind schedule.

REMEMBER

Metrics enable you to quantitatively evaluate performance.

It's hard to imagine running an organization or a project now without using extensive metrics. But it still happens. (Why you don't see metrics embraced is the subject of a different book.) I strongly recommend that relevant and actionable metrics accompany your smart city work — no ifs, ands, or buts. (I can't believe I found a way to use that expression in my book. Score!)

Metrics that are used to support business goals, called *key performance indicators (KPIs)*, are often tracked on a KPI dashboard. These terms are also relevant to projects and programs. For an example of a city KPI dashboard, check out the city of Los Angeles:

```
https://sites.google.com/a/lacity.org/mayors-dashboard
```

Spend time with your teams to identify the KPIs for your smart city program. This isn't discretionary work. It's *essential.* You'll thank me later.

For many organizations, the following are typical KPIs:

>> Sales revenue

>> Net profit margin

>> Sales growth

>> Cost of customer acquisition

>> Lead-to-client conversion rate

Each of these KPIs helps leaders understand how their business is performing. A leader without this information is effectively blind to what is going on.

These KPIs are often used on projects:

>> Budget-versus-actual spending

>> Number of open issues

>> Number of tasks completed

>> Number of issues behind schedule

>> Deviation of planned hours

Organizations and projects have a lot of standard KPIs. The ones in this list represent just a sample. In addition to standard KPIs, every leader and project manager typically has the option to add their own.

Different metrics may have different audiences — and the same is true for your smart city program. It's intuitive that the metrics that might be important for your community might be different from the day-to-day granular metrics that a project manager needs for a specific project. The same goes for elected officials and city management. This also suggests that metrics can be strategic or operational in nature. You need to determine which metrics you want to provide to each audience as you develop your KPI dashboard and communications plans.

You and your teams will identify KPIs that are relevant to your smart city work. Some of it is at the project level, and some is at a more macro level. You want some notion of whether your city is growing "smarter" over time — specifically, in the areas relevant to your smart city vision.

Here are a few simple examples for different domain areas:

>> **Transportation:** Number of electric charging stations deployed

>> **Energy:** Number of homes with solar energy panels

>> **Connectivity:** Percentage of homes with broadband access to the Internet

>> **Buildings:** Number of city buildings with LEED certification

>> **Digitalization:** Number of city services available via a smartphone app

You don't need to determine every metric on Day 1. For your strategic plan, identify a few meaningful metrics for each goal area. Then, as initiatives go online and the work matures, add more. This happens by demand anyway, but take a proactive approach, too.

TIP

Your KPI dashboard and reports should only include metrics that matter, so remove any when it becomes apparent that they are no longer adding value.

Communicating the plan

So you and your teams have worked diligently on a strategic plan. You've captured the core information you need and have attained appropriate approval to move to the next stage. This is a significant accomplishment. Hopefully, however, the celebrations are brief, because it's now time to make some progress.

KPI FRAMEWORKS

You can leverage one of many existing KPI frameworks for measuring smart city efforts. Here are two examples:

- **CITYkeys,** a project funded by the European Union's HORIZON 2020 program and developed and validated with the assistance of a number of cities, offers KPIs of smart city solutions across Europe. Learn more at www.citykeys-project.eu/citykeys/home.

- **The International Telecommunications Union (ITU),** an agency within the United Nations (UN), created the United for Smart Sustainable Cities (U4SSC) initiative, which has a set of international KPIs for smart sustainable cities. Notably, this work was done to also help city leaders understand their cities' performance in order to help meet the UN Sustainable Development Goals (SDGs). Learn more at www.itu.int/en/ITU-T/ssc/Pages/KPIs-on-SSC.aspx. (For more on the UN SDGs, check out Chapter 2.)

With the approved version of the strategic plan in hand, you have a roadmap for the work ahead. Assuming that it's referenced often (and I hope you and your teams make that a habit), this document reminds you of the vision, the motivation, the goals, and — by way of metrics — makes you accountable. By using this strategic plan, though, you also have a communication tool. It's a valuable and essential mechanism for sharing your progress with a broad set of stakeholders.

REMEMBER

Your smart city strategic plan is one of the most powerful communication tools you and your teams have as the work unfolds and progresses.

After you've completed this version of the plan (you'll have many more), it's time to think about how to use it to communicate to a wider audience that will be impacted by the smart city work ahead.

Both the steering committee and the operations team should, at minimum, weigh in and help determine the communications plan. Here are five tasks to consider:

- ≫ Providing the strategic plan online and on hard copy.
- ≫ Enabling mechanisms for feedback from anyone.
- ≫ Ensuring that, for the online version, the smart city KPI dashboard is clearly accessible.
- ≫ Illustrating progress and challenges online via stories, posts, videos, and photos.

>> Insisting that outreach includes regular updates in a newsletter, for example. Take advantage of all channels, such as Facebook, Twitter, the city website, and local media. (I discuss the use of social media in Chapter 8.)

Let's take a look at three leading global smart cities and how they're communicating their smart city plans and progress online.

Melbourne, Australia

Melbourne has a smart city microsite as part of its broader city website. It provides some introductory narrative and then highlights a number of initiatives. The site features videos and contact information for any of the work and its associated initiatives. (For a list of current initiatives, see Figure 5-3.)

Explore more here:

```
www.melbourne.vic.gov.au/about-melbourne/melbourne-profile/
    smart-city/Pages/smart-city.aspx
```

FIGURE 5-3: Melbourne's smart city website.

Moscow, Russia

As with Melbourne, the Moscow smart city online presence is a microsite of the city's website. This one highlights the main focus of the work — validating the argument that every smart city has its own priorities. It emphasizes the benefits that have been delivered and uses facts and photographs to support the team's priorities, as shown in Figure 5-4.

Explore more here:

```
www.mos.ru/en/city/projects/smartcity
```

FIGURE 5-4:
Moscow's smart
city website.

Barcelona, Spain

Barcelona is often cited as a model for smart city work. Its team has been at it for a while and has pioneered ideas that are being adopted worldwide. They are now using the term *digital city* to capture the theme of their current work. Plans and projects are available in detail on the city's website:

```
https://ajuntament.barcelona.cat/digital/en
```

The site has featured stories (see Figure 5-5), a blog, and links to additional social media channels.

FIGURE 5-5:
Barcelona's smart
city website.

Review a number of smart city websites and note the things you like. Build a site that you'd be equally proud of, keep it current, and communicate it often.

TIP

IN THIS CHAPTER

» Developing policies and regulations

» Identifying funding sources

» Choosing options for procurement

» Implementing governance

» Reporting on progress

Chapter **6**

Enabling a Smart City Strategy

Establishing a smart city involves more than just identifying technology and deploying it to your community, and the task is certainly more diverse in the range of implementation options available. Smart city work is also about having smart regulations in place, improving training for city staff, and creating policies for improved environmental management. Whatever it is that you do to make your community smarter — whether it's as a city official, community member, vendor, or some other stakeholder — it has to begin and end with people, and it has to focus on improving the quality of life for everyone. To make this happen, you first need a vision and a strategy, and then you need the tools to enable a successful program to be implemented.

When it comes to tools, I'm not simply referring to the software and hardware required in your projects — although those elements are vital. Instead, you also need some of the bureaucracy that comes with proper regulations and policies, a variety of options for procurement, and the adoption of mature governance practices. These aspects may not be the most glamorous ones in smart city work, but they're essential.

In this chapter, I help you explore each of these areas in detail so that you can gain a greater appreciation of their value. With the stakes and the risks high in building sustainable and smarter cities, you need all the right tools and best practices available to you, to increase your chance of success.

Putting the Building Blocks in Place

Cities are complex beasts. Even a medium-size city might provide, and support, hundreds of different types of services. For the community member, the expectation is that the services just work. Sure, they may not always be seamless or even the most efficient, but the baseline expectation is that they have to deliver. Behind the scenes, people, processes, and systems must work together in order to acquire, process, and execute on requests. Every single day, this may happen hundreds or even thousands of times.

It's not just the high number of necessary services, and the variety of supporting technologies and processes, that add to the complexity of urban life. What elevates the delivery of city government a few notches in difficulty is that everything must take place in the context of rigorous and comprehensive rules. These rules have evolved over a long period, and they represent, for example, guidance on making decisions, protections for people, and a way to enforce law. Of course, a smart city must adhere to these rules, but the requirements of a smart city may necessitate updates to certain rules and even the creation of new rules. Without a doubt, building a smart city requires attention to rules.

The building blocks of a successful smart city strategy also include many other, nontechnical requirements. The smart city team needs to consider how the work will be funded. The money may come from the city's general fund, but in a tight financial environment, might other sources of funding be available? The team also needs to look at the procurement process and determine how it can support the goals of the work. For example, are there mechanisms to move faster or to support experimental work? Finally, a smart city team will be well-served by ensuring that they have the right project management structure and processes in place. After all, a smart city strategy is about execution. Great project management is a vital ingredient of success for any effort.

Developing policy

The basic role of government is to help provide services that benefit the well-being of a community and to work toward increasing quality of life. (Though I encourage you to explore the large body of knowledge on the role and purpose of government, the definition I provide here should suffice for this book.) Governing is a daunting and complicated task. Government bodies that are made up of people with different backgrounds and perspectives typically have principles that guide decision-making. All decisions have consequences and must be deliberated carefully. To support this deliberative process, governments develop and enforce something called policies.

A government *policy* is a rule that guides decisions in order to benefit the community. A policy documents the reasons that things are done a certain way. Policies lead to the development of procedures and protocols that describe the How, Where, and When of how the policies will be delivered. Though policies are not laws, they can often lead to the creation of laws. By extension, the enforcement of laws is often guided by policy.

Here are some examples of government policies that guide how decisions are made in a city jurisdiction:

>> Recycling requirements

>> Crime reduction

>> Poverty remediation

>> Affordable housing

>> Public transportation

>> Public safety

>> Urban innovation

The need to update and create policies is driven by many factors — new ideas, new needs, federal laws, and an evolving culture, for example. The introduction of innovation and technologies related to the smart city movement is a driver of policy work. For example, cities have had to respond to the emergence of ride hailing services such as Uber, Grab, and DiDi. This policy development is often reactive because many of these new services emerge and descend on cities quickly. Given the original nature of many of these urban innovations, there's a low likelihood that existing policy will suffice. As a result, once a new service arrives, policymakers scramble to respond.

REMEMBER

An emerging characteristic of smart cities is the need to quickly develop policies in response to completely new innovative services in order to reduce risk and meet community expectations. Because cities don't generally have a history of being able to respond quickly to change, this new phenomenon requires enhancements to current processes.

Creating and updating city government policies has become a core smart city strategy requirement. It's not easy work, but having relevant and supportable policies is essential.

Getting started

These steps succinctly spell out the process for developing government policy:

1. Understand.

First, fully determine the need for the policy. It may involve interviews and discussions with many stakeholders. Because policy-driven issues can be complex, it's essential to secure agreement on the core of the problem. Understanding context is vital, as is identifying and agreeing on the outcome of the policy.

2. Research.

After the need has been established, those tasked with policy development conduct research, ranging from understanding existing policy to digging deeper into the challenge. You should conduct a thorough analysis and, by all means, ensure that all stakeholders are actively involved.

3. Develop.

With all the information gathered, it's time to develop the policy itself. As with every step of policy creation, be sure to involve all relevant stakeholders. Development should be based on evidence and data. It's often important to consider the wider context of political, economic, technological, and environmental trends.

4. Approve.

Each government entity has (or should have) an approval process that must be followed. This process is smoother when you involve all the right stakeholders in earlier steps. Approval may undergo several iterations before final acceptance. Receiving feedback and editing requests from decision-makers is normal.

5. Communicate.

After the policy is completed and approved, it's time to determine the communications strategy. The policy should be posted in a central policy database that is open and searchable. In addition, other communication channels should be used that are relevant to the policy. For example, it doesn't make sense to include a new policy in an email to the community when the policy will be used by only one city department.

Figure 6-1 gives you a graphical illustration of this process.

Many of the steps in the preceding list can be conducted in a workshop setting. All steps should include as many stakeholders as possible. In this instance, it may be better to have too many cooks than too few.

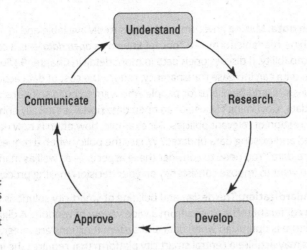

FIGURE 6-1:
The basic steps
in creating a
government
policy.

Understand

Research

Communicate

Approve

Develop

WARNING

There's a subtle difference between public policy and the policies I describe earlier in this chapter. It's completely unintuitive given the terms, but it's important for me to clarify. *Public policy* is the process of converting political intentions into outcomes in the real world. It focuses on the decisions of politicians that result in actual policy change related to such areas as a public healthcare system, defense forces, transportation, and education. Public policies come from all governmental entities and at all levels: legislatures, courts, bureaucratic agencies, and executive offices at national, local, and state levels.

Examining a few examples of smart city policies

Need some concrete examples of smart city policies? Here you go:

REMEMBER

>> **Data protection and usage:** The collection and use of data are central to the delivery of smart services in a city. For example, one could use Internet of Things (IoT) sensors on light posts to collect air quality samples or measure noise levels or count vehicles at an intersection. (See Chapter 8 for more on IoT.) Capturing this data and delivering meaningful results to decision-makers and other interested stakeholders can have real value.

Collecting data can also mean inadvertently capturing sensitive data. For example, a camera at an intersection may be used for dynamically changing the light signals, but it may also record the license plates and occupants of a vehicle. To protect any data that's collected, determine how it may only be used. To protect privacy, policies should be developed to help manage the design and deployment of data collection technologies.

>> **Open data:** Making government datasets freely available and in machine-readable form — a concept known as *open data* — is a core smart city capability. (I discuss open data in more detail in Chapter 9.) For example, open data can increase transparency, reduce the cost of data acquisition for requestors, and be useful for people who want to build solutions based on city data. Governing the use of an open data portal is typically enhanced by the creation of relevant policies. For example, how often is new data published and existing data updated? What's the policy when a request is made to delete data? You need to consider these aspects — as well as many others — if you want to impose consistency on your decision-making process.

>> **Standardization:** The design and building of smart city solutions involves many different technologies from a wide variety of vendors. A digital infrastructure is optimized when data and system functions are integrated. Some cities may acquire a central smart city platform that requires the integration of other systems. It's advisable for the technical architecture underlying smart city solutions to be scalable and supportable for a long time to come. For this reason, you need to establish technical standards early on in the process. Standards may include file formats, naming conventions, back-end database systems, and application programming interfaces (APIs). Policies are a great way to support the adherence to, and adoption of, standards.

Establishing regulations

Both regulations and policies are rules created by city governments; however, they differ in important ways. Though a policy is created to help make decisions and to achieve outcomes, a *regulation* is a rule that is made to ensure compliance. It's comparable with a law and imposes some form of a restriction to ensure that people follow a specific set of rules. Unlike laws, which typically require elected officials to pass, regulations are can be created by professional staff within a city. In addition, regulations often describe in greater detail how laws are implemented in a local government. Finally, regulations are administrative and are used to enable successful operations within an organization.

Here are some examples of city regulations:

>> **Zoning:** This involves the process of designating land in a city into zones in which certain land uses are permitted or prohibited. It's the most common regulator for cities to carry out their urban plans. Examples of items regulated in zoning include buildings, parking, signs, walls, factories, and commercial entities.

>> **Business licensing:** Many cities do not permit a business to operate until it has been issued a certificate of occupancy. Attaining the certificate may

require the business meeting regulations, which may include vetting that the business type is allowed, that safety concerns are addressed, and that accessibility accommodations are made.

» **Building improvements, construction, and remodeling:** Cities require strict adherence to regulations governing areas such as electrical, plumbing, and mechanical work. In addition, those hired to do the work may be required to have a city business license and worker insurance.

» **Drones usage:** The use of drones for both recreational and professional use is growing quickly. In addition to countries that have federal laws and regulations on drone use, some cities have adopted their own, more restrictive rules. Regulations may include how drones are used, where they are used, whether a permit is required, and limits on video recording to protect privacy.

Developing regulations

Fortunately, the process of creating a regulation largely follows the same pattern as a policy. (Refer to Figure 6-1.) Though regulations can be created as a stand-alone set of rules, often it's the result of the passing of a new law. As a result, in this instance, developing a regulation is based on the content of the law. As with a policy, comprehensive and regular engagement with stakeholders is essential to capture feedback and evolve the regulation. How regulation is created depends on each city's agreed-on processes, so it's important to understand the local approach when considering this topic. In addition, many larger, noncity government agencies have specific mechanisms in place when it comes to formulating regulations.

Ensuring regulations support smart cities

Clearly, city rules are an important part of the context of smart city efforts. Regulations impact strategy and implementation decisions, and the opposite is also true: Smart city work can result in the modification or creation of regulations.

TIP

Smart city planning work must be viewed comprehensively through the lens of regulation. Teams must determine whether they need to heed any existing regulatory considerations and whether they may require the creation of new regulations. Rather than consider this a burden, new regulations may bring about better outcomes and foster more support. Of course, understanding existing regulations and making appropriate strategic choices also helps to avoid serious compliance risks.

REMEMBER

Even if a new service may look like a whole new kettle of fish, thus requiring a host of new regulations, you should make the effort to determine whether existing regulations currently in place for a relatively similar service might work for you.

The traditional model of public regulation is being challenged by the nature of smart cities as they drive a new relationship between technology, government, and society. Specifically, the rapid emergence of new urban innovation presents the question of whether existing legal mechanisms can strike the right balance for the current and future needs of smart cities. Simply put, recognizing and accommodating the benefits of new solutions in response to city needs and also encouraging the right level of innovation should not be limited by traditional regulatory considerations. City leaders may need to be open to modifying and creating regulations to support the realities of 21st century smart and sustainable cities.

To understand the seriousness of the challenges and considerations outlined here, let me briefly discuss regulation through the lens of economic and social issues.

In the case of economics, regulations should avoid *regulatory asymmetry* — different rules for different players in the same market, in other words. New innovation creates new business models. For example, a ride hailing service such as Uber provides the same service as taxis do, but in a completely new way. Regulation may support the old model of taxis and punish the new model of ride hailing. (With this example, I don't mean to trivialize the important debate about the potential destructive nature on incumbents from new business models such as ride-hailing.)

Older rules should be evaluated to ensure that all permissible participants in a marketplace have equal and fair competitive access. In a related matter, regulation must not create barriers to entry for new players by continuing to enforce old and outdated standards and rules. In fact, regulation should encourage more entrants, in order to increase urban innovation.

In the case of social issues, regulation must protect society from the potential harm of any new technology. Though innovation brings solutions, it can also introduce new problems. For example, increased threats to personal privacy and digital exclusion are real possibilities in smart cities.

These examples of the economic and social aspects of government regulations in the age of smart cities point to a need for city leaders to evolve and embrace the changes necessary to respond to new realities on the ground.

Smart cities need smart regulation.

Evaluating funding models

There's one consistent truth when it comes to working in city government: There are always more projects to be completed than there are available resources, such as talent and money. Demands for government services continue to increase as communities expect more and operating a city becomes more complex. Simply meeting existing operating costs can consume most of a municipality's annual budget. In the worst case, some even run an annual deficit. A few fortunate cities have revenues that enable them to comfortably meet all operational needs and also build for the future, but for most, the reality is more sobering. These cities can meet most operational needs, but choosing which projects to fund and tackle each year is a matter of rigorous prioritization. Many projects will be deferred or may never be completed. They'll just be declined. All this takes place during the annual budgeting process.

Now that cities are beginning to focus on developing smart city strategies, the central question of how the attendant projects will be paid for has quickly risen to the top of the agenda. In fact, in several surveys, a lack of available funding is cited as the main reason that smart city efforts aren't being pursued. Smart city projects often require significant investment in existing or new infrastructure. Beyond deployment, there's also the need to ensure that funding is available to support the long-term operation and maintenance of the solutions.

For many cities, the smart city strategy and its related annual project requests are processed via the normal annual budgeting cycle. This means acquiring funds from the city's revenue that is derived from taxes, service fees, and other sources of income. The team responsible for the smart city effort is required to participate in the budgeting process, just like every other city department. They need to write up the business case and make a compelling pitch for funding approval. Gaining agreement is more likely when those making the budgeting decisions have already bought into the smart city strategy. Extensive planning, preparation, and stakeholder engagement prior to the budgeting process — particularly of relevant leadership — is of paramount importance here.

Though the annual budgeting process is the primary source of funds for many smart city projects, many cities may find that this avenue either isn't an option or will fall desperately short of what is required to support an expensive, multiyear effort. As a consequence, alternative funding and financing options need to be explored.

Such funding can be grouped into these four categories:

>> **Private:** Here, funds for the project come from a private enterprise source. A privately owned city service organization, such as a power utility, funds its own upgrades and innovations, for example. Some of the reasons they're motivated to do this is to meet customer expectations, improve safety, and reduce operational costs.

Another example is the large and continual investment that telecommunication companies make in communities to ensure support for wired and wireless communications. Many telecommunication companies now also provide smart city services such as digital signage, Wi-Fi, IoT services, and sensor networks.

Private enterprises can also engage in contract operations for cities. This means that the upfront design and build costs are absorbed by the private company, and the city then pays a monthly or annual fee for them to provide the service. For the city, such an arrangement means that it avoids capital costs and is responsible only for an operating fee.

Other private sources may include grants that are nonrepayable funds given by a charity, foundation, or corporation. Though grants may be difficult to win because of their competitive nature, they can often be worth the effort.

REMEMBER

>> **Public:** In this model, funds are sourced only from government entities. In addition to the local government funding projects in the annual budgeting process, money can come from regional and national governments. These funds may be used for major infrastructure upgrades, such as those related to transportation and water systems. Regional and national governments often make available funds in the form of subsidies to poorer areas to improve economic and social conditions. National governments are also investing in smart city efforts to encourage community innovation, conduct city-scale urban improvement experiments, and kick-start compelling city projects.

Another way that public funds can be made available is through projects that reduce operational costs. Smart city projects often create efficiencies that result in lower costs. The money saved can then be used for other smart city projects.

Though not popular for obvious reasons, cities can increase a tax or impose a temporary tax or tariff to raise specific funds.

Where relevant, a city can also impose a service fee on a new smart city service. The fee repays the cost of the project and supports the ongoing operations and maintenance of the solution. Fees can also be applied to existing services in order to raise funds for a project. For example, one could increase street-side parking fees or costs for city permits.

>> **Public-private partnership (PPP):** Here, funds are derived from both private and public organizations, which allows private enterprise and local government to collaborate so that they can provide input as well as funds for a project. Such partnerships are often favored approaches because risk is shared among participants. An example of a PPP is a shared revenue stream. If the smart city project generates revenue, such as from a new parking system, the government and the private company agree to split any revenue from the service.

PPPs are gaining popularity in experimental urban innovation work as well. In this model, the city may provide some funds and resources in order to incentivize an innovative technology company to experiment in the community. I discuss this approach in detail in Chapter 7.

Smart city projects funded by advertisements are often PPPs but can also be privately funded exclusively, depending on the arrangement with city hall. For example, a private company may get permission to build modern bus stop shelters with digital signage. They will then sell add space on the digital signage which can produce significant funds depending on location. A city might negotiate a revenue-share in this example as well.

Community members working alongside their local government can crowd-source funds for special projects. *Crowd-sourcing* is a method of raising finance by asking a large number of people for a small amount of money apiece. Though possible as a private approach, collaborating with your city is a better way to increase the chance of success.

Given the effort it takes to win large grants, a PPP approach is often preferred because it means sharing the burden and having each partner exercise their strengths.

>> **Financing:** In this model, funds provided by a financial institution are borrowed on the understanding that they must be repaid under an agreed-on plan. An example is acquiring a long-term loan from a bank.

Another popular form of financing is the issuance of a bond. A government bond is issued to investors that promises to pay periodic interest payments and then to repay the full amount of the investment on the maturity date of the bond.

Financial organizations can offer cities a variety of loan services. However, raising money for smart city projects this way can result in push-back from financial institutions. These are some reasons they may cite:

- *Bad municipal credit ratings*
- *The risks of new technology*
- *A lack of a clear business case*

REMEMBER

Sooner rather than later, the question of funding your smart city strategy comes up. Deciding which path to take varies based on each city's circumstances. You may also choose a blended approach, depending on the project, need, and timeline. For many cities, the funding model that's adopted requires leadership and creativity. Whatever approach you take, deeply involve your community and a broad set of stakeholders.

Handling procurement issues

You've addressed the source of funding for some or all of your smart city strategy. Yippee! Now it's time to spend it. Beyond identifying funds for delivering smart city projects, another priority area that can be challenging is the procurement process. Intuitively, particularly with a private sector mindset, it may seem like identifying and purchasing solutions would be one of the easier processes. However, the important qualities of being transparent and enabling the marketplace to have a fair shot at competing requires a notable amount of bureaucracy and regulation. There is a high degree of responsibility and accountability when spending large sums of public money, and it's important to openly demonstrate prudent and diligent processes and behavior. In a 2019 survey of city leaders, 44 percent of them maintained that procurement was a significant challenge in building a smarter city.

LinkNYC: FREE WI-FI IN NEW YORK CITY

Back in the 2010s, New York City recognized that their 13,000 public telephones were getting little use, given the popularity of mobile phones. The availability of power and telecommunication connections at each booth gave city officials an idea. They decided to explore what it would take to replace each public telephone with a multipurpose kiosk for high-speed Wi-Fi, Internet access, and city information.

City leaders opted for a public-private partnership (PPP) approach. They issued a request for proposal (RFP) to solicit vendors to propose a solution with the condition that it be provided at no cost to the city. The provider would be required to identify a business model to build, deploy, and support the solution over the long term. The city would provide the infrastructure, permitting support, and other municipal resources.

The winning bid was for CityBridge, a New York-based group of companies made up of Qualcomm, CIVIQ, and Intersection. Indeed, the $200 million project would not cost the city any money, because it would be entirely funded by advertisements on the new kiosks. With 8 million people roaming the streets of New York, those ads on each device would occupy prime real estate.

Finally named LinkNYC, these kiosks, at 9½ feet tall, feature two 55-inch displays. (See the sidebar figure.) An Android-based tablet computer can be used for accessing city maps, finding directions, and making video calls, plus using two USB charging ports. There is a phone for calling all 50 US states for free and one button to call emergency services. Each kiosk offers an encrypted, gigabit-speed Wi-Fi hotspot. The goal is to eventually deploy 7,500 kiosks across the five boroughs of New York.

For more on LinkNYC, check out www.link.nyc.

REMEMBER

The requirements for procurement differ, particularly between countries. Some places don't require the rigor of others. You should consider the specifics of your city and region's processes when exploring your procurement options.

In general, the traditional procurement process requires that an agency builds out a detailed request for proposals (RFP) document and submits it to the market-place. An RFP typically includes exhaustive details on the solution required, the requirements expected from the vendor, and the context of the need. Vendors are then expected to submit their responses within a specific timeline. Respondents who meet the requirements of the RFP are invited to demonstrate their capabilities. A panel of evaluators, largely made up of city staff and perhaps other stakeholders from the community, scores each proposal. Several rounds of evaluations may occur until a winner emerges and a contract is awarded. It's a thorough and detailed process. In terms of fairness and careful deliberation, this RFP process is effective. It's by far the most common approach adopted by public agencies. Rules that go back many years govern the process. There's no doubt that many of your smart city projects are procured this way.

WARNING

The biggest and most obvious limitation of the traditional RFP procurement process is the length of time it takes. Sure, it's a great way to buy something, but a bad way to buy something if you want it quickly. You may not want to spend many months or even years procuring and deploying something that may be obsolete by the time it's ready for use. Because many smart city projects have qualities of experimentation and a desire to rapidly demonstrate the value of new innovation, a slow process may not be optimum. Additionally, a traditional procurement process may impose limitations that make experimentation with particular vendors more difficult or even impossible because of the need to ensure an opportunity is open to any qualified vendor.

So, what options may be available for a more creative procurement process to support the innovative nature of smart city efforts?

Public-private partnerships (PPPs)

The days of choosing a go-it-alone strategy for public agencies is largely over. It's just no longer possible for governments to achieve their goals by themselves. Increasingly, efforts are delivered through partnering with such players as those in private industry, academia, nongovernmental organizations (NGOs), and community members.

By partnering with innovative urban technology companies, particularly start-ups, cities can evaluate new solutions to solving problems well in advance of a full-scale procurement — a try-before-you-buy approach, in other words. For example, this may take the form of a vendor collaborating with an urban innovation lab (see Chapter 7) or demonstrating their capabilities in an innovation district (see Chapter 7). Because the vendor gains the benefits of piloting its solution — which may include positive marketing and real-world showcasing — the costs involved may be low, or there may even be no cost to the city. Though an RFP may be required at the end of the process regardless, this partnership approach enables considerable learning and other benefits for both the city and vendor. A completely novel solution may also qualify for a sole source — a procurement approach that supports the acquisition of a solution when there's only one provider.

Another partnership approach was pioneered by the city of San Francisco in 2014. The city created a Startup-in-Residence (STiR) program. Start-ups are solicited to compete for a limited number of city slots to try to help solve identified challenges. Over 16 weeks, city staff and the matched start-ups work together to co-create solutions for the community. Called *challenge-based procurement,* this type of RFP specifies only the desired outcome of the solicitation rather than all the details. Start-ups typically offer a substantial discount to the hosting city so that if a sole source is not an option, the cost can fall below the open market solicitation requirement. For more on the STiR program, check out www.cityinnovate.com.

Innovative procurement methods

Here are seven alternative innovative procurement approaches:

» **Piggybacking on another agency's procurement:** In some jurisdictions, it's permissible to use the existing vendor contract work of another agency to negate the need for an RFP.

» **Create procurement processes specifically for innovation:** An agency may create a separate set of rules specifically for the purpose of supporting the rapid procurement of innovative technology while still adhering to the principles of transparency and accountability.

» **Performance-based contracting:** Rather than base procurement on upfront pricing, contracts use vendor-and-solution performance to determine cost based on the quality of execution.

» **Incentivize private innovation:** Create and communicate opportunities for the private sector to deliver solutions directly to the community. In addition, make open data available for private enterprises to use to create solutions. (For more on open data approaches, see Chapter 9.)

» **Create an independent organization to deliver the smart city strategy:** Here, a city creates a separate and independent entity that executes the smart city work. Because they aren't subject to government procurement rules, they have more freedom when it comes to identifying and buying solutions. The city pays the entity an annual management fee. A variation of this approach involves engaging a third-party program management company to run the smart city strategy.

» **Contract to multiple vendors:** Create an RFP that identifies vendor capabilities rather than specific deliverables. Contract with multiple vendors in each capability area. Then utilize the vendor that best meets the need for a particular round of work at a specific time.

» **Open source software:** Though not technically a procurement strategy, an agency can determine whether open source software may meet an organizational need. The upside is that a great deal of high-quality open source software is available, and it may be freely used without procurement costs and modified without restrictions. For example, WordPress (https://wordpress.org), an open source content management system, is used by almost 35 percent of all websites in the world. The downside to open source is the hidden costs. For example, third-party support may still be required.

Managing projects and carrying out business analyses

The topics of project management and business analysis may not be the first things you think about when you consider the development of a smart city. Of course, you and I recognize that it's essential to have strong leadership and a big vision. It's also vital to have community support and access to funding. However, all too often we overlook giving sufficient focus to how the work is executed and the necessary talent to achieve it. I've worked in various organizations over the past 30 years delivering hundreds of projects, and I can firmly attest that performing quality business analysis and then delivering through high-performing project management are essential ingredients to success. This is why I'm including these areas.

Project management

In Chapter 5, I discuss the steps to create and codify a smart city strategy. I explain how to get to the point where the strategic vision, goals, and objectives are defined and agreed on. After the plan is approved, it's time to create the projects that will deliver the desired outcomes of the strategy. Next, the projects are identified, prioritized, and then scheduled. You can use a Gantt chart to visualize and manage project schedules. (Check out this overview of Gantt charts: http://bit.1y/2vuk8Ug.) Finally, assuming that funding has been established, you assign projects to specific project managers in accordance with the schedule.

The projects then begin. Good luck.

TIP

Depending on the scope and scale of project activities, it may be worth considering the establishment of a project management officer (PMO) to provide oversight and assistance. I discuss the role of the PMO in Chapter 4.

Though you have many different methods for conducting a project, ranging from the traditional waterfall approach to the current popularity of agile approaches, projects generally include the same major milestones. For technology-related projects, Figure 6-2 illustrates the universally acknowledged systems development lifecycle (SDLC).

According to the Project Management Institute (PMI), at https://www.pmi.org/, these six criteria must be met for a project to be considered successful:

>> It's on time.

>> It's on budget.

>> It works as specified.

>> People actually use the solution.

>> The people who funded the work are pleased.

>> All objectives have been met.

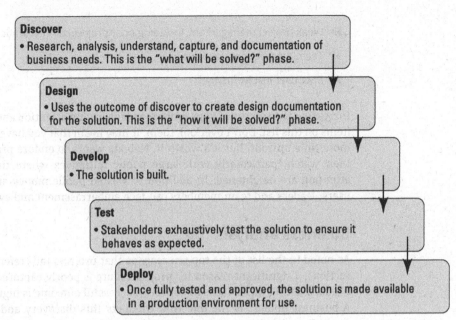

Discover
- Research, analysis, understand, capture, and documentation of business needs. This is the "what will be solved?" phase.

Design
- Uses the outcome of discover to create design documentation for the solution. This is the "how it will be solved?" phase.

Develop
- The solution is built.

Test
- Stakeholders exhaustively test the solution to ensure it behaves as expected.

Deploy
- Once fully tested and approved, the solution is made available in a production environment for use.

FIGURE 6-2: Systems development lifecycle (SDLC).

Meeting these criteria is a lot harder than it sounds. In fact, the data on project success is rather sobering: The research shows that, overall, 71 percent of projects fail to deliver. They fail to meet at least one of these three project criteria: It's on time, it's on budget, and it works as specified. The number jumps to a staggering 94 percent with really large projects.

Specific to technology-related projects, a 2017 PMI report about IT projects stated that 31 percent failed to meet their goals, 43 percent exceeded their budgets, and 49 percent were late.

Why do so many projects fail to deliver, and what should you focus on to ensure greater success for your smart city work?

Here are the top ten reasons that projects fail:

- » Poorly captured organizational needs
- » Lack of leadership support and involvement
- » Changing project objectives
- » Overpromising on timelines and underestimating costs
- » Failing to confront unidentified risks
- » Dependency delays
- » Lacking a sufficient number of skilled people to complete required tasks

- » Weak project management, including poor project communications

- » Team member procrastination

- » Poor user involvement

Increasing the success of your projects means paying attention and addressing the items on this list. Don't overlook them. It may mean that you have to invest a little more time upfront, but it's worth it. Nobody wants to endure project failures on their watch, particularly with large public initiatives where the visibility and attention are heightened. In addition to wasted public money and disappointed users, leaders and team members can face embarrassment and even termination.

Business analysis

As noted in the list of the top ten reasons that projects fail (refer to the previous section), a significant reason for project failure is poorly captured organizational needs. Eliciting these needs to deliver a successful outcome is highly skilled work. A business analyst is the one who conducts this discovery and documentation work. Knowing how to capture requirements, recording the right information, and then gaining approval from decision-makers makes a significant difference in project outcomes.

Project managers and business analysts must work closely together, particularly in the early phases of a project. (Refer to the Discover and Design phases in Figure 6-2.) Remaining engaged until the project ends is important too, in order to ensure that the business analyst can provide, to the project manager and team members, timely insights that are relevant from early analysis work.

A business analyst captures requirements from relevant stakeholders via methods such as interviews (the most popular) and observations and user surveys. This process answers the question, "What city need will be solved?" These requirements are documented and approved by decision-makers.

TIP

Have your smart city program sponsor sign off on the analysis documentation to ensure that they have read it in detail and understand that any needs that are not captured might not be delivered. Adding a new requirement later in the SDLC is hugely disruptive and costly. Of course, it happens, but it should be rare.

Requirements documentation is then used to create the design specifications. In this phase, you're answering the question, "How will the problem be solved?" Many design methods can be used, including modeling, which is simply a way to represent some aspect of a system. The model can be text-based, graphical, or mathematics-based. A popular form of modeling, particularly for building software, is called Unified Modeling Language (UML). You can learn more about it at www.uml.org.

TIP

Getting the early phases of a project right sets you up for success. High-quality business analysis is important. In addition, having an experienced and talented project manager makes a world of difference. Finally, as with every phase of your smart city journey, involve as many relevant stakeholders as possible. Identify the right people, engage them, communicate often, and embrace open collaboration. This isn't simple work, but by making good choices early on and adopting quality practices, you can increase the likelihood of meeting the expectations of your smart city strategy.

Governing the Strategy

A smart city strategy is only as good as the degree to which it is followed. A strategy that is written and agreed on and then never referenced again is worthless. Success in reaching goals relies on having a roadmap and a set of guiding principles that everyone can follow. But even with the best of intentions, individuals and teams can veer off course and, before long, find themselves way off track. Pulling the team and projects back into alignment with the strategy is then expensive and will incur delays. The risk of failure also increases. For this reason, to keep focused and aligned to the strategic goals — allowing, of course, for modifications along the way — requires an agreed-on management framework, a process for decision-making, and methods of enforcement. This is called *governance*.

In Chapter 4, I suggest how you can design an organizational structure to support the creation and implementation of your smart city strategy. Each layer of the organizational chart has a mandate and a specific set of roles and responsibilities to execute against it. Each team contributes in some way toward ensuring that the work is being governed. After all, the assumption is that all participants are focused on achieving the same goals and have agreed-on rules to get there. This requires a common understanding of why something is being done, what is being done, how it will be done, and when it will be done.

In the next few sections, I describe and recommend models for both the strategic and project governance of your smart city efforts. Finally, I share suggestions on communicating the status of your strategy.

Defining strategic governance

The term *strategic governance* is most often used to describe how entire organizations are managed from the top all the way to the bottom. But it can also be used to help define the management and decision framework of large organizational programs. A smart city strategy falls into this category.

As such, my definition of strategic governance runs as follows: It's the process of envisioning a future and then managing the decisions and efforts to realize that vision. It encompasses the development, implementation, and monitoring of the strategic plan.

Strategic governance drives how each team executes the vision, mission, values, policies, and processes of their respective work. It's a top-down approach, with leadership and guidance coming from the strategy/steering committee. Governance flows down through the various organizational layers and is executed in a way that's appropriate to each team's responsibilities. Figure 6-3 summarizes the role of leadership in strategic governance.

These are the core responsibilities of strategic governance:

>> Defining, agreeing on, and revising your goals and objectives

>> Creating and enforcing policies that provide guidance on execution

>> Approving and allocating resources

>> Leading and controlling activities and tasks

>> Insisting on accountability for quality delivery

>> Monitoring performance

>> Reporting on progress

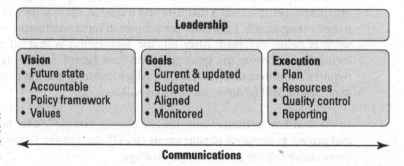

FIGURE 6-3:
Basic strategic governance framework.

Leadership		
Vision	**Goals**	**Execution**
• Future state	• Current & updated	• Plan
• Accountable	• Budgeted	• Resources
• Policy framework	• Aligned	• Quality control
• Values	• Monitored	• Reporting

Communications

Managing projects with project governance

Though recognizing that creating and governing a smart city strategy is essential work, the real outcomes actually happen through your smart city projects. Even when you use the best strategy, results are bad if projects are poorly managed. Projects must meet the minimum requirements of being on time and on budget and meeting the expectations of users. There's a vast chasm between simply managing a project and managing a project well.

TIP

You will be well served by hiring skilled project managers *and* investing in developing the skills of your existing project managers.

Project managers and their team members require the necessary organizational conditions and environment to excel. A priority ingredient when it comes to repeatedly managing successful project outcomes is an agreed-on framework for project decision-making — project governance, in other words. It's a direct descendant of strategic governance. Though project managers and their team members focus on the details of running a project, project governance provides them with valuable guidance, oversight, and timely decision-making.

For your purposes in this book, think of *project governance* as a structured system of processes and rules used to manage a project. It provides a decision-making framework to ensure alignment between the project team members, executives, and the rest of the organization. Project governance can also be used to decide the sequence and timing of projects, including the identification and assignment of project managers and team members. Figure 6-4 summarizes the core components of project governance.

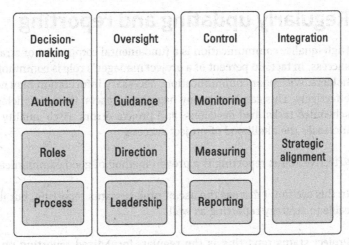

FIGURE 6-4:
Four central
project govern-
ance functions.

These are the core components of project governance:

>> **Team structure:** Establish the organizational structure and reporting relationships between all relevant project stakeholders. (I cover this topic in detail in Chapter 4.)

>> **Role definitions:** Provide all stakeholders with detailed information on their role and responsibilities. Decision-making authority can be defined here as well.

>> **Project management plan:** This formal document gets approved by all who define exactly how the project will be executed, managed, monitored, and controlled.

>> **Project schedule:** This list of dependent and independent project milestones, activities, and deliverables is coupled with their estimated and actual start and finish dates.

>> **Issue review process:** This agreed-on guide specifies how different types of issues encountered during the project will be handled.

>> **Reporting plan:** This plan designates a process and a set of agreed-on methods and channels for ensuring clear and frequent communications to all stakeholders. I tell you more about this topic in the last section of this chapter, "Regularly updating and reporting."

>> **Risk register:** This one acts as a repository for logging and managing project risks. It also documents what actions were taken to mitigate or directly address the risk, if any.

Regularly updating and reporting

High-quality communication is a fundamental component of strategy and project success. In fact, 80 percent of a project manager's role is communicating to stakeholders. With poor communication, necessary information may not be exchanged effectively. This can have many negative impacts, including delays, omissions in scheduled tasks, bad decisions, and project errors. High-quality communication increases the likelihood of project success.

Effective status reporting is a proven method of good communication.

In this section, I discuss the use of project status reporting, but it's just as applicable to strategy reporting as well.

REMEMBER

Project status reporting is the regular, formalized reporting on the health of a project. It's a project management monitoring and controlling function. Project managers typically perform this reporting responsibility, but really large projects can benefit from a dedicated person or team.

GOOD GOVERNANCE AT THE SOCIETAL LEVEL

The United Nations (UN) defines *governance* as the process of decision-making and the process by which decisions are made or not made. They further define *good governance* as the processes and institutions that produce results that meet the needs of society while making the best use of resources at their disposal.

The UN defines these eight characteristics of good governance:

- **Participation:** Decisions must involve both men and women, through either direct engagement or representation. Those involved must be informed and organized.

- **Consensus oriented:** Society represents many points of view. Mediation can be used to capture different interests in order to reach a broad consensus on what is in the best interest of the whole community.

- **Accountability:** Government organizations, the private sector, and civil society must be accountable to the public and to their institutional stakeholders. Accountability can be enforced only by way of transparency and the rule of law.

- **Transparency:** With transparency, decisions and enforcement are made in a manner that follows rules and regulations. Information on such decisions must be available to those affected.

- **Responsiveness:** Institutions and their processes must serve stakeholders within a reasonable time frame.

- **Effectiveness and efficiency:** Institutions must produce results that meet the needs of society while making the best use of resources. Processes must be sustainable and also protect the environment.

- **Equity and inclusiveness:** All members of society must feel that they have a stake in decision-making and do not feel excluded from the mainstream.

- **Rule of law:** This is the requirement that legal frameworks are fair and enforced impartially.

Reporting is used as a vehicle to communicate to stakeholders in order to keep them informed, solicit feedback and questions, elicit action, and assist with timely decision-making. The frequency of reporting is typically decided on and documented when the project management plan is created. Not every report is sent to every stakeholder. The right report should be created for the right people. As always, *know your audience*.

Keep in mind that electronic project status reporting is one important form of communication, but all other channels should be kept open and used. Project managers can still speak to their colleagues as well. Yes, that means visiting their offices or picking up the phone.

TIP

Consistent, quality reporting helps to avoid surprises to stakeholders.

Status reports also comprise a historical record of a project. The reports can be used to attain lessons learned, serve as a reference for any questions, and capture the strengths and weaknesses of various aspects of the project.

Project status reporting can include

>> Overall project health

>> Schedule and budget status relative to a specific stage of the project

>> Project summary and milestone status

>> Significant-accomplishments status

>> Challenges-and-risks summary

>> Open issues that must be handled

>> Change requests

>> Project metrics

Finally, when it comes to writing up a status report, here are some best practices you should follow:

>> **Consistency:** Establish and maintain a uniform format, distribution frequency, and method.

>> **Metrics:** Create and report on metrics decided during the planning phase of the project.

>> **Process:** Develop and communicate the reporting process to team members with reporting responsibilities.

>> **Simplicity:** Ensure that reports are clear and effective.

>> **Verify:** Regularly confirm that distributed reports are adding value and are reaching all the right people at the right time.

>> **Tools:** Identify and use reporting tools that lower the burden of report development and distribution.

3

Using Smart City Technologies

Explore techniques to enable urban innovation and transform communities.

Discover a wide range of technologies that are powering smarter cities.

Delve deep into the value that data can bring to every city.

Understand and explore the opportunities open data provides.

Chapter 7

Embracing Urban Innovation

The art and science of applying new ideas to solve urban problems has existed since the first human settlements. When confronted with an unrelenting and often unforgiving flow of challenges, city leaders throughout history have been forced to evaluate options, experiment with ideas, and deploy creative responses. Every day presents another hurdle to overcome, and many times it's new and confounding. That's the nature of running a city in the 21st century. Cities may be humans' greatest invention, but they require exhaustive attention, maintenance, and support in order to thrive. With bigger and more complex problems, higher expectations from residents, and a sense of urgency in many areas, discovering and acting on new ideas —*innovating,* in other words — is being elevated as a priority by cities all over the planet. A city can innovate without having a smart city strategy, but it can't have a smart city strategy without innovation. In this chapter, I discuss various aspects of urban innovation, including a few approaches to get results.

Defining Urban Innovation

In my experience, there's often confusion and disagreement about the term *innovation*, so here are a couple of definitions to help you understand this topic:

>> **Innovation:** Converting ideas into value

>> **Urban innovation:** Discovering and implementing new ideas to meet city challenges

Okay, now that I've spelled out the definitions, let me talk about water.

All living things on Planet Earth need water, and wherever you find water, you'll find life. To survive, humans need regular access to drinking water. In their early nomadic times, as they wandered, they would need to find streams, rivers, and lakes. Later, when humans began to settle in small gathering places, they needed to be close to sources of water. Wells were dug into the water table, which provided a reliable water supply. Cisterns were created that gathered rainwater. In other instances, where water was relatively close, it was transported by people carrying baskets and other containers on their backs or heads or in their hands. Later, animals were used to pull carts. In some parts of the world, water is still transported by humans and animals.

As human settlements grew, demand for water for drinking and agriculture also increased. Systems were required in order to bring larger volumes of water predictably from the source. To solve this problem, humans invented the *aqueduct* — an elaborate combination of tunnels, surface channels, canals, clay pipes, and bridges — to move water to wherever it was needed.

Aqueducts that covered short distances were used in the earliest days of civilization, beginning with the Minoans on Crete, over 4,000 years ago. More sophisticated, longer-distance systems were developed during the Assyrian Empire. Later, the Babylonians, the Greeks, and communities across Persia, Egypt, and China all constructed elaborate aqueduct systems, including communal drinking fountains.

Finally, it was the Romans who mastered the building of aqueducts. Ambitious projects overcame all kinds of difficult terrain, including engineering, to move water upward. Many forms of aqueduct construction could be seen across the Roman Empire. The water supplied not only all basic needs and agriculture but also large public baths, fountains, and private homes. Many remnants of these systems can still be seen, scattered across the landscape. (See Figure 7-1.)

FIGURE 7-1:
The Pont du Gard Roman aqueduct, in southern France, from the first century.

Aqueduct systems were essential for enabling communities to grow and thrive. In particular, major Italian cities such as Rome were able to prosper over the centuries because of the regular supply of water. Aqueduct engineering can be considered one of the most important urban innovations of its time. Human ingenuity brought to bear on a pressing and essential need resulted in nothing less than a transformation.

REMEMBER

History is replete with these game-changing innovations in an urban context. Humans have solved many intractable issues over several thousand years (though many more remain to be solved). The results have been nothing less than miraculous, enabling them to design and build dense urban environments such as the greater area of Tokyo, Japan, which now is home to over 35 million residents.

Here's a list of some of the most important urban innovations:

>> Roads and railways
>> Harbors and airports
>> Electricity
>> Skyscrapers
>> The Internet
>> Sanitation systems

- >> Traffic signals
- >> Street lighting
- >> Urban planning
- >> Drainage
- >> Parks
- >> The grid system
- >> Public transportation
- >> Telecommunications

Each one of these items, and many more (alone and together), has made cities smarter, and typically better, places to live.

Urban innovation now continues at an accelerated pace. In fact, you can't separate this topic from the topic of smart cities. Urban innovation is largely driving the pace of change in cities.

Relying on urban innovation networks

Solving the problems of the world's communities requires the participation of a wide range of stakeholders. It's not possible for a local city agency to solve every issue: No single organization has the budget, time, or talent. The challenges are just too large, often regional, and highly diverse for any single entity to tackle. Solving these challenges today requires a network of participants. Fortunately, a movement of urban innovators in cities all over the world are rolling up their sleeves and making things happen. Disparate stakeholders are joining forces to solve some of the world's most intractable urban issues.

Urban innovation networks are clusters of various people and organizations who are connecting and collaborating on solving challenges. They're interested in, and invested in, game-changing, new ideas, often (but not always) technologically driven. These networks are trying to make a difference in areas such as sustainability, transportation, inclusion, climate, governance, equity and equality, public safety, waste management, and more. Fundamentally, efforts have one large-scale focus: improving quality of life (QoL).

Here are just a few of the areas where participants in urban innovation networks come from:

- >> Academia
- >> Vending

>> Local government

>> Regional and national governments

>> Student

>> General community

>> Specialized institution

>> Regional, national, or international organization

The ways in which these disparate players connect and collaborate are as diverse as the cities and participants themselves. An urban innovation network can be a formal organization with a charter and rules or an ad hoc collection of entities that tap into each other's skills and resources as necessary. It can be centralized by way of city hall or a motivated vendor. Universities have been particularly active in building out urban innovation networks, to tackle a single-focus issue or a suite of challenges.

REMEMBER

Urban innovation networks reflect an acknowledgment that the world's biggest urban problems will be solved when people work together. Done right, they are powerhouses for creating and sharing knowledge.

If humans are going to create cities that they aspire to live in, their future will be built on networks of motivated, empowered, and talented participants. Cities are now too complex and interdependent for any single entity to lead efforts alone. The best solutions won't necessarily spring from government buildings (although a few will); instead, support and success for smart city efforts, powered by urban innovation, will come from entrepreneurship, the exchange of ideas, the synergy of resources, and the energy of a diverse community.

Creating urban innovation labs

Solving today's tough urban problems in the years ahead will require a variety of new approaches. Albert Einstein, the German-born physicist, is reported to have said, rightly, "We can't solve problems by using the same kind of thinking we used when we created them." To create urban innovation, we humans will need new, dedicated processes and talent to experiment and test original ideas and technologies.

One approach is the creation of *urban innovation labs,* which are entities tasked with developing leading-edge ideas for a city's most intractable challenges. The labs are typically physical locations that support the experimentation, testing, and — assuming success —deployment of new solutions. They're laboratories of urban innovation.

There's no agreed-on blueprint for creating an urban innovation lab. The first step for a city is to agree that such a lab has value and then to either build one or collaborate with an external party in delivering its value. Many cities create their own labs and house them in city-owned or -leased buildings. Others collaborate with private entities and universities that partner to provide capabilities as a service. Cities that support these labs share at least two common — and still quite rare — qualities: They have a higher tolerance for risk and are comfortable granting some autonomy and freedom to innovate to these innovation teams.

Urban innovation labs can work in alignment with smart city activities or they can be independent of those activities. Either way, their work is typically focused on pressing city issues. Their independence from the requirements to support core city functions gives them the flexibility to experiment and not be constrained by regular city operations. Regardless, the lab gets no free pass when it comes to abiding by all city rules and regulations.

To embrace urban innovation labs, cities must have a higher tolerance for risk. This is because innovation, by definition, is riskier. Specifically, innovators must be allowed to try strategies that have a higher likelihood of being unsuccessful. Being able to approach problems with this mindset increases the chance of a unique solution emerging and — in the case of a failure — creates continuous opportunities for learning. Unlike in the private sector, where some amount of experimentation and failure is expected relative to advancing new, proposed products and services, the public sector isn't historically predisposed to this approach. Public officials have an enormous obligation to be fiscally responsible when managing taxpayer funds, and, with so many priorities to serve a community, the appetite for risky bets is always low.

It's fair to say that the proposal for an urban innovation lab is a hard sell. That's why you don't yet see many of them. But the tide is turning: A broader recognition that innovation is essential to solving the world's greatest challenges is helping communities and city officials recognize the benefits of paying more attention to, and focusing on, processes that are game-changing. In addition, the success of urban innovation labs in several cities is providing good evidence for making the case.

TIP

In developing an urban innovation lab, city leaders must emphasize the focus on experimentation, learning, and efficiency. Though these labs can exist independently of a smart city strategy, there appears to be important value in determining whether they can accelerate and improve the performance of smart city efforts. Aligning their goals may be a good approach for some agencies.

Implementing Urban Innovation

Even if cities don't formally call it "urban innovation," many agencies are engaged in some form of idea generation and development. For example, in a 2019 survey of 581 public officials from different governments in the United States, over 40 percent said they were experimenting with urban innovation. Agencies have to innovate — community needs and challenges aren't getting easier. In fact, intense issue complexity and creative responses will be defining characteristics of most cities in the years ahead. It's not even a matter of size or location — the need for innovation spans all types of cities. There's pressure to discover new ideas, explore them, test them, and decide whether to implement them. The challenges of cities demand it. Urban innovation can be applied in every aspect of a city's operations.

Though some local governments have formalized and developed multi-year innovation agendas, many have not yet made that decision. They certainly innovate, but they haven't yet carved it out as a deliberate part of their city's strategic plan, with an attendant set of approved processes. Of course, it's fair to say that, for many, the absence of formality isn't caused by a lack of enthusiasm. There are many legitimate reasons that plans don't exist: insufficient budget amounts or a lack of time and talent or other, more pressing priorities. However, my guess is that, for most, the time will come for developing a formal urban innovation program. It's a question of *when*, not if — and then a follow-up question of *how*.

Engaging in urban innovation means discovering and implementing new ideas to meet city challenges. So it's okay to acknowledge that urban innovation may be part of many projects in a city. Lots of innovative staff are agents-of-change in their agencies. They also use innovative tools to implement and support solutions. Bravo to them! But urban innovation is also often understood to mean the process of trying new things in an experimental manner. Being experimental suggests, by definition, that the work has a higher likelihood of failure. That's clearly different from engaging in work where the anticipated outcome is success. That's what is expected from most projects: Identify a need, determine the budget, create a plan, and then perform and complete the work. For the purposes of the discussion in this chapter, urban innovation — the experimental kind — typically doesn't follow that comfortable and predictable path.

Here's the general path for urban innovation:

1. Discover: Understand the problem and engage in a process to find viable solutions.

2. Pilot: Develop a small but sufficiently viable implementation of the solution to test.

3. Share: Document and provide the insights gained from the discovery and pilot phases to a large stakeholder group, including internal and external parties.

There are many flavors when it comes to this sequence, but this is the gist of it.

Figure 7-2 illustrates the process. It's a cycle because there may be a need to repeat it several times before a viable result emerges. I cover moving from an experiment to a project later in this chapter, in the section "Converting ideas into projects."

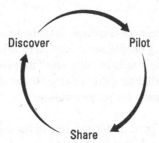

FIGURE 7-2:
The basic cyclical
process of urban
innovation.

Discover   Pilot

Share

Examining the discovery process

Let's look at what triggers the discovery process. Remember that this phase concerns itself with both understanding the issue to be solved and the exploration of solutions.

At least seven triggers can act as an impetus for starting the discovery process, as described in this list:

>> Required implementation (a new regulation, law, or policy, for example)

>> Necessary upgrade to a process or technology

>> Response to a community need

>> Implementation of new service

>> Solution to a specific problem

>> Support of an urban innovation agenda

>> Implementation of a project within a strategy, such as the smart city initiative

In this section, I'm mainly concerned with the last two triggers, which, for simplicity's sake, I collapse into a single trigger. In your city, the innovation agenda may be the consequence of the smart city strategy or simply an agenda in support of advancing the city's broad goals. Either way, the process is the same.

In Chapter 5, I discuss how a smart city vision is translated into goals. These goals then become objectives, which in turn typically manifest as projects. These projects trigger discovery work. An objective to reduce road flooding may be perfect for the urban innovation process because the solution is unknown and many new technologies may be worth exploring. You have to decide, case by case, what's appropriate.

So you have a project that requires discovery. Now what?

First, ask yourself whether you fully understand the scope of the project, its objectives, and its metrics. If not, interview the teams responsible for the objectives as well as the project.

TIP

Document your understanding of the conversations, and then present that info to the teams you've spoken with. Being on the same page here is essential. The last thing you want is to work on discovery, only to "discover" that you were researching the wrong issue. It's worth highlighting this strategy because poor communication is often cited as a leading reason for project failure.

Now, I'm assuming that you have a good understanding of the scope of the project and that you're now ready to engage in discovery. You have two main tasks:

>> Investigate potential solutions.

>> Determine whether identified solutions potentially meet your project objectives.

When it comes to carrying out your investigation, here are a few options to consider:

>> Conducting a web search

>> Talking to colleagues in other cities

>> Tapping into professional networks

>> Researching industry groups

>> Consulting industry publications

>> Searching an online solutions catalog

>> Eliciting solution providers to submit their solution for consideration

After you've identified a short list of potential solutions, you might request an informal discussion with each of the potential vendors. The purpose of this meeting is to better understand their offering and compare it against your project objectives. Using a checklist is beneficial so that you can easily compare products against each other. Because this isn't a formal elicitation process, the normal rigor of vetting the vendor and the product is less necessary (though you might choose that option). The experimentation and piloting process enable an understanding of the functions and performance of solutions.

WARNING

The entire urban innovation process *must* align with the vendor engagement and procurement rules of your agency. Don't even begin to think about initiating this work until the permissible rules are established. In government agencies, these rules are specific and enforceable. Make sure your legal, financial, and procurement team leaders are all onboard and have formally approved the approach.

Running pilots and experiments

I make a differentiation between pilots and experiments. Others may not.

A *pilot* is an effort that tests a solution with a decent expectation that it might be a candidate for later full deployment. Given that it's defined as a small implementation — a few users, a limited geographical area, and a short time frame (three to six months is reasonable), for example — it should provide ample evidence to the project team that it's worthy of further exploration and potential use.

An *experiment* is work that is highly speculative and risky. It's usually done when the project team has a lower level of confidence that the right solution has been found. It's also a more learning-intensive approach, and its timeline may be even shorter than a pilot.

TIP

Though not always the case, another clarifier that may be useful is that an experiment often tests a hypothesis, whereas a pilot tests a specific solution.

Just to keep it confusing, some people also use terms such as *proof of concept* and *prototyping* to describe the same type of project methods. All are relevant, and the available literature goes to great lengths to describe all the subtle differences. Just know that each is a way to test an idea, a product, or a service in order to make informed decisions.

Though the overall approach to running pilots and experiments may be largely identical, my differentiation helps you set expectations for stakeholders. Also, an experiment may not be subject to quite the same rigor as a pilot. For example, in a pilot, the project team may decide to also test the training for the solution. In an experiment, the team may pass on the training and be hyperfocused only on the functionality of the potential solution.

A pilot and an experiment, hereafter called the *innovation pilot*, may follow the typical stepwise project methodology, such as the waterfall model, where the project is completed in the following five distinct stages and moved, step by step, toward an ultimate project launch:

1. Plan

2. Design

3. Develop

4. Deploy

5. Test

You can choose the project methodology most appropriate to your organization and preferences. For example, *agile* methods — those that emphasize collaboration and skills — are increasingly popular. Mostly though, it's about maintaining some level of rigor. An innovation pilot isn't the same as permission to take an ad hoc approach. You'll want to keep all participants on the same page and also clearly document the results along the way.

A variety of stakeholders have differing interests in innovation projects. Solution providers, which can range from start-ups to large corporations, are often particularly enthusiastic about partnering with a city on an innovation project. This partnership can provide them with vital, on-the-ground test data and also be an opportunity to draw attention to their product or service. And, of course, the corporations are pleased that the work might eventually translate to a full sale. The interest in an innovation pilot for a solution provider may mean that it's prepared to be accommodating on cost. At minimum, the costs should be low, given the limited scope of the work, and, in the best case scenario, the provider might be prepared to engage in the innovation pilot at no cost. This is certainly no guarantee, and is determined case by case. It's also subject to procurement rules for your agency.

For the city, an innovation pilot provides insights into whether a solution is right for a specific challenge. There are benefits to being able to test in a real environment without a lot of risk in terms of costs and time lost, and it always helps to learn about the performance of a product and vendor in advance.

Other regional parties may benefit, by either participating in the innovation pilot or receiving any insights gained from the work. Participating means that costs can be shared and a larger variety of conditions can be explored. For example, a solution for public safety may be well informed by having several regional agencies participate in terms of data sharing and coordination.

Finally, as with all activities related to smart cities, collaboration between departments in a city agency is a proven approach to success. Having multiple, impacted teams engage in the innovation pilot provides essential data to inform the larger deployment; it improves learning and identifies potential gaps as well as provides the basis for achieving any decision consensus.

Setting up living labs

Urban innovation leaders may want to consider the development of a *living lab* for their pilot and experimentation efforts. In the context of a city, a living lab is a real-world environment, often in a defined geographical area, where community members and other stakeholders can either participate in co-developing solutions or experience an innovation pilot and provide feedback. Many stakeholders can participate and learn from these labs, including service providers, government staff, media, and constituents. In this way, they're said to be public-private-people partnerships (PPPPs). Both the participation and feedback from partnering members have enormous value in helping to evaluate an innovation. The candid feedback from community members — typically, those who will be impacted by any new urban innovation — is particularly important.

REMEMBER

You need to build a distinct program around the living lab, one that may include facilitators and mechanisms for feedback. The living lab can be entirely a city-operated endeavor or an outsourced capability — or a mix of the two.

A smart city with an urban innovation capability would be well-served to explore the development of a living lab.

Living labs have these benefits:

>> Co-creation of innovation with various stakeholders

>> Discovering uses, behaviors, and unanticipated consequences

>> Encouraging the participation of citizen scientists

>> Experimentation of different scenarios in a real environment

>> Research opportunities for academia and other interested parties

>> Evaluation of a pilot or experimentation from many different perspectives

Engaging in hackathons

To be successful when it comes to urban innovation, you need the input of many stakeholders. It's a mistake to see it as the domain of a few dedicated folks. Assigning a team to innovation and not encouraging collaboration from disparate players can result in others believing that they can wash their hands of innovation by simply believing it's the responsibility of a single team. You don't want that. Sure, you may want a team that's designated to take the lead when it comes to innovation, but you also want to make it easy for lots of people to be engaged.

REMEMBER

With the extent of urban challenges confronting humans, cities need all types of people and organizations to be involved in creating solutions. Cities should provide a variety of platforms for participation. You never know who will come up with the next great idea for your community.

Hackathons and challenges are two creative ways to engage a broader community in the process of urban innovation. I discuss each one individually in this section.

INNOVATION DISTRICTS

The innovation district, a brand-new model for urbanization, has emerged over the past two decades and is fast becoming a distinctive feature of smart cities. The district acts as a well-defined, walkable area in a city where public and private sector participants work to attract economic opportunity and development with the general aim of revitalizing an urban location. These districts are typically populated by research-oriented institutions, high-growth firms, and tech and creative start-ups. They include or are surrounded by a variety of amenities as well as residential and commercial properties. Unlike unplanned innovation regions such as Silicon Valley, right from Day 1 innovation districts deliberately focus on integrating quality housing, public transport accessibility, work opportunities, and recreation. Innovation districts are carefully planned and are the opposite of naturally occurring innovation districts (NOIDs).

The first district was launched in the year 2000 in Barcelona, Spain. Today, there are thought to be over 100 around the world, including districts in Berlin, Cambridge, London, Medellín, Montreal, Seoul, Stockholm, Toronto, and even Aurora, Illinois.

Innovation districts support the creation and commercialization of new ideas, thus encouraging economic growth by increasing employment and by generating profitable business activity. Jobs can then be created for the low-income neighborhoods that often surround these districts. Educational and training opportunities are often baked in. Innovation districts have the unique potential to encourage productive, inclusive, and sustainable economic development.

To succeed and create an innovation ecosystem, innovation districts have three distinctive components: physical, networking, and economic. The intersection of these components, together with a risk-taking culture, can result in increased idea generation and faster commercialization.

The three components, shown in the figure below, are described in this list:

- **Physical:** The idea here is to insist on beautifully designed buildings (or restored structures), open spaces, recreation areas, and streets that create opportunities for collaboration.

- **Networking:** By mixing the environment with academics, entrepreneurs, students, innovators, and a wide range of eclectic stakeholders, relationships can be generated that generate and push ideas forward.

- **Economic:** This refers to the businesses, institutions, and other organizations that support, finance, and encourage the pursuit of innovation.

Innovation districts present a compelling economic proposition to mayors and city leaders. After all, who wouldn't want a solution for bringing economic activity to a run-down part of the city? The big caution is this: Just because you build it doesn't mean they will come. The last thing a city needs is another project to encourage economic develop-ment that ends up digging a bigger economic hole. Certainly, cities must ensure that they have the economic, physical, and networking components in place, but they also require consistent and determined governmental, institutional, and business leadership.

The Global Institute on Innovation Districts (www.giid.org) may be a good starting point to learn more on this subject. Another resource is the Atlas of Innovation Districts, which explores the secret recipe for high-performing Innovation Districts, unlocking economic potential in communities around the world. You can find it at www.aretian.com/atlas.

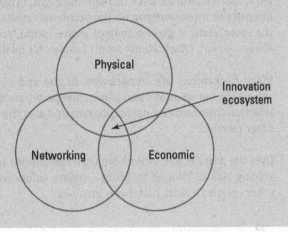

What exactly is a hackathon? The word itself comes from the combination of *hack* and mar*athon*. Straightaway, you might wonder why *hack*, which typically has a negative connotation, is being used here. Hacking does have a rather shady repu-tation when it comes to the cybersecurity world, because it's used to describe the act of breaking the security of some product or service. You've seen it on the news, and maybe you've even been a victim, if someone hacked your email or bank account. However, the *hack* in hackathon doesn't have that meaning. You can find several stories about its origin; I'm sharing my favorite here:

During World War I, planes returning from battle would land at their base having sustained damage from gunfire, such as in the fuselage, wings, and tail. Engineers on the ground used spare parts and parts from destroyed planes to fix the planes that were capable of returning to the skies. They would "hack" apart the broken planes to assemble new, reconstructed parts quickly — thus, the rise of the word "hacking." In the modern context, it means throwing together a solution quickly and crudely, but in a way that works.

The -*athon* part of the word *hackathon* comes from the word *marathon*. It reflects that the event has a specific duration and that the activity is rigorous: hack + athon = hackathon.

But, again, what is a hackathon? It's a private or public event that brings together solvers to work on one or more problems. Historically, these solvers have been software programmers, but that's no longer the case. These events can attract all sorts of talent to solve tricky issues.

The event can last from a few hours to a few days; they typically don't run longer than five days. Participants usually form small teams, dive deeply into the problems, and sometimes work through the night. (They often sleep at the event.) The intensity of those working on the problems results in full exhaustion by the time the event ends. A good supply of coffee, pizza, soft drinks, and other snacks is always served. (Hackathons aren't famous for quality nutrition.)

Many hackathons are competitive. At the end of the event, a group of judges selects the top solutions and teams, and prizes are awarded. Participants gain satisfaction from creating useful projects and also the possibility of receiving cash or other rewards.

Over the past decade, cities have used hackathons to engage their communities in solving issues. Though building software solutions has largely dominated, these other creative events have been involved:

>> Writing policies

>> Cleaning up documentation

>> Organizing data

>> Drafting budgets

>> Building hardware

Creating software solutions to solve city issues often requires city data. The emergence of open data, as discussed in Chapter 9, creates a superb intersection of value. Hackathon developers can easily access city data via the city's open data portal, either by downloading data in a standard format or, preferably, a real-time connection called an application programming interface (API). I explain APIs in Chapter 8.

Many cities hold hackathons to draw attention to their open data initiatives. Providing the data in this way also enables many events to encourage participants to solve problems that interest them, rather than tackle problems the event imposes on them.

City-based hackathons are excellent platforms for community involvement. Though the practical outcomes may not always meet expectations, the networking, collaboration, learning, and civic engagement of the participants is often enough to make the events worthwhile. Sometimes, though, a brilliant solution may in fact emerge.

Here are a few quick tips for running your own hackathon:

>> **Make the invitation inclusive.** Though the solutions may require software development, there are roles for lots of different types of people and talent. You can assist by splitting participants into diverse teams (unless they show up as a team).

>> **Find a suitable facility.** You need a large, open space and, possibly, areas for sleeping. The size depends on the number of participants. On average, space to accommodate between 30 and 100 people is reasonable.

>> **At the event's kickoff, describe the problems that need to be solved.** Though keeping goals open is an option, focused hackathons often get better results. Solving the problems should be attainable in the allotted time frame.

>> **Offer plenty of food, drinks, and snacks.** As I mention earlier, don't expect much nutrition. Can I suggest throwing some fresh fruit into the mix?

>> **Invite dignitaries to attend at certain times.** Having these leaders participate can boost morale and add cachet to the event. In my experience, having the mayor attend, perhaps at the start as well as later during the event, is extremely helpful.

>> **If permissible by your agency, consider acquiring sponsorship from local companies and technology vendors.** This lowers the cost burden to the city but also allows for better facilities, food, and prizes.

>> **Ensure that plenty of power sockets are available.** How embarrassing would it be to have this type of preventable problem?

>> **Ensure that the event has excellent Internet connectivity.** This is an absolute must-have item.

For more great advice, check out `https://hackathon.guide`.

Participating in urban challenges

Finally, another type of event, similar to a hackathon, is the urban challenge. You don't need to limit yourself to the constraints of a hackathon to engage different stakeholders in developing urban innovation. You can explore other options.

An *urban challenge* is typically a longer, more focused process. Distinct from a hackathon, it typically has the following qualities:

» Participation that comes from solving a single complex issue

» A longer duration, perhaps three to six months

» Larger rewards for winners and runners-up

» Participation from people all over the world

» Possibly one or more major sponsors from public and private sectors

» A large number of participant teams

The successful technology behind self-driving cars is the result of a challenge.

Check out www.challenge.gov, shown in Figure 7-3, a service of the United States government that works to engage citizens in competitions to solve issues of national importance. At the local level, San Francisco's Civic Bridge (www. innovation.sfgov.org/civic-bridge) and Chicago's Civic Consulting Alliance (www.ccachicago.org), are examples of solicitations for pro-bono talent to solve community challenges.

FIGURE 7-3: Examples of challenges at the US government site, challenge.gov.

Open innovation versus closed innovation

Both hackathons and urban challenges embrace the idea of engaging a wide range of participants. This concept, known as *open innovation*, functions as an alternative to conventional methods that limit participation only to specific people and groups. Intuitively, such a conventional approach is called *closed innovation*. The thesis is that, with open innovation, you can increase the volume of ideas and engage the best original thoughts from a broad and diverse group of innovators. This is particularly important when it comes to solving tough problems.

Open innovation is highly beneficial to cities because it can reduce the cost of research, bring novel ideas and practices into the mix, leverage existing innovation ecosystems, and encourage productive collaboration among diverse teams.

There are a few downsides to open innovation in a local government context. In the private sector, the main concern for organizations is being afraid of their ideas being stolen. For public agencies, the downside to open innovation is that it's more complicated to manage. You may have to coordinate a large number of people and ideas. In addition, open innovation can be a lengthier process. You'll determine the approach based on your needs.

GLOBAL CITY TEAMS CHALLENGE

The Global City Teams Challenge (GCTC) program is a collaborative platform for the development of smart cities and communities, led by the US National Institute of Standards and Technology (NIST) in partnership with other US federal agencies, including the US Department of Homeland Security Science and Technology Directorate (DHS S&T), the National Science Foundation, the International Trade Administration, and the National Telecommunications and Information Administration. It enables local governments, nonprofit organizations, academic institutions, technologists, and corporations from all over the world to form project teams — also known as action clusters and SuperClusters — to work on groundbreaking Internet of Things (IoT) and cyberphysical system (CPS) applications within the city and community environment.

The long-term goal of the GCTC program is to establish and demonstrate replicable, scalable, and sustainable models for incubation and deployment of interoperable, secure, standards-based solutions using advanced technologies s and to demonstrate their measurable benefits in cities and communities.

For more on the GCTC program, check out https://pages.nist.gov/GCTC.

Sharing urban innovation

In the process of urban innovation, you'll create and document a lot of data and information. This output is valuable to a whole host of stakeholders, from city leaders to community members and from department heads to vendors and many others. At the conclusion of an innovation pilot, the core project team will likely present its findings. At minimum, the question arises of whether the pilot was a success, based on the desired outcomes. Information needs to be presented that supports the project findings as well as any recommendations stemming from the pilot. If the pilot didn't succeed, you have to determine what lessons were learned.

TIP

Make the results of your urban innovation efforts broadly available, particularly to the community to which you are accountable. Consider posting the results on the city website and, if appropriate, the urban innovation or smart city microsite. Document the highlights of the work, post relevant reports, feature actual-versus-budgeted spending, consider data visualizations (a popular way to communicate information), summarize the conclusion, and include next steps, if any.

The opportunity exists to share even more broadly. Consider making the results available to other communities, particularly those who are interested in solving the same problems as you. Find a platform that enables the sharing of urban innovation in your region or country. In the private sector, sharing the work of innovation isn't generally embraced, because this work is highly competitive in nature. But in the public sector, where cities generally aren't competing (with some exceptions, say, for talent), sharing ends up benefiting everyone. With the focus on quality-of-life improvements, shared urban innovation can help more people and can be magnified when applied at a regional level. This is what's at the core of serving the public's interest.

REMEMBER

People in the public sector are reticent to broadly communicate failures. Of course, an innovation pilot that doesn't succeed must be discussed and shared internally in an agency. This is essential learning for the organization. But the data on this topic suggests that cities aren't inclined to broadly share these failures with other agencies. Because it's a public record, this information can of course be acquired by anyone. The question becomes whether a city wants to proactively communicate its poor results. Recognizing the value in lessons to other agencies of why a project failed, though, should encourage more cities to share their urban innovation endeavors. I, for one, would encourage this, despite any embarrassment. At the end of the day, piloting innovation and limiting risks and costs should take the sting out of any failures. Those expensive, high-profile projects that, after full deployment, fail to meet expectations — well, that's another story.

Converting ideas into projects

Fundamentally, an urban innovation program is about sourcing new ideas for solving intractable city issues. As I discuss in this chapter, piloting and experimenting with new ideas before full deployment is a smart risk mitigation strategy. But don't lose sight of the intent. If an innovation pilot is successful, the opportunity exists to convert it to a full-blown project.

After the innovation pilot is complete, the team must document all its findings, and the results must be compared to the original objectives and desired outcomes. This work should make for some robust discussions. In the end, the team needs to determine, with supporting data, whether the innovation pilot was a success. If it has succeeded, further decisions need to be made.

A successful innovation pilot doesn't automatically turn into a full deployment. For example, the project may have been exploratory or demonstrable only, or a way to gather more data for input into a higher-level decision. The project may also be lower on the priority list.

However, the innovation pilot may need to be moved to a full project. In this case, the effort will likely be moved to a project team or project management office (PMO). Any decision surrounding how a project is handled is the subject of *project governance*, a topic I discuss in Chapter 6.

If an urban innovation pilot results in an actual full-scale deployment and then goes on to solve what once was an intractable community issue, that's the definition of success. Cities all over the world are quickly learning the value of urban innovation, pilots, and experiments. This work isn't restricted to large and wealthy communities. All types of communities are seeing the benefits of applying rigor to eliciting and identifying new ideas.

REMEMBER

In the 21st century, cities are demanding creative solutions. These won't come if you continue business as usual. Smarter cities are those that approach the future differently. They're open to possibilities, and they're ready to take some risks and try new things — even if it means that failure is an option.

Chapter **8**

Enabling Change through Technology

In his book, *WTF?: What's the Future and Why It's Up to Us*, the notable Silicon Valley technology pundit Tim O'Reilly, the founder and CEO of O'Reilly Media, says that "reinventing government to bring it up to date with the rest of society is one of the grand challenges of the twenty-first century." I think he has it exactly right. For a whole host of reasons, city governments find themselves playing catch-up in terms of contemporary processes and technologies. By 2022, it's predicted that there will be a global market for smart city technology and services of around $158 billion annually. China alone is anticipated to spend approximately $333 billion by 2025 on transforming 80 percent of its cities into smart cities.

You can find lots of great exceptions — cities pushing the envelope on what's possible — but they represent a small number relative to the hundreds of thousands of cities across the globe that are behind the curve. And yet, I think it's best not to concentrate on past or present failures. To be sure, it's important to learn from the past, but only if it helps you better focus on what cities can do now and in the future.

You might have turned to this chapter first because so many people see smart cities as a product of technology innovation. You might be wondering what kind of cool new technology you can apply in your city to improve the quality of life for the community. It's not an unreasonable assumption or question. Technology is a driving support mechanism for building better cities. In fact, technology has become *the* driving force across economies. What enterprise isn't a technology organization today? Though it's entirely fair to want to understand the new tools that are available to bring about positive change, tools alone won't get the job done. This book is replete with guidance on additional and essential focus areas that include strategy, governance, data, community engagement, and communications. You have to consider the broader context of the environment in which you're working. For example, what might be the outcome of considering aspects such as demographics, education, topography, income, commerce, and infrastructure in influencing your smart city strategy?

REMEMBER

Though technology is at the core of the smart city movement, don't let it entirely guide the important choices that need to be made. Consider technologies as enabling a strategy that has been designed with your community's characteristics and qualities in mind. Most of all, make sure that the target goal is to improve the quality of life for your community members.

With that reminder in place, let's focus on this chapter. Over the next few pages, I help you explore a wide variety of new and emerging technologies that are beginning to make a positive difference in communities all over the world. It's not an exhaustive list. It can't be. I'd need another book just for that. However, based on surveying the main innovative technologies being adopted in smart cities, these are all at the top of a long list. For each technology, you should understand what it is and how it's being applied. If you're inspired and curious, dig deeper into that area. Fortunately, an abundance of quality content on all these technologies is available online to you as well as in other books.

Okay, enough of the prologues — it's time to jump in and take a look at both the drivers of technological change and the cool (wait, I mean important) technologies themselves.

Recognizing Technological Change in Modern Cities

The world is evolving at great speed. (This assertion isn't lost on anyone.) It doesn't matter where you live — everyone is observing and experiencing the shift that is underway. Some of it's economic and political in nature, other aspects are tied to changing demographics and scientific discoveries, and a lot of it's technologically driven. A data-driven, hyperconnected, and digitally and physically transforming world is impacting so much of how humans live, work, and play.

Taken as a whole, these changes are readily apparent in the cities of the world.

The drivers of technological change in cities are multidimensional in nature. Of these dimensions, the most important to mention are hyperconnected constituents and devices, increased expectations when it comes to government, aging systems and infrastructure, digital transformation, and a fourth industrial revolution. In this first section of the chapter, I dive deeper into some of these drivers of change. Understanding these dimensions can help put matters in context and inform your smart city strategy and plan.

From analog to digital

In the technology world, anything that isn't digital is considered analog. The core functions of cities are (and have been since Day 1) the definition of analog. Think about roads, bridges, water systems, buildings, parks, hospitals, and airports. These are the big, physical components of the urban world. Of course, regardless of other changes occurring in the economy, these elements will remain. In fact, as many cities continue to grow, they'll need a lot more analog elements.

What must be recognized, though, is that the role of digital is increasingly important in the world. By *digital,* I mean electronic technology that generates, stores, and processes data in terms of 1's and 0's — the language of computers. As the primary driver of the third industrial revolution, which began in the 1950s, digital has transformed much of how things get done. However, even though it feels like the world has come a long way and is reaching the peak of digitalization, I believe that the reality is far different: Society is just getting started in realizing the full extent of the possibilities of going digital. As the third decade of the 21st century begins, the vast majority of organizations are only now embarking on their digital transformations. That is, they are completely rethinking how they function and what they deliver, by examining these crucial aspects through the lens of the Internet and digitalization. A simple example is what has happened with newspapers: Not only have many publications succumbed to digital, but news is also now consumed entirely differently, by way of video, tweets, blogs, and other methods.

REMEMBER

Digitalization is destroying and creating industries. That's why it's nothing less than a revolution.

As this digital transformation has emerged within the private sector, consumer expectations have changed. People want their services and products to be provided and delivered faster and at a higher quality. They want services on their smartphones, and they expect deeper engagement with providers. Send a complaint email? A quick response is anticipated. Providers are embracing digital in order to meet these expectations and to lower the cost of production. Radical changes are happening rapidly on both sides of the consumer-provider equation.

These same trends are beginning to be evident in cities. Communities often want to interact with city hall electronically. They want apps on their phones to request permits, find recycling centers, book community centers, check the quality of air, and so much more. For example, the city of Moscow in Russia now offers over 300 digital government services to its residents and completes over one billion of these digital requests per year.

Cities, too, are at the beginning of a wide-ranging digital transformation. Done right, this situation can be a win-win for the public agency and the community. Digitalization is a pillar of smart city efforts. If cities embrace digital solutions — many of which I discuss in this chapter — they can do all of this and much more:

>> Lower costs

>> Improve efficiencies

>> Increase service quality

>> Add new services and value

>> Capture and share meaningful data

>> Magnify citizen engagement

>> Create innovative public-private partnerships

(Figure 8-1 highlights some of the areas that might benefit from a digital transformation.)

Customer focus	Personalization
All efforts put customer at the center of decisions.	Service and product focused on each customer.
Digitalization	**Leadership**
Migrate from analog to a transformed digital business model.	Leaders are prepared to take bold risks and transform the organization.
Organizational structure	**Supply chain**
Table of organization is designed around customer focus.	Focused on improving efficiency, transparency, and reliability.
Data integration	**Cybersecurity**
Enable data to easily flow between systems.	Prioritize matters of information security and privacy.

FIGURE 8-1: Common areas of digital transformation.

THE US DIGITAL SERVICES PLAYBOOK

In October 2013, the website in support of US President Obama's signature legislative achievement, the Patient Protection and Affordable Care Act (or just Affordable Care Act), was launched. History records that the website did not perform well. In fact, it was an embarrassing failure. Though the website was eventually fixed, the US federal government was determined to put in place steps to prevent a similar disaster in the future.

In August 2014, Obama announced the creation of the US Digital Service, or USDS (at www.usds.gov), one of several steps to improve the outcomes in the creation and delivery of federal technology services. The service brought together talented engineers, designers, product managers, bureaucracy specialists, and others to change the government's approach to technology projects. Today, the USDS brings best practices and new approaches to support government modernization efforts.

To apply consistency and to influence good practices across the entire US federal government (and to encourage state and local agencies), the USDS created a playbook of 13 key "plays," drawn from the private and public sectors, that, if followed together, would help in the effective design and creation of digital services.

Here are the 13 digital services plays:

1. Understand what people need.

2. Address the whole experience, from start to finish.

3. Make it simple and intuitive.

4. Build the service using agile practices.

5. Structure budgets and contracts to support delivery.

6. Assign a single leader and hold that person accountable.

7. Bring in experienced teams.

8. Choose modern technology components.

9. Deploy in a flexible hosting environment.

10. Automate testing and deployments.

11. Manage security and privacy by taking advantage of reusable processes.

12. Use data to drive decisions.

13. Default to open. Make non-protected data easily accessible.

You can find the details of each play at https://playbook.cio.gov.

Cities are the ultimate intersection of the analog and digital worlds.

In smart cities, digital rights must be protected. Cities Coalition for Digital Rights (`https://citiesfordigitalrights.org`) is a joint initiative launched initially by Amsterdam, Barcelona and New York City that has the support of UN-Habitat: United Nations Human Settlements Programme, EUROCITIES, United Cities and Local Governments (UCLG), and other participating cities to protect, promote and monitor residents' and visitors' digital rights.

The fourth industrial revolution

Though I argue that the world is still in the early innings of a third industrial revolution — the electronics, digital, and Internet age — the signs of yet another revolution are becoming visible. First coined in 2015 by Klaus Schwab, the executive chairman of the World Economic Forum, the *fourth industrial revolution* is defined as an emerging period of rapid technological innovation and societal change. (Figure 8-2 illustrates the major developments in each of the four industrial revolutions.) These new technologies are advancing the intersection and capabilities of hardware, software, and biology — collectively called *cyberphysical* systems. In addition, many of these systems are being enhanced by developments in communications and connectivity. Breakthroughs are being made in megatrend areas such as robotics, artificial intelligence, quantum computing, biotechnology, nanotechnology, neurotechnology, the Internet of Things, blockchain, fifth-generation wireless (5G) and other communications protocols discussed in this chapter, 3D printing, and autonomous vehicles (AVs). Societal changes include the transforming nature of work, shifting global demographics, exploding consumer expectations, varying technology ethics (*technoethics*), and expanding global economics.

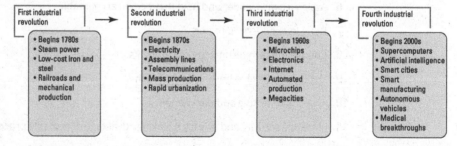

FIGURE 8-2: The four industrial revolutions.

In addition, these technological and societal changes are being shaped by four major drivers: velocity, impact, scope, and convergence. I cover each of these drivers in the next few sections.

Velocity

Velocity refers to the speed of change — the fact that the introduction of new innovation is happening at a faster rate and that the rate continues to increase. Looking at the length of time it took for various products to reach 50 million users over the years provides a few examples of increasing velocity:

>> **The telephone,** first introduced in the late 1800s, took 75 years to reach 50 million users.

>> **The television,** beginning in the 1920s, took 13 years.

>> **The Internet's** availability to the general public, beginning in the 1990s, took 4 years.

>> **Pokemon Go,** the popular smartphone game introduced in 2016, took just 19 days.

Being able to quickly reach large global audiences is now mainstream for providers of successful products and services. Marketing through online channels can reach millions of people within a day — particularly if a message becomes viral. Rapid communications and product adoption have significant positive and potentially negative consequences. On one hand, large sales can bring in sizable revenues quickly, but on the other, bad news or a fake story that spreads rapidly can badly damage a brand. Fast technology deployment has pros and cons as well: For example, a software upgrade can bring more capability to lots of people quickly, but an accidental deployment of bad software can cause significant problems.

Scope

Scope refers to the extent of introduced change. In the fourth industrial revolution, the scope of change is quite expansive. Take software distribution as an example. Years ago, installing software required purchasing a box with discs and then installing the software from those discs on each computer you wanted to put the program on. Later, installation was made easier with the introduction of client-server technology, which enabled software to be accessed from a single computer — a server on a network. Today, software for smartphones is distributed over the air, sometimes to millions of users in a few hours. An Apple or Android operating system can be made available to billions of devices over the course of just a few short days. Coupled with velocity, scope means reaching and affecting large global audiences quickly.

Impact

Impact refers to the magnitude and consequences of the effects of the change. For an example, take a look at how music distribution has evolved. It wasn't so long ago that music was purchased on a physical medium, such as a record or tape. Later, in the third industrial revolution, the format at first became digital but remained on a disc. Soon after, it became a file accessible over a network. Downloading music to a device was popular and convenient — but then it changed again. Rather than downloading, the model changed to streaming the music. Today, several solutions provide massive catalogs of streaming music that can be accessed anytime, and from anywhere, quite simply with just an Internet connection. Rather than a simple incremental change, the shift from file downloads to streaming has reimagined the distribution of music and the music business as a whole. This kind of impact, coupled with velocity and scope, has no precedent. It's the fourth industrial revolution in action.

Convergence

Though technologies alone are important, when combined, the outcomes are far more interesting. For example, artificial intelligence (AI) is a significant technology that has the possibility of being a game-changer in many industries, including government and cities. But it's not AI alone that typically changes the game. It's when AI is combined with, say, data, GPS, cloud, and fast networks that it becomes considerably more powerful. The combination and intersection of technologies is called *convergence*. Ride-hailing solutions such as Uber and Grab are the products of convergence. These solutions require AI, online payments, GPS, smartphones, cloud computing, data optimization, and other technologies to converge in order to function. In addition, each of the converged technologies must be at the right level of technological maturity. A tried-and-tested technology converged with an emerging, unproven technology may be a recipe for failure.

The fourth industrial revolution and cities

As it ramps up, the fourth industrial revolution will have material consequences in every aspect of the world. This is the context in which urban communities will evolve and your smart cities strategies get executed. The technologies and societal changes of the fourth industrial revolution will directly and indirectly impact cities in terms of both function and operations. They will expand the toolkit available to city planners and technologists, creating enormous new benefits and, at the same time, plenty of risk. In addition, cities will continue to be shaped by societal forces — the future of work, for example, or shifting demographics — but at an even faster pace and with even bigger consequences in the years ahead.

The fourth industrial revolution represents an environment of change unlike any other time in human history. The future is both exciting and unpredictable, and this directly applies to the future of cities. The remainder of this chapter explores many of the emerging technologies of the fourth industrial revolution and how they may be applied in designing and developing smarter cities.

The Internet of Things (IoT)

When the Internet emerged from the lab and was made available to the general public in the 1990s, it enabled people to easily access information and other resources over a standards-based global network. It was a seamless online medium for person-to-person (P2P), business-to-consumer (B2C), and business-to-business (B2B) interactions. In time, the Internet was also used to connect people to machines. For example, it became possible to check the status of a hardware device at a distant location. A machine on a network simply became another type of user. If a backup device completed a backup job, it could send a notification to a person or to another computer. At this point, participation on the Internet included both humans and machines. By the early 2000s, the first references to the notion of an IoT emerged.

The *Internet of Things (IoT)* is a network of physical objects that can be equipped with sensors, software, and other technologies that connect and exchange data with other systems over the Internet.

Though the number of people who can use the Internet has a finite size, an IoT has no upper limit. Billions of "things" are already connected over the Internet, and by 2025 the number is projected to exceed 22 billion.

REMEMBER

The definition of the IoT goes beyond simply connecting hardware devices over the Internet. It's a convergence of technologies — you might recall that convergence is one of the four dimensions of the fourth industrial revolution. The IoT includes low-cost wireless connectivity and sensors, machine learning (a form of artificial intelligence), cloud and edge computing, and other control systems. The IoT helps to derive data-driven insights in many contexts. It also connects the physical world to the digital world, enabling new innovation and value. (Figure 8-3 illustrates the basic architecture of the IoT.)

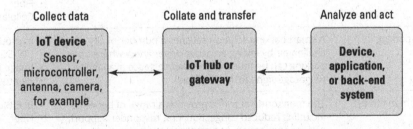

FIGURE 8-3: The basic architecture of the IoT.

IoT devices can already be found in homes, businesses, factories, and hospitals, and they're increasingly finding an important, growing, and lucrative market and application in smart cities.

In the home, many smart devices are also IoT devices, such as digital assistants, thermostats, audio speakers, and security cameras. When applied in a factory context, IoT is better known as the Industrial Internet of Things (IIoT). For example, embedding this technology in a manufacturing setting can improve operations by helping to predict production and maintenance problems before they occur. Connected sensors can detect and report on characteristics such as temperature levels, cog movements, pressure, and air and oil flow. The IIoT improves quality control, sustainability practices, and supply chain operations. Improved outcomes — such as optimizing resource deployments, energy management, and asset tracking — are also clear benefits.

Both the IoT and IIoT are central technologies of the fourth industrial revolution. The IoT is quickly becoming a useful set of tools in a city context. As I explain later in this chapter, a growing number of IoT applications can be applied in cities. In addition, Table 8-1 illustrates some common uses of IoT devices in the city context. Each IoT solution has a connectivity type. You can learn more about one by referencing Table 8-2 later in this chapter.

TABLE 8-1   ## Examples of IoT Solutions for Cities

IoT Solution	Description	Technology Examples
Smart street lighting	Streetlights are targeted at commercial and residential streets for energy efficiency purposes (LED and solar, in other words), sensor attachments, as well as public safety functions.	• Wi-Fi • Mesh • NB-IoT • Weightless
Smart area lighting	Area lighting is targeted at commercial and citizen locations — shopping malls, parks, and garages, for example.	• Wi-Fi • Mesh • NB-IoT • Weightless
Environmental monitoring	The monitoring of city environments for pollutants, dust, and various gases benefits the community and provides health metrics for the city.	• Bluetooth • NB-IoT • Wi-Fi • Fiber • Cellular
Smart parking	A smart parking solution satisfies a number of city challenges by letting an active driver know where open parking can be found (by displaying space availability on garage signage, for example).	• In-ground pucks • LTE/5G • Image sensors + ML/AI • Bluetooth/BLE
Traffic monitoring	The monitoring of traffic provides a range of benefits, including reduced congestion, first responder support, accident mitigation, and transportation planning.	• BLE/Bluetooth • Fiber • Radar/LIDAR • DSRC • Magnetometer and inductive loops • Traffic management systems • Detection cameras

IoT Solution	Description	Technology Examples
Counting • Pedestrians • Cars • Bicycles	The movement of people and vehicles in an urban environment can be monitored. City and transportation planning is assisted through the analysis of traffic patterns.	• Image sensors and cameras • Radar/LIDAR • Bluetooth/BLE • LTE/5G
Curbside management	Curb space is a valuable city asset, optimized by monitoring and management capabilities to improve safety and reduce congestion.	• Image sensors and cameras • Radar/LIDAR • Bluetooth/BLE • LTE/5G
Digital signage • On the street • Area/parking/parks	Digital signage provides dynamic content that includes community messaging and engagement, advertisements, traffic notifications, and wayfinding.	• LTE/5G • Wi-Fi • Fiber • Image sensors • Content management system (CMS)
Water monitoring and metering	Water monitoring and metering helps detect leaks and other forms of water loss, manages billing, and improves energy efficiency and flood detection.	• LPWAN • NB-IoT • LTE/5G
Security monitoring	Security monitoring provides the public safety team with improved situational awareness, deters criminal acts, stores a record of activity as evidence, and often assists with a faster response.	• Image sensors and cameras • Radar/LIDAR • Bluetooth/BLE • LTE/5G
Gunshot detection	Gunshot detection can provide real-time notification of a gunshot occurrence and its location. It improves response time and citizen safety and can even be used as evidence.	• Acoustic sensors • LTE/5G • Fiber
Smart trash cans	Notification of real-time trash levels in order to optimize servicing of the cans. The cans are often solar-powered and have automatic trash compacting.	• Wi-Fi • Level sensors

Table created in collaboration with Bill Pugh and Smart Connections Consulting LLC (www.smartconnections.io).

REMEMBER

The IoT is enabling new opportunities for innovation and automation, capabilities in a wide range of industries, increased efficiencies, and the possibility of reinvention. This technology is still in its early days, but the promise of the IoT is quickly coming into focus.

Exploring a Variety of Urban Technologies

Okay, this is the fun part — the new and emerging technologies section. You may be familiar with some of these technologies or, perhaps at minimum, you've heard the terms *blockchain*, *digital twins*, or *machine learning*. What exactly are these technologies, and why should you care?

Each of the following technologies is at some stage of urban development and deployment. Some might still be experimental in a city context, and others may be moving into the mainstream of smart city expectations. For example, smart lighting and smart signage are already relatively mature, whereas delivery drones and self-driving cars are still in the early stages. Understanding this continuum of urban innovation can help you manage risk. Proven technologies provide some additional project comfort that an emerging technology may not. That shouldn't stop you from experimenting with, or even implementing, a newer solution, but it does mean that you should deploy it differently. For example, assuming that the business case has been made for smart lighting, a project can embrace a phased, full-city deployment. However, if you're looking to implement a blockchain solution, you might have a more extensive evaluation and pilot phase.

REMEMBER

Tolerance for risk in the public sector is low relative to other industries, which has made many agencies risk averse. It shouldn't. Knowing that you face more risk may mean moving forward in a more deliberate and conservative manner. Though the riskier route may be less appealing, the upside is that higher-risk projects that succeed often bring bigger rewards. For example, upgrading a system may be safer and less risky, but replacing a system may transform the service of a government division.

Ladies and gentlemen, I present to you [drumroll, please] the technological enablers of change in cities.

Social media and communication tools

In the early days of the White House in Washington, DC, the home and office of the president of the United States, anyone could walk up to the front door — and even into the lobby — and ask to see the president. If the visitor had a complaint or an idea and the president wasn't available, they could pass it to a messenger to give to him. In some instances, the president would even welcome the guest so that he could hear directly from the person.

Today, communicating with government officials has changed just a little bit since those quaint early days of the White House. For a long time, in-person meetings and events, letters, and phone calls were the only channels available.

These methods are still important now, and in some smaller communities it's still relatively easy to find an opportunity to talk directly to the mayor and other government decision-makers. Even in larger cities, if you're prepared to wait a while, most city leaders will meet with you. Listening directly to community members, reading their emails, and checking voicemail are all essential ways for leaders to understand what's important to their locality.

REMEMBER

Surprisingly, even in the third decade of the 21st century, letter writing is still considered to be one of the most powerful ways of communicating a message to government. Partly it has to do with tradition, but it also demonstrates that someone has made an effort. Quality letters require thought and reflection.

In the past several decades, the number of channels to communicate to, and hear from, government has expanded considerably due to the advent of your friend the Internet.

Email has become the de facto primary communications tool in almost every industry, including government. The accessibility, immediacy, and speed of email make it an obvious choice. Despite many efforts to replace email with innovative alternatives, email remains the "killer app," to use the currently fashionable techie parlance.

It would be unusual for any city to not provide a list of email addresses relevant to areas of interest. What might be less unusual is the difficulty in finding those email addresses!

TIP

Make access and visibility to your city's essential email addresses glaringly obvious on your city's website and other communications channels such as social media. The information can be as obvious as a large Contact Us button or some hypertext on the home page that says, "Click here to find city email addresses." In addition, every department and division home page should list of relevant email addresses. Most importantly, make sure that a process is in place to check and respond to emails that arrive in these inboxes.

REMEMBER

It's okay to add contact forms as well, because they're quite popular on city websites. I recommend having an email option, too. I'll say it again here: Make sure you have a process in place to check and respond to information submitted by a contact form.

The Internet has provided a lot of new communication tools for cities. Municipalities have embraced email newsletters, online surveys, and forums for community engagement and discussion. Choosing the right platform for the right message is a critical decision. If your city can afford it, a communications leader combined with a coherent strategy can do much to ensure the success of your smart city initiative.

Perhaps the biggest change to city communications in recent years is the introduction of social media. In the same way that cities have websites, many now have a presence on the dominant social media platforms, such as Facebook, Twitter, LinkedIn, Instagram, and YouTube. These platforms, in addition to being largely without cost for basic functionality, lower the barriers to communications in both directions: from the community member to the city and vice versa. They enable a city to communicate and engage in different formats, ranging from text to video. Recent research has shown that the use of social media by local government triples the number of people who feel connected to their city.

Here are some other uses of social media in smart cities:

>> Recruiting

>> Marketing

>> Crisis management

>> Gauging the emotional temperature of constituents

>> Community analytics

>> Polling

>> Idea management

>> Event management

The impact of social media exceeds just the definition of "another" media channel. It has the power to win elections and motivate social revolutions.

On November 4, 2008, Barack Obama became the 44th president of the United States. His campaign was the first to completely embrace social media applications to raise money, champion proposed policies, and win followers. During the campaign, President Obama's activities could be found on over 15 social networking sites. His usage of Internet services, and in particular social media, has been compared to President Franklin Roosevelt's adoption of the radio and President Kennedy's use of television as "firsts" in the engagement of the White House and the American public. Today, Obama has the highest number of Twitter followers, now exceeding 117 million.

From 2010 to 2012, a wave of revolutionary demonstrations and protests, called the Arab Spring, took place across the Middle East and North Africa. These activities resulted in much bloodshed and the overthrow of several governments. The impact of the Arab Spring is still being felt, especially in terms of many ongoing unsettled conflicts. Social media was used by protestors to facilitate communications and interactions. They also used it to organize demonstrations, disseminate information, and raise local and global awareness. Highly heated social media discussions frequently preceded demonstrations, and it often helped to shape the political debate. Governments used social media to communicate their own messages to communities and the protestors. They also used it for monitoring communications for anti-uprising activities. The conclusion of academics is that social media played an important role in the mobilization and empowerment of the Arab Spring.

For all its remarkable benefits, social media has some big challenges as well. As of 2020, it remains largely unregulated — in other words, it's basically the wild west, where almost anything goes. It's used for (among other nefarious activities) promoting hate, bullying, and harassment, and it accelerates and amplifies misinformation. Social media also creates inclusion issues by, for example, limiting the participation of those without easy access to the Internet, and also dividing people into those who understand and know how to use the technology and those who don't. Careful attention is required in order to manage privacy. From knowing what to publish, how to manage posts, and how to handle the threat of plain old hacking, ensuring privacy presents a formidable challenge.

TIP

For governments to succeed in using social media for smart city channels requires a coherent strategy, the appropriate prioritization, experienced talent, and supporting tools. Anything less may result in poor value being derived, unmanaged costs, higher risks, privacy challenges, and a disappointed community.

Artificial intelligence (AI)

The capability of a machine to imitate intelligent human behavior is the dictionary definition of artificial intelligence (AI). The concept that a computer can simulate human actions is at the core of current use, research, and development. For now, I'll put aside the notion that the goal of AI is to create computer consciousness and emotions. That work continues, but it will be a long time — if ever — before anyone sees real results.

A more reasonable near-term view of AI is, for example, the use of a computer to study a digital photograph and being capable of accurately identifying a person or an object. Although it has been a tough challenge, current AI is getting good at it. Using machines for visual and audio identification has achieved some remarkable results in the past few years.

Hey, Siri. Okay, Google.

Based on all the recent news surrounding AI, it would be easy to believe it's a new topic. In fact, AI research dates back to the 1950s. However, it's only in the past few years — as a result of high-performance computing, big data, and advanced software code — that major leaps have been made. It's not yet C3PO from *Star Wars*, but AI is already delivering a wide range of value across the world's economies. You may not realize the subtle ways that AI is supporting humans' day-to-day activities already, such as receiving directions on their smartphones, email spam filtering, ride hailing apps, mobile check deposits, friend suggestions on Facebook, and online search. Already, AI is enabling cars to complete several autonomous tasks, such as self-parking.

When IBM's efforts to build a computer that could beat a chess grandmaster finally succeeded, it was a major milestone in AI. A computer capable of repeatedly defeating a human at a game that was thought to require unique human ability was a sobering moment in the realization of the power we humans had unleashed.

When you hear talk of AI, you often hear the term *machine learning* (ML) used. This is a type of AI that uses data to train a computer to complete specific tasks. For example, if you want a computer to identify a bicycle in any digital picture, you would populate the system with a lot of pictures of bicycles. ML then uses an *algorithm* — calculations based on a set of rules — to process the training data and make predictions on pictures it hasn't already seen. In other words, if it looks like a bicycle, it's probably a bicycle. The system learns and improves with more data and confirmations of success. A subset of ML is *deep learning* — it's an even more accurate predictor than ML and uses the information processing patterns that are emulated on how the human brain works.

Current research and progress areas in AI include problem solving, perception, planning, and the management of robotics.

As you can imagine, AI is already being used in cities and new applications are quickly emerging. Smart cities are embracing the benefits. For example, when used in combination with IoT technologies, AI is already helping with traffic-related challenges. Los Angeles, California, which has the unfortunate title of having the world's worst traffic congestion, is using a smart traffic solution to inform drivers of traffic congestion and signal issues. Road surface sensors and closed-circuit cameras send real-time updates to a central traffic management system. The data feed is analyzed and then information is distributed to vehicles. IoT and AI are also helping drivers find open parking spaces. A variety of apps and implementations are able to determine parking space availability and send notifications.

In Barcelona, Spain as well as in many other cities around the world, smart waste management systems use AI and IoT technology that is fitted on trash cans and can notify waste collectors when full. In this way, waste collection routes can be optimized for trucks, and trash cans be assured of being available for use.

AI is being used in many other areas, including smart streetlights, video surveillance, data analytics, improved resource utilization, and public safety.

The topic of AI isn't without some significant challenges. The use of AI in several contexts, including public safety analytics and surveillance, raise serious questions and concerns about privacy. AI coupled with robotics has the ability to displace human workers. Though the long-term effects are unknown, some experts are concerned that these technologies might create a lot of unemployment. It has emerged that AI adopts the biases of society and, in fact, can exacerbate them. A recent example was an AI system for reviewing resumes that favored male applicants.

REMEMBER

With all new technology, you have to weigh up the advantages and challenges. The future is less about whether humans can achieve something and more about whether they should do something. Careful evaluation of AI solutions is required as you move forward with your smart city strategy.

Combining AI with other technologies from the fourth industrial revolution — such as IoT, big data, cloud computing, digitalization, robotics, and quantum computing — introduces a whole new generation of urban innovation capabilities. Today, humans are just scratching the surface of what is possible. Tomorrow's smart cities powered by AI have the potential to be *amazing*.

Blockchain technology

In 2008, the paper "Bitcoin: A Peer-to-Peer Electronic Cash System" was published on an online discussion board. (You can read it at https://bitcoin.org/bitcoin.pdf; it's quite short and relatively understandable.) The paper described a proposal for a digital form of money, Bitcoin, that could be exchanged quickly and seamlessly between people and with no intermediaries. Bitcoin is believed to be a response to the failure of the financial system in the great recession of the late 2000s. Though the concept of digital money wasn't new and people had made many attempts to make it work, the paper offered for the first time a novel solution to the problem known as *double-spend*, which was an issue inherent to digital: It's far too easy to duplicate something in the digital world. If digital money is simple to duplicate, then it's going to fail. Though a detailed explanation of how the paper solved the problem is beyond the scope of this book, let's just say the idea required agreement from many participants for each digital money transaction, and computing processing power and some clever mathematics were thrown into the mix.

Surprisingly, though the paper is attributed to Satoshi Nakamoto, to this day, nobody knows who that is or whether they're even a real person. One hypothesis suggests that the paper was written by a group of people who decided to remain anonymous.

In 2009, a year after the paper appeared, Bitcoin was launched into the world. Because it used encryption as part of its design, it was called a *cryptocurrency*. (*Crypto* means "hidden" or "secret.") Now, you may be thinking, "I thought this was a section on blockchain, not cryptocurrency." Well, this is where the story gets interesting.

Though Bitcoin stole the show in 2009, the underlying technology that made it work — its inner workings, in other words — proved intriguing to many people after its launch. Bitcoin uses a technology called a *distributed ledger (DLT)*. It turns out that the form of DLT used in Bitcoin is called a blockchain. Voilà! Blockchain had arrived.

Blockchain is a type of database that stores transactions. Each transaction that is recorded in the database is tied to the previous transaction. (Instead of *tied*, you could, of course, say *chained*.) Because the entries in the database cannot be deleted, the database is said to be *immutable*. It turns out that the immutability of a blockchain database can be applied in many contexts. Blockchain out of the box supports peer-to-peer, consensus-based, high-integrity transaction processing. (Figure 8-4 outlines the process.)

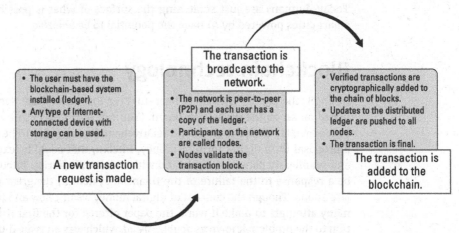

- The user must have the blockchain-based system installed (ledger).
- Any type of Internet-connected device with storage can be used.

A new transaction request is made.

The transaction is broadcast to the network.

- The network is peer-to-peer (P2P) and each user has a copy of the ledger.
- Participants on the network are called nodes.
- Nodes validate the transaction block.

- Verified transactions are cryptographically added to the chain of blocks.
- Updates to the distributed ledger are pushed to all nodes.
- The transaction is final.

The transaction is added to the blockchain.

FIGURE 8-4: How blockchain technology works.

REMEMBER

Blockchain elegantly increases trust and efficiency in online transactions. Its design makes fraud and transaction manipulation difficult — nearly impossible, in fact. In many contexts, this kind of integrity is superior to traditional databases.

At its core, blockchain eliminates the need to rely on traditional, human-brokered trust; it's a trustless system. It eliminates intermediaries and distributes system logic in a more efficient manner.

Many blockchain variants have been introduced. A popular solution called Ethereum can capture rules in the database known as smart contracts. These *smart contracts* trigger events whenever certain conditions are met, which can enable the creation of serverless, distributed applications called DApps. *DApps* reduce the bottlenecks of traditional hierarchical system architectures and create increased efficiencies.

Today, blockchain is being used in a large variety of industries and applications, ranging from supply chain to financial services and food safety and from health-care and retail to the IoT, identity management, and, of course, government and cities.

As an industry, governments collect, store, and manage high volumes of data. In the best case scenario, this data is stored in an information system, but all too often it's still paper based.

Here are several examples of documentation that governments and cities store:

>> Government personnel data

>> Appropriated funds

>> Patents

>> Trademarks

>> Copyrights

>> Property deeds

>> Professional licenses

>> Fines, including payments and processing

>> Criminal records

>> Birth and death certificates

>> Voting records

>> Identity management

Might the storage of these types of documentation in a blockchain database improve integrity and access management?

According to a recent survey conducted by IBM and the Economic Intelligence Unit, government interest in blockchain is high. Nine in ten government organizations plan to invest in blockchain for use in financial transaction management, asset management, contract management, and regulatory compliance.

To see the potential that's out there, have a look at actual blockchain applications in government and cities. The governor of Delaware, John C. Carney, Jr., recently signed a bill amending Delaware's incorporation law. The initiative enables blockchain to store corporate records to increase speed and efficiency in incorporating companies and start-ups in the state. Nearly half of publicly listed companies are incorporated in Delaware.

The small Baltic country of Estonia is working with blockchain provider BitNation on its e-residency program, which will allow anyone around the world to take advantage of the secure authenticated online identity that the Estonian government already offers its 1.3 million residents.

The city of Zug, in Switzerland, has become the first to offer its citizens the opportunity to acquire a digital identity. They consider it a type of digital passport for a variety of applications in the city, and they hope to eventually use it for online voting. It's not based on a look-up against a central database at city hall. Instead, identities are stored in the blockchain. In this instance, the system is based on Ethereum using a Dapp called uPort.

The government of the Republic of Georgia is using blockchain to register land titles and validate property-related government transactions. A custom-designed blockchain system has been integrated into the digital records system of the National Agency of Public Registry (NAPR). The system will boost land title transparency, reduce the prevalence of fraud, and bring significant time and cost savings in the registration process.

The crown prince of Dubai has announced a strategic plan that will see almost all government documents secured on a blockchain. The Dubai government estimates that this blockchain strategy has the potential to save 25.1 million hours of lost economic productivity each year.

Samsung, using its enterprise blockchain called Nexledger, announced an agreement with the South Korean government to create a new platform for welfare, public safety, and transportation by 2022. The hope is to increase transparency for all government services.

In one of my favorite applications, the United Nations World Food Program is using the Ethereum blockchain to distribute cash more cheaply and quickly and with less risk. The transparency and security of the blockchain eliminated the fear of potential misappropriation of funding or tampering with transactions. In the pilot program, vulnerable families in Pakistan were able to receive food and cash assistance that World Food Program personnel were able to authenticate and record with smartphones. The pilot was a success and is now being expanded.

The state of Illinois is experimenting with a variety of blockchain-enabled solutions. One solution will work with health provider registries to enable patients to easily check doctor's licenses and insurance; another will start an energy credit marketplace to track renewable energy credits; and a third will create a pilot for recording births at a hospital as a way to initiate digital identity.

I've provided these examples to illustrate the vast range of possible blockchain use cases in government and, by extension, in cities. Though several are in full development, many remain experimental in nature. There's emerging support for blockchain applications in government, but, understandably, there is also caution. With any new technology, a wise approach is to first experiment and test. This approach couldn't be more important in government, where criticism can be particularly harsh when taxpayer money is expended on efforts that fail.

It's still early, but in the near future blockchain technology may create a lot of new value in making cities smarter.

To learn more about blockchain technology use in government, visit the Government Blockchain Association at `www.gbaglobal.org`. You can also explore a 2020 report on the state of implementation and regulatory treatment of blockchain by the public sector around the world at `https://govchain.world/`.

Autonomous vehicles (AVs)

A few years ago, when I would give talks on the future of cities, I would discuss self-driving cars, also known as *autonomous vehicles (AVs)*. My view then was that cars that were capable of sensing the environment and moving safely with zero human input seemed like a good idea, but I wasn't convinced that a fully autonomous car would be possible. I recognized that partial self-driving was possible, and in fact many cars at the time were already demonstrating that capability by parking themselves and performing other maneuvers.

Today, I've changed my mind. I am now fully convinced that full AVs are coming to the masses — and sooner than most people believe. What changed my mind? As a city leader in Silicon Valley, I had an opportunity to experience many AVs, and each time I did, their capability was better. Finally, I sat alone in an AV as it drove itself confidently in an urban area. It felt right, and my confidence in the technology skyrocketed.

Engineers have been trying to build cars that drive themselves since the 1920s. The fantasy of a car that frees the occupants from the burden of driving so that they can do other activities — such as working, watching a movie, or just catching up on some sleep — has been a preoccupation now for almost a hundred years. However, for much of that time, the dream of a full AV has been an elusive goal.

Early efforts included embedding technology in the road in order to interact and guide the car. However, as with a lot of innovation, many concepts simply failed.

It took technological breakthroughs in several areas, from the 1960s through the early 2000s, for major progress to occur. These areas include computer vision and LIDAR, which stands for *light detection and ranging*. It uses a pulsed laser to illuminate a target and then measure the reflected pulses with a sensor. The differences in laser return times and wavelengths are then used to construct a 3-dimensional representation of the surrounding areas. You might recognize one or more LIDAR spinning enclosures on the top of an AV. They look similar to police car beacons. LIDAR isn't the only AV technology available, but it now dominates as the central enabling technology of self-driving cars. (See Figure 8-5.)

FIGURE 8-5:
Autonomous vehicles are already on the road, including providing public transport.

The major milestone for AV innovation was the result of a highly publicized competition. Between 2004 and 2007, the US Defense Advanced Research Projects Agency (DARPA) funded a series of AV challenges. After many stops and starts (literally), a competing team achieved a series of self-driving obstacle and distance milestones.

By the 2010s, all major car manufacturers were actively working on fully viable AV models.

THE SIX LEVELS OF AUTONOMOUS VEHICLE (AV) AUTOMATION

To classify and manage innovation in the AV space, the Society of Automotive Engineers has established descriptions for six levels of automation:

- **Level 0, no automation:** All controls are made by a person.

- **Level 1, driver assistance:** Under certain circumstances, the car can control steering or acceleration, but not both simultaneously. An example of this is cruise control.

- **Level 2, partial automation:** The car can steer, accelerate, and brake itself in certain circumstances.

- **Level 3, conditional automation:** Under the right conditions, the car can manage many aspects of driving, including monitoring the environment. The driver must be able to take over at any time.

- **Level 4, high automation:** The car can operate without human input or oversight, but only under select conditions defined by factors such as road type or geographic area.

- **Level 5, full automation:** The driverless car can operate on any road and in any conditions that a human driver can negotiate.

Though there are production versions of levels 0 through 3 and, as of 2020, engineers are close to reaching level 4, they have some distance to overcome to achieve a viable level 5. In a level 5 AV world, humans are simply occupants of the vehicle with few control capabilities. The vehicles have no steering wheel or pedals, which opens up a world of completely rethinking what the interior of the vehicle may look like and the kinds of things that can be done during the journey.

Based on progress by the car manufacturers, the opinions of automobile analysts, and my own personal experiences, it appears that reaching and adopting level 5 is inevitable. The reduction in accidents and the potential for better utilization of the roadways seem like motivations enough.

AVs may also enable humans to redesign cities, building them around people and not around cars. A cityscape occupied by AVs has little need for traffic signals, signs, and even lanes. These artifacts were made for humans — computer-driven cars won't need them. AVs will communicate and negotiate with each other via wireless vehicle-to-vehicle (V2V) interactions. They will also send and receive data with urban infrastructure and the environment via vehicle-to-infrastructure (V2I) communications. A medley of supporting wireless communication devices will need to be deployed in cities. I discuss these urban wireless technologies later in this chapter, in the section "Wireless communications."

It has been said that AVs may be the most important societal innovation in the first 50 years of the 21st century. But there's much work to do when it comes to regulations, the change management involved, the economics of making it all work, and the process of dissolving many people's love affair with driving. Engineers also face the challenge of ensuring good security so that AVs can't be hacked. Society will need to address the consequences of displaced workers who drive for a living. This category of work represents millions of jobs around the world. Many ethical questions will need to be resolved. For example, if faced with an inevitable accident, should an AV optimize for the occupant of the vehicle or the person on the street, if it's certain that one or the other will be killed?

REMEMBER

Despite all the challenges ahead, it's likely just a question of when, not if, the world will see the end of human driving.

City leaders would be well served to dig deeper into the topic of AVs and to evaluate what it means to their communities and urban infrastructure.

Drones

The 15-year-old Luke Bannister had a proud and exuberant smile on his face. He had just flown the flight of his life, hurtling at stunning speeds while taking steep corners, avoiding obstacles, and outthinking all his opponents. In doing so, he walked away with the $250,000 first prize at the inaugural World Drone Prix in Dubai. His success was witnessed by 2,000 spectators and envied by his 250 competitors.

All around the world, competitions are being held with participants of all ages and with drones of all types, big and small. Drone racing requires exceptional attributes, such as the ability to create an excellent strategy, razor-sharp reflexes, and nerves of steel. Leagues are sponsored by brands such as AIG, DHL, and Mountain Dew. The Drone Racing League has a TV rights deal with ESPN. It's starting to be big business.

Almost unknown to most people until the end of the 1990s, drones have emerged as a serious industry in the first two decades of this new century. *Fortune* magazine estimates that, over the course of the years 2015 to 2025, the drone industry will have an economic impact of more than $82 billion and will create over 100,000 high-paying jobs. What's responsible for the explosion in drone use? Primarily, the cost of the technology that's used has dropped. Drone options range from just a few dollars to thousands of dollars, depending on use and interest. (See Figure 8-6 for an example of a reasonably priced drone.) Innovation also made leaps driven by military needs and research and growing use in the industrial sector.

FIGURE 8-6:
Flying drones may soon become a familiar sight in cities.

Drones have become highly attractive across the economy due to the broad range of applications appropriate for them. They're used for live-event filming, delivery transportation (to get a sense of the possibilities, check out Matternet: `https://mttr.net`), weapons, emergency support in cities, and, soon, people transport. (Don't believe me? Check out `https://ehang.com`.)

The following examples explore some of these and other uses of drones:

>> A few years ago, I attended a smart city event in Yinchuan, China. One evening at an outdoor dinner, the post-meal entertainment included what initially appeared to be a fireworks display. Instead, it was an illusion. In place of explosions, a fantastic, highly choreographed aerial dance was performed by what appeared to be tens, if not hundreds, of small synchronized drones. In addition to colorful sequences set to music, the drones spelled words and completed gravity-defying stunts. It was spectacular.

>> US Air Force First Lieutenant James Klein arrives for his piloting shift in Las Vegas. His workday starts with a briefing, and then he takes his position inside a featureless building for the next ten hours. He'll spend the day flying a Predator XP drone somewhere over the Middle East, looking for persons of interest. He describes his job as 99 percent boredom and 1 percent adrenaline rush. Today he's piloting alone but knows that in a few months he'll be joined by a copilot — not a human, but instead artificial intelligence (AI). Military leaders are betting that a human and AI can be more effective than either one alone. On this day, if Klein does launch a missile at a target, he'll have to head to his suburban home that evening and keep it to himself as he shares dinner with his family. Such is the nature of drone warfare in the 21st century.

» Hurricane Matthew made US landfall on October 8, 2016. Though only a Category 1 storm, it nevertheless caused significant damage, with the worst of it coming days later in the form of flooding. Paramedic Andrew Miller of Horry County Fire Rescue was sent to help evacuate stranded residents. Throughout his engagement, he used a drone to help with operations. The drone developed a 360-degree, real-time overview of Miller's flooding area. He was able to gain a more complete understanding of the incident, looking at where the floods were, determining the best way to deliver services to those in need, and providing critical information to rescue crews — not just verbal information but also visual information about the situation they were being deployed to. For emergency workers of all types, drones are transforming emergency response. It's happening in industrial settings and in cities all over the world.

» In early 2017, ground drones, otherwise known as unmanned ground vehicles (UGV), started to appear on the streets of Redwood City, California. These drones were delivering takeout meals to residents. According to their maker, Starship Technologies, the ground drones are about 15 inches high, can carry three bags of groceries, and weigh about 50 pounds when full. Their maximum speed is 4 mph, and they have nine cameras and proprietary mapping software that's accurate to the inch. Its creators hope that, among its anticipated advantages, the experimental deployment will reduce traffic as well as delivery costs.

» In April 2020, during the COVID-19 pandemic, the police department in Elizabeth, New Jersey, used drones to play recorded messages that told residents to practice social distancing and stay indoors. The drones flew around the city with an automated message from the mayor telling people to stop gathering, disperse, and go home. Anyone who violated the rules was potentially fined up to $1,000. The practice of using drones in this way was first seen in China during the same crisis.

WARNING

Drones are offering cities many benefits, but you still need to consider some glaring challenges. Imagine this scenario:

Unbeknownst to hundreds of workers who are busily making their way to work on a typical workday morning, a small drone with its noise drowned out by the hustle-and-bustle is flying overhead and collecting the private information from the smartphones in people's pockets and purses. It uses software called Snoopy to leverage any of the phones that have Wi-Fi turned on. The drone captures an abundance of content, including the websites that people visited, credit card information entered or saved on different sites, location data, usernames, and passwords.

The technology in this scenario exists, and it may be only a matter of time until it's deployed in this manner. Perhaps it's already happening.

Consider the urban consequences resulting from a mix of the IoT, drones, and malicious software. Research teams from Israel and Canada demonstrated how a drone can exploit a software vulnerability in wirelessly connected lightbulbs and turn them on and off from a distance. Imagine for a moment a drone attack that turns off city lights in neighborhoods or citywide or worse — it might flicker them to elicit mass neurological responses.

Of course, as you'd expect, in response to the threats posed by drones used for nefarious reasons, a whole new defense industry is emerging that includes hardware and software solutions as well as risk management services. Dedrone (www.dedrone.com), which sells RF sensors to track drone movements and jammers to incapacitate them, provides a good example of these types of emergent enterprises. New innovation will be required as the threats continue to speed ahead of the solutions.

Regulation is finally catching up with advancements in drone technology, and in many countries and cities, drone rules are on the books. Some communities are fighting against drones as a noise nuisance, as a danger to humans, and as an expansion of privacy intrusion. Sure, there's plenty of contention between enthusiasts and legislators, and I'd bet that will continue for a long time. Make sure you know the rules, and if the use of drones in cities interests you, consider becoming engaged in the debate.

REMEMBER

For many people, drones have been a sideshow — an interesting concept but not necessarily high on the priority list. For city leaders, those days are over. Drones must be considered a part of your smart city strategy, whether as a tool to provide support for city services or to understand and mitigate the potential risks they may pose for your community in the years ahead.

Wireless communications

Connectivity is one of the most basic enabling components of a smart city — it allows electronic communication and interaction from machine-to-machine (M2M), machine-to-person (M2P), and person-to-person (P2P).

Cities use a variety of existing and emerging connectivity technologies — from Wi-Fi to 5G — to connect people and machines. (I refer to these as devices from now on.) There's no single one-size-fits-all connectivity technology option that can support all city devices and applications. For example, a video-based city application can typically be supported well only by high-bandwidth connections (big data pipes), such as fiber, cellular, and Wi-Fi. A low-data-rate network, such as Semtech's LoRa network protocol, cannot support video. Similarly, city applications transmitting and receiving small amounts of data, such as an air quality sensor system, are well suited for a low-data-rate connectivity option instead of a costlier, high-bandwidth network. Figure 8-7 illustrates the variety of wireless options available depending on bandwidth and range (distance) requirements.

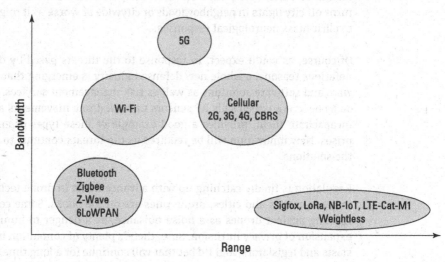

FIGURE 8-7:
A variety of
wireless
communications
solutions, based
on bandwidth
and range.

As you build out your smart city solutions and deploy devices such as air sensors or parking spot monitoring, you'll likely have to make choices when it comes to the type of connectivity required. Multiple connectivity options support a myriad of operational uses. To determine the types of connectivity that are needed, consider, at minimum, the answers to these questions:

>> **Is the solution used indoors, outdoors, or both?** Different connectivity technologies are optimal for indoor and outdoor applications. (There's some overlap in which indoor technology, such as Wi-Fi, can be used for outdoor applications.)

>> **How much data do you anticipate being transmitted, and how frequently?** For example, continuous video feeds require the most bandwidth, and messaging data requires the least. Some connectivity options can support only very low data-transfer rates.

>> **What is the distance (range) from the receiver to the *gateway* — the device that connects all the receivers to a central system?** This number can range from a few feet to tens of miles. As an example, air quality sensors in remote locations send data to a base station that's miles away, whereas an indoor thermostat only needs to send data to a wireless access point less than 20 feet away.

>> **How are the connected devices powered?** Device power sources can include external AC or DC line power, solar panels, and internal batteries. The availability, or lack of availability, of particular power sources determines what the device or sensor can or cannot do. Devices that do onboard processing and send and receive large amounts of data need continuous access to power. Devices without access to continuous power, or lacking the ability to recharge internal batteries, must operate intermittently. The more frequently they operate, the more data they transmit. The more data they transmit, the more power is consumed.

The licensed-versus-the-unlicensed wireless spectrum

Smart city sensors and other network-connected devices can operate on either the licensed or unlicensed frequency bands. Government regulatory agencies, such as the Federal Communications Commission (FCC) and National Telecommunications and Information Administration (NTIA) in the United States, specify which frequency spectrums licensed and unlicensed connectivity options can use. Telecommunications companies offering connectivity in the licensed bands must first apply and then pay to use part of the frequency spectrum over a specific geographic area. In contrast, the unlicensed frequency bands — such as those used by Wi-Fi, Bluetooth, and LoRa — are open to everyone. They don't require an application or a payment to operate.

The main advantage that licensed band connectivity has over unlicensed band connectivity is that potential interference is greatly minimized and, in cases where interference occurs, the licensee has the right to assert claims against the sources of interference. Because licensed operators in the same coverage area are operating on different frequencies, there's little likelihood of their networks interfering with one another. This is important for applications that are mission critical, latency- or time-sensitive, or in need of high uptime or availability, such as a broadband network service being sold in subscription models — retail cellular plans, in other words.

In contrast, the unlicensed band is open to anyone, with no consideration for aligning frequency occupancy — meaning future interference is a distinct possibility. For example, Wi-Fi, microwave ovens, Bluetooth headsets, baby monitors, and smart meters all operate in the same 2.4 GHz spectrum. Each new device that's added increases the likelihood of interference, which can cause signal degradation and possibly result in some devices failing to connect altogether. This interference, then, can clearly impact the operation of the applications using the connectivity service and require more network tuning and controls to operate together.

Open-versus-proprietary connectivity

Connectivity options can be based on open standards or proprietary technology. Each has its own set of advantages and disadvantages.

Open standards have been developed by a consortium of major communication vendors in order to provide a measure of flexibility and ensure maximum interoperability with compatible devices. They do not lock you into a particular solution vendor for service and hardware. Open standards benefit from continuous updates, innovative capabilities, and enhancements faster than any single vendor can do on its own. In addition, free access to the technology increases the pool of experts, developers, and support resources that you can potentially tap into when the need arises.

However, open-standards-based options may not work in every situation. You may have IoT applications that have specific or unique requirements, such as security, that haven't been incorporated into the standard. You may have mission-critical applications requiring robust and dedicated engineering support that you cannot get from a consortium. A proprietary technology might come packaged with vendor or third-party support, giving you lower risk and liability. In addition, your city may not have the expertise to support an open standard and thus may prefer a proprietary, vendor-backed alternative.

Proprietary connectivity may incorporate approaches that work better than the current open-standards-based technologies for security, latency, and throughput. Solution providers of these technologies may provide a more robust level of customer and technical support. Depending on the technology, some proprietary connectivity solutions have an ecosystem of third-party devices and applications that support their technology. In other cases, cities may have limited options if they want to use a particular device (for example, smart water meters) that work only with a particular connectivity technology.

Table 8-2 summarizes the common (current and emerging) types of wireless connectivity that are now available for use in smart cities and specifies whether the technology is open or proprietary.

Smart street lighting

The first use of elevated street lighting dates back to Antioch in the fourth century BC. Oil was used as the burning fuel. During the Roman Empire, wealthy Romans made sure their slaves kept the oil lamps burning in front of their villas. In medieval European towns, often the lights were stationary, although sometimes streetlighting was provided by an escort who would guide people through the town's dark, winding streets. After several hundred years, candles were used for lighting. A lamplighter would illuminate each candle at dusk and then extinguish them at dawn.

TABLE 8-2   Common Wireless Connectivity Options

Connectivity	Indoor or Outdoor	Data Transmission Rates (Theoretical)	Range	Open or Proprietary	Licensed or Unlicensed
Wi-Fi 4 (802.11n)	Both	300 Mbps, 2 spatial streams, 40 MHz channel width	150 feet (indoor); 300 feet (outdoor)	Open	Unlicensed
Wi-Fi 5 (802.11ac Wave 2)	Both	3.5 Gbps, 4 spatial streams, 160 MHz channel width	150 feet (indoor); 300 feet (outdoor)	Open	Unlicensed
Wi-Fi 6 (802.11ax)	Both	9.6 Gbps, 8 spatial streams, 160MHz channel width	150 feet (indoor); 300 feet (outdoor)	Open	Unlicensed
Bluetooth (Version 5.x)	Indoor	2 Mbps	800 feet (theoretical)	Open	Unlicensed
Bluetooth Low Energy (Version 4.x)	Indoor	1 Mbps	200 feet (theoretical)	Open	Unlicensed
Z-Wave	Indoor	9.6 Kbps 40 Kbps	30 m	Open	Unlicensed
Zigbee	Both	20 Kbps (868 MHz) to 250 Kbps (2.4 GHz)	10 to 100 m	Open	Unlicensed
LoRa	Outdoor	250 bps to 50 Kbps (EU); 980 bps to 21.9 Kbps (North America)	10 km	Open	Unlicensed
NB-IoT (Release 14)	Outdoor	127 Kbps (downlink) 159 Kbps (uplink)	40 to 100 km	Proprietary	Licensed

(continued)

TABLE 8-2 *(continued)*

Connectivity	Indoor or Outdoor	Data Transmission Rates (Theoretical)	Range	Open or Proprietary	Licensed or Unlicensed
Sigfox	Outdoor	100 to 600 bps; 600 bps (down)	10 km (urban); 40 km (rural)	Proprietary	Unlicensed
LTE–Cat M1	Outdoor	1 Mbps (up); 1 Mbps (down)	30 km	Proprietary	Licensed
Weightless	Outdoor	0.625 to 1 Kbps	2 km	Open	Unlicensed
Wi-SUN	Outdoor	50 to 300 Kbps	2 to 3 km	Open	Unlicensed
Cellular (2G/3G/4G/LTE)	Outdoor	0.1 to 0.3 Mbps (2G); 7.2 to 42 Mbps (3G); 150 Mbps (4G)	30 km	Proprietary	Licensed
6LoWPAN	Outdoor	20 Kbps (868 MHz); 250 Kbps (2.4 GHz)	10 to 100 m	Open	Unlicensed
CBRS	Both	Greater than 150 Mbps	Low range (In-building) to miles (outdoor)	Proprietary	Licensed
5G	Outdoor	Greater than 10 Gbps (high band); 100 Gbps possible in the future	500 m (small cell, mm wave)	Proprietary	Licensed

This section on wireless connectivity was created in collaboration with Benson Chan, Renil Paramel, and Strategy of Things (https://strategyofthings.io).

USING SIGFOX'S 0G NETWORK TO CONNECT URBAN MOBILITY

Self-service bicycle fleet INDIGO weel, a subsidiary of the INDIGO group, has been fitted with sensors, supported by Sigfox's 0G network, that can accurately pinpoint their location at any given time. As the number of shared vehicles in circulation increases, this integration of Sigfox technology will help to better protect the fleet from damage or theft.

The Sigfox solution offers multiple benefits for INDIGO® weel:

- **An easier customer journey:** Pinpointing the location of bicycles more accurately, in real-time, allows users of the service to locate bikes on the street faster and more easily.

- **Better protection against damage and theft:** Understanding where the high-risk areas are is half the battle.

- **A reduction in repair costs:** Thanks to reusable sensors that can easily be transferred from a damaged bike to a new one, the fleet can be maintained efficiently.

- **Durable sensors that consume very little energy**

Together, INDIGO weel and Sigfox are providing a solution to the public that addresses a number of the current challenges facing mobility services. Population growth in cities as well as increasing environmental awareness now requires you to reconsider the way you move around each day. Innovative private sector services are therefore needed in order to be able to offer a wider range of mobility solutions to the public. These must, however, complement the existing public transportation offerings, with those in charge working closely with city authorities in metropolitan areas.

Any change involves some risks and challenges, but the association between Sigfox and INDIGO weel is already reaping benefits. Since the fleet was equipped with connected sensors, improvements to the geolocation system have reduced bicycle damage by a factor of 4. In addition, bicycle repair/replacement is now also faster than in the past. These improvements benefit INDIGO weel, but also, more broadly, the inhabitants of cities where the connected vehicles are available, providing them with a high quality, sustainable service.

In the 1500s, the lantern — a lamp with a glass case to protect the flame and improve light quality — was invented. Lanterns began appearing all over Europe. Again, though many were hung on posts, they were still relatively rare, so lantern–bearers also escorted people. Paris was early in deploying thousands of lights by order of the Sun King, King Louis XIV, in the 1670s. It wasn't until the 1700s that another great city, London, embraced lanterns along all major thoroughfares.

Gas-based lighting began to appear by 1800, and once again Paris was the first to embrace this much brighter-and-whiter illumination. These gas lamps lined the grand boulevards and city monuments of Paris, and it was from this situation that it took on the nickname "the City of Light."

The first electric streetlights were installed in the city of Newcastle, in England, at the end of the 1800s. These lights used incandescent bulbs (the type most people are familiar with), which are still in use in many homes. This type uses a glass-enclosed wire filament that glows when heated.

Today, the most common form of streetlight along streets and roads uses high-intensity discharge (HID) lamps. These lamps create light by producing an electric arc between tungsten electrodes housed inside a tube. These streetlights provide a large amount of illumination with low use of electricity.

The newest form of streetlighting uses a technology called light-emitting diode (LED), which uses a semiconducting material that emits light when an electrical current flows through it. Many cities are in the process of migrating to LED lighting. But why? There are several reasons. LEDs have extremely long lives. They can last up to 100,000 hours, which means maintenance costs can be reduced because the lights need to be replaced less often. LEDS are also highly energy efficient. With a long life span and heightened energy efficiency, LED streetlights can reduce carbon emissions, which can be further enhanced with the addition of solar panels. In this way, these lights become self-sufficient and, in some cases, can send excess energy back to the electrical grid. LED lights require no warm-up; they turn on immediately and can be easily dimmed. They can produce directional light — light emitted in a specific direction — rather than be diffused. This capability can be used to illuminate specific areas or objects.

LED streetlights aren't without some concerns. Though directional lighting is an advantage, it does mean that they can't produce a glow in all directions, which means that they have to be positioned hanging down rather than in lamp-type lights. Issues and complaints have come along with brightness, but recent innovation is improving this situation.

The initial cost of using LED lights is high, but costs are recouped through longer use and lower-cost energy bills. That said, the cost of a full city conversion may be restrictive for many communities. In fiscally tight municipalities, turning off streetlights is used as a way to reduce electrical bills.

The ubiquity of city streetlights, pole elevation, and the presence of a power source in each light post means that they're ideal for the addition of new functionalities. In other words, streetlights provide the necessary power and connectivity for new technology to be tethered to them, such as a sensor.

Streetlighting is becoming a smart and intelligent element of infrastructure. The addition of sensors opens up a vast opportunity for innovation. Smart streetlights can be programmed to turn on only when traffic or the presence of pedestrians is detected. The lights can communicate together in order to illuminate the path of a person or car, turning off in sequence as the traffic proceeds. Smart streetlights can be used to monitor parking spaces and send information to smartphone apps. Smart streetlights can listen for gunshots and produce evidence for investigators; determine the speed, type, and direction of traffic; and even detect particulates in the air in order to monitor air pollution. They can monitor air temperature, humidity, and vibration and report back to a central collection point for analysis. Some even serve as Wi-Fi hotspots.

Based on collecting data from a variety of sensors, smart streetlights are helping cities improve dangerous intersections by better understanding challenges. Safety is also improved due to better lighting conditions for drivers.

Migrating to smart LED-based streetlighting is becoming popular with cities pursuing their smart city strategies. Cities such as San Diego, Singapore, London, Chicago, Copenhagen, and Chongqing, China, are among the early adopters.

Given that smart streetlighting can be used for a variety of sensors and communication devices, it can form the backbone of a smart city network. Depending on need and ambition, building this network can be complex and expensive. Considerations must be made for return on investment (ROI), data security, privacy, system redundancy, and scalability. Weigh the benefits and determine whether smart LED streetlights are part of your smart city strategy.

Smart grids and microgrids

Let's talk about the electrical grid. What is it, exactly? The *grid* is a network of transmission lines, substations, transformers, and other technologies that deliver electricity from a power plant (shown in Figure 8-8) to your home, office, factory, or anywhere else that power is needed. The common electrical plug socket on the wall is the endpoint of the grid.

The first electrical grids began to be built in the late 1800s. Though these engineering feats have been upgraded over the years and continue to serve people relatively well, they're certainly showing their age.

FIGURE 8-8:
The electrical grid is a common sight in cities around the world.

Traditionally, utilities have had no insight into how consumers actually consume electricity. When a utility detected increased demand, it ramped up production from a power plant and supplied more power to the grid. It's a fairly crude and inefficient system. In addition, the nature of the grid has evolved. Today, for example, millions of homes have solar panels on their properties, so they're no longer just consumers, but rather homes that both produce and consume electricity.

The 21st century demands a new, improved grid to support today's needs and to manage the increasingly complex nature of electricity optimization and energy sustainability in cities.

Say hello to the smart grid.

A *smart grid* uses digital technology to improve the communication, automation, and connectivity of the components of a power network. It enables detailed, real-time, two-way communication between the power distributor and the consumer.

An essential element of this new system is the use of the smart meter in buildings — also known as an advanced metering infrastructure (AMI). These meters replace the older, analog meters with digital devices that can relay supply-and-demand data between the power distributor and the consumer. Data collected and analyzed by the power company can be used to better predict and respond to changes in demand. Specifically, this capability enables the power producer to reduce distribution when less power is needed and to increase it during peak periods.

Building and supporting a smart grid will require that cities replace many components across the network. It's an expensive and lengthy process.

But what's in it for cities?

Smart grids offer the following advantages:

>> Improved efficiency in electricity transmission

>> Faster restoration of power after an electrical disturbance

>> Reduced cost of utility operations and management, which can result in lower cost for consumers

>> Increased integration of large-scale renewable energy systems

>> Improved security

For consumers, a smart grid enables enhanced access to information about energy use. For example, it's possible to understand your energy use at any point. Homeowners don't have to wait until the end of the month to check their energy usage details on their electrical bill. At any given moment, they can see how much energy is being used and how much it's costing them. Consumers are provided with more control over their power usage and costs by way of real-time information.

Smart grids enhance the ability to deliver a demand response strategy. *Demand response* is a way to reduce stress on the grid and high electricity prices: By reducing the demand for electricity during certain periods, demand response programs can lower prices by reducing the need to run high-cost generators. Rather than supply more energy, demand is lowered in response to higher prices. As an example, a factory is incentivized to run its machines at times when the cost of electricity is lower and the stress on the grid is less.

Are smart grids the same as microgrids, you ask? There's some overlap in that they use similar technologies and processes.

A *microgrid* is a small, self-contained version of the electrical grid, but typically smarter and more efficient. It serves a smaller geographic area, such as a college campus, a military base, an industrial area, or an area that might contain critical services — say, a hospital, police station, or grocery store. Put all the pieces together and you have something called a *community microgrid*.

A microgrid offers a way for power to continue flowing when the larger grid is down. It's a form of smart city resiliency. Intelligent software and controls can detect a broader outage and then "island" the microgrid from the main grid. The microgrid can then separate and protect itself from the issues occurring with the main grid. The microgrid stops relying on other power and depends on its own (often renewables), thus providing continuity of services to critical sites.

A microgrid and the main grid support each other as well. If a microgrid fails, it can turn to the main grid for power. Similarly, if the main grid requires a boost of power, it can turn to the microgrid.

Both smart grids and microgrids are effective tools designed to make your city smarter and more resilient.

Smart water

Needless to say, a city's water system is critical infrastructure. (See Chapter 7 for a brief history of aqueducts.) With city populations growing, water consumption continues to increase as well. In addition, many of the world's city water systems (see an example of dated and decaying water infrastructure in Figure 8-9) are old, poorly maintained, and in desperate need of upgrades. It's not unusual for a city water system to lose 25 percent of its water volume during its transport from source to destination. Some cities in the world even experience significantly higher water loss.

FIGURE 8-9:
Many municipal water systems are old, poorly maintained, leaky, and inefficient.

Smart water is a term that describes the efficient management of water and wastewater infrastructure as well as the energy used to transport it. Areas of management include water sourcing, treatment, and delivery.

A smart water system is built to harvest actionable data about flow, pressure, and distribution. It also accurately records consumption levels and forecasts water use. The system typically includes tools to identify and analyze abnormalities in consumption patterns for both the water utility's organization and its users. Unsurprisingly, water loss management is a particular priority. Smart water technologies, such as IoT sensors, can help to find leaks. System software can also use modeling to compare actual-versus-predicted use. A large variance can indicate water loss in the system.

REMEMBER

A water system often consumes 50 percent of a city's energy, meaning that it's also the largest controllable expense in water operations. Yet water systems are often overlooked as an opportunity to reduce costs and free up cash for other uses. Implementing smart water systems can help optimize water energy use and deliver energy savings of up to 30 percent.

To summarize, these are the benefits of implementing a smart water system:

>> Reduced water consumption

>> Reduced leakage

>> Increased productivity

>> Pipeline monitoring

>> Water quality monitoring

>> Preventive maintenance

>> Reduced costs and increased revenue

>> Safety improvements

>> Reliability improvements

>> Assisted sustainability goals

>> Improved water metering

Digital twins

Imagine for a moment that you've been tasked with building a new, complicated factory machine. Before you build it, you and your team will want to design it on a computer that can accurately simulate all manner of future usage scenarios under a variety of conditions. For example, how might this new machine operate under different temperatures? What design choices may make sense to make it run more efficiently?

Being able to accurately answer these questions, and many more, before a product or service is built is now achievable by creating and simulating a fully functioning digital version. It's called a digital twin — a data-driven virtual replica of a physical item.

The value of digital twin technology isn't limited to simply the design phase of products and services. A digital twin has a role in a number of areas, including planning, design, building, operations, maintenance, and optimization.

Digital twins are particularly valuable in the operations of a solution. Imagine for a moment an energy-producing wind turbine deployed in a remote location. The wind turbine is equipped with a range of IoT sensors placed in strategic locations. Critical performance information about the turbine is sent back to a receiving station, where a digital twin is used as a monitoring tool for engineers. Any issues that are detected will immediately show up on the digital twin. Continuous improvements can also be applied through analysis of real-time data. In addition, using artificial intelligence, the digital twin can predict maintenance issues, thus enabling preventive actions to be taken in advance.

Addressing a problem before it happens has a significantly lower cost than addressing it after the issue has occurred. For example, General Electric (GE) has over 1.2 million digital twins for around 300,000 different types of assets that range from individual pieces of equipment to entire power plants. By analyzing real-time and historical data, the company can identify maintenance issues in advance and thus reduce downtime and expensive repairs.

Digital twins are becoming particularly popular in the world of the Industrial Internet of Things (IIoT). These Internet-connected electronics collect and produce data and services and interact and communicate between each other and central systems. An IIoT infrastructure in a manufacturing setting, for example, can build out a digital twin of an entire factory floor.

Though the vast majority of digital twin implementations that exist today are in an industrial setting, they're beginning to show up in an urban context.

Digital twins of cities offer urban planners, policymakers, and city leaders more tools and information than static data models. Areas such as scenario-testing and strategic planning are greatly enhanced by accurate, data-driven, visual simulations. (See Figure 8-10.) Stakeholders can monitor construction progress, traffic, environmental conditions, public safety, energy consumption, and building occupancy. They can query information regarding live and historical traffic data, zoning regulations, property transaction data, building permits, county parcel records, and IoT devices and their attendant sensor data.

FIGURE 8-10:
An example of a city's digital twin with real-time building operational data.

Image provided courtesy of https://cityzenith.com.

Digital twins can enable constituents to explore the impact of different city projects directly. For example, visual simulations can illustrate how a particular construction project would change the view from a building or impact traffic.

In India, the state of Andhra Pradesh is building the first city created from the start with its own digital twin as it establishes its new capital, Amaravati. The digital twin will enable government leaders to manage the permitting process, monitor construction progress, and evaluate design plans. They will be able to understand information such as how buildings will respond to the hot-and-humid climate.

Singapore has developed a $73 million data-powered, real-time replica of the city-nation. City leaders and planners can gather a more detailed view of things like planning for the installation of solar panel roofs or emergency evacuation routes. With just a click, city staff can see how much energy a building is using. The possibilities are wide-ranging. In the not-too-distant future, you'll likely see digital twins help build and maintain all types of smart cities and even national infrastructures across the world.

A pilot project has been established by the Association of Southeast Asian Nations to build a network of digitally twinned smart cities, which, in addition to Singapore, will include Jakarta, Indonesia, and Cauayan City, Philippines. The goal of the project is for participating cities to use their shared resources and capabilities to collaborate on solutions to major urban challenges.

Other cities that have developed digital twins include Glasgow in the United Kingdom, Boston in the United States, and Jaipur in India.

REMEMBER

Digital twins appear to offer great value in the development of smart cities. Benefits include urban planning, land use optimization, and scenario studies through analytics. They can simulate any type of plan before implementation and reveal problems before they become reality. Architectural aspects that can be planned and analyzed include housing, wireless networks, antennas, solar panels, urban aesthetics, movement of people, and traffic support.

TIP

Consider planning and building your smart city first as a digital twin and use it as one of the ways to get input from the community. As the smart city is built, you can use the twin to monitor and operate various aspects of it. Your city would join a growing list of cities doing just that and gleaning all the benefits for the community.

Digital signage

Throughout the Roman Empire, stone columns were erected to provide information on the distance to Rome. Known as *milestones,* these markers were placed along a road or path at intervals of one mile. They were some of the earliest road signs. During the Middle Ages, multidirectional signs giving directions to towns and cities became common. In the years that followed, signage became more common and complex as more people and goods were transported and as cities began to grow.

The arrival of cars ushered in a new era of complex signage systems. By the turn of the 20th century, international signage standards were being established. As car use grew, road signs became a much more common sight across towns, cities, and rural areas. Most were made from stone or wood. Until the 1930s, most road signs were text-based. Then pictures began to be used because they removed language barriers and also simplified the message. (Signs that are easy to understand assist with traffic safety.)

A wide range of signage was gradually introduced that included warnings, street names, guides, welcome banners, areas of interest, schools, railroads, and bicycle signs.

In urban areas, another type of signage, known as *wayfinding,* became increasingly popular — it's an information system that guides people through a physical environment. It can enhance an understanding and experience of a space. As cities have become more complex, increased wayfinding has been required in order to provide visual cues — such as maps, directions, and symbols — to help guide people to a destination. Navigating an urban environment, particularly one that you're not familiar with, is a high-stress experience. Effective wayfinding systems contribute to a sense of well-being and safety. (Ineffective wayfinding tends to confuse; see Figure 8-11 for an example.)

FIGURE 8-11:
An example of
city wayfinding
that perhaps
needs a
little work.

Similar to traditional traffic signage, wayfinding has traditionally been an analog experience. It has served cities well. One obvious limitation with analog signage and wayfinding is that it's static. After it's created and deployed, it cannot be changed unless it's updated or replaced. In addition, it's constrained to a single purpose.

Electronic signage — which primarily uses different forms of illumination, such as fluorescent, LED, and neon — was an upgrade on wood and metal. Broad use is expensive but has found a sizable niche in outdoor advertising. Electronic signage has created more opportunities for dynamic displays, and large installations are popular in city centers.

The latest incarnation of signage — digital signage — has quickly become a signature component of a smart city. Digital signage is considered a subset of electronic signage. It uses a variety of technologies, including liquid crystal display (LCD), to display pictures, video, and all sorts of other text and graphics. LCD signage is beginning to show up on sidewalks in urban centers. Because it's digital, the display is entirely dynamic and can be controlled and updated over the Internet. Content displayed can include wayfinding, informational and emergency notices, event calendars, and advertising, for example. Content can be localized and change depending on the time of day. The signage can also be engaged via a touchscreen, enabling a user to enter information in a search box or tap an icon to find more information, make a restaurant reservation, call the police, or request transportation. Some digital signs even offer free Wi-Fi. A good example of an interactive kiosk is the LinkNYC project in New York City. I provide details on this solution in Chapter 6.

Many advanced digital signs are *context-aware:* They use technologies such as sensors, cameras, and other IoT devices to monitor the environment and deliver content based on external conditions. For example, by detecting the approximate age and gender of an individual, the screen can display relevant content to that specific demographic. In addition, ambient data that's captured can be collected and analyzed by the city to better understand information such as traffic patterns, shopper profiles, and air quality at various times of the day. Digital signs for traffic can deliver real-time information about traffic conditions, available parking spaces (including numbers available and their location), alternative route suggestions, alerts, and advertising.

For a city, digital signage enables the development and deployment of richer content. Information can be quickly updated and distributed to multiple digital signs over a large geographic area directly from a single application. In addition, if permissible, advertising can constitute a source of revenue for the city. In a world of tight budgets, this income can be a welcome addition to the city's coffers.

REMEMBER

Digital signage offers many advantages to a city and its community. It represents the definition of a smart city technology that can add value and quality of experience. If you're reluctant to pursue digital signage because of its cost, keep in mind that advertising, if permissible in your city, might not only pay for the digital signage project but also bring in a continuous stream of revenue. I recommend taking a closer look.

Application programming interfaces (APIs)

Okay, you might be inclined to skip over this section because it sounds a little too much like techie-talk. But don't skip it. It's an important area of technology. I do my best to make it easy to understand. Seriously, I limit the use of complex terms (and explain any that I introduce), and I don't assume that you have a technology background.

To give the topic of application programming interfaces (APIs) some context, consider a simple use where you're sure to have some familiarity. In this example, you use your computer to browse the web and find the time when a movie is showing at your favorite theater. The first thing you do is open your browser — Internet Explorer, Safari, Chrome, Firefox, Opera, or another one. You type the address to the theater website in the address bar. Your computer then sends a request over the Internet, and it reaches the computer that hosts the website. That computer is called a *server*. The theater server then responds to the request by sending information about the home page to your computer. The website then shows up. Then you locate your favorite theater and the movie you want to see. Another request is sent over the Internet, and the server responds with the movie and the show times. When your request arrives at the server, specific software analyzes the request and decides what to do with it. This software is called an *application programming interface, or API*.

What's cool about APIs is that software developers can use them to perform all sorts of functions without knowing how the function works. For example, in the theater scenario, your browser made a request for a particular movie to the theater server computer, and it was able to find the movie and its times and return them to you. Your computer didn't need to know how the theater server performed the search. You could say that the software magic is hidden. All your computer needed to know was to send a request, and the API on the theater server would do the rest.

FIWARE

FIWARE was created in 2011 as part of the European Commission's Future Internet Public Private Partnership (FI-PPP) program to encourage the development of digital, sustainable, open source platforms and solutions.

Over 140 cities worldwide are using FIWARE to power their smart city strategies. FIWARE is becoming a standard information model to enable the development of smart solutions in a faster, easier, interoperable, and affordable way.

The specifications of FIWARE's APIs are public and royalty-free.

FIWARE Foundation was founded in 2016 as a non-profit organization to drive the definition and encourage the adoption of open standards. Over 8,000 subject matter experts, entrepreneurs, start-ups, academic and industry associations have been contributing to developing market-ready FIWARE-based solutions. FIWARE has over 330 members, from South America to East Asia. Among its Platinum members are Atos, Engineering, NEC, Telefónica, and Trigyn Technologies.

FIWARE's mission:

- Driving standards for breaking information silos
- Making IoT simpler and cheaper to implement

(continued)

(continued)

- Transforming large volumes of data into knowledge

- Unleashing the potential of open data

- Creating business value and innovation paths for the FIWARE Community via the 15 FIWARE global iHubs, FIWARE labs, and the FIWARE Marketplace, which has over 165 solutions

The mission is achieved through:

- Providing standard APIs to easily connect to the Internet of Things

- Reducing the complexity of context information management

- Linking subject matter experts and enterprises to open calls of funding programs that support research and innovation projects

- Promoting the use of FIWARE technology in local and global projects

- Ensuring a presence at leading events

As the digital revolution has dramatically changed the way organizations conduct businesses, having standard APIs — crucial if you want applications that can easily communicate with other programs and devices — is of paramount importance. The core component of any "Powered by FIWARE" platform is the Context Broker (see details below) — selected by all European member states as the new Connecting Europe Facility (CEF) Building Block in 2018. This component supports the FIWARE NGSI API, a simple yet powerful API that solves an essential function in any smart solution: how to gather, manage, and provide access to context information. The FIWARE NGSI API enables the integration of FIWARE platform components, the interoperability of smart solutions or services running on top of "Powered by FIWARE" platforms, as well as their portability across different "Powered by FIWARE" platforms.

Coupled with a set of additional FIWARE components, FIWARE Context Broker facilitates:

- The interface with IoT devices, robots, and third-party systems, capturing updates on context information and translating required actuations

- The monitoring, processing, and analysis of current and historical data using event rules, advanced data and AI algorithms, dashboard and analytical support tools that support smart decisions and the smart automation of processes

- The management, publication, and monetization of context data and services, preserving defined access and usage control policies

FIWARE has been used to create many smart city solutions, including smart parking and air quality measurements.

Cities in countries such as Finland, Denmark, Belgium, Portugal, Italy, Spain, and Brazil are committed to using FIWARE to power their smart city strategies.

Learn more at www.fiware.org/community/smart-cities/.

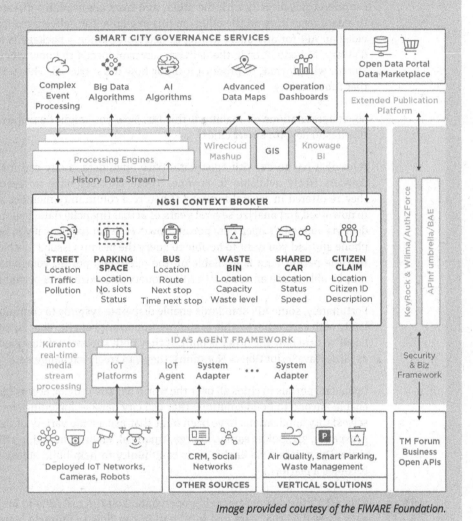

Image provided courtesy of the FIWARE Foundation.

When you run software on your computer, open an app on a smartphone, or access a cloud application in a browser (assuming that you're connected to a network), each time a request is sent, it's likely hitting an API. Modern software is typically made up of modules of functionality that work with APIs. These are called *microservices*.

In particular, APIs make accessing data much easier for computer applications (and for the developers who build them). For example, if you order an item online and want to know the delivery time, the online service can query the delivery company server and extract just the data about the delivery time. Each server communicates directly with the other, and from application software on one side to a data repository on the other. In this example, the delivery company has provided an API for any query asking to determine when a package is scheduled for delivery. Nobody outside the delivery company needs to know where the data is stored, what format to produce it in, or how it's retrieved. The API performs all that functionality.

So, congratulations on making it this far. Now you might be wondering what all this has to do with smart cities?

A lot of it has to do with open data. With open data, a city can make particular datasets freely available to anyone. These datasets have no restrictions, and they're offered in several formats. If you're a community member and you want to download and analyze several years of actual financial data, you may be able to do it via your city's open data portal. However, what happens if you build a smartphone app and you want to be able to query the permits issued in a city? Assuming that the permit data is available on the open data portal, your smartphone app may be able to use an open data API to query and extract the permit data.

Fortunately, some API standards enable disparate systems to communicate seamlessly with each other — this is another important benefit. That is, neither system needs to care how the other is built. If they both support a data API standard such as JSON (JavaScript Object Notation), they can freely exchange data.

Open data portals in cities all over the world list and provide accessible APIs. These enable anyone to build solutions that use city data — including the cities themselves! City applications have been built that use a wide variety of data, including geospatial, 311, public safety, energy, financial, environmental, traffic, and much more. Open data APIs enable your community to help build solutions. Your city becomes a platform.

REMEMBER

APIs aren't just about leveraging open data. You can use APIs to break down city silos as well so that data and information can flow seamlessly between systems that belong to different departments.

Cities are complicated, often disjointed entities. They provide many services, and those services are increasingly delivered using information technology. The capability for systems to work together and improve efficiencies has been elusive. City systems are provided by a large variety of vendors, and they're often highly specialized. In addition, departments usually focus on their needs and don't necessarily collaborate with colleagues that perform completely different functions.

There are many times when sharing data and functionality between systems is extremely beneficial. Look, don't get me wrong — connecting disparate systems is something we've been doing for a long time. It's just been messy and often unreliable. If you've ever opened a web page that's blank after making a request, it's probably because a connected system failed to transfer data.

Smart cities focus on connecting systems and data such that city staff and the community can have a greatly improved experience. For example, there are many times that geospatial data may be useful in some departments' application. That application should be able to call up an API on the geographic information system (GIS) and easily embed a map or set of directions. Perhaps a city application needs to populate an address. Rather than have to type an address, an application in one department can call the API of an address book in another department. These integrations don't need to stop at the city's borders, either. Systems can talk with other cities and organizations anywhere that it makes sense.

FIWARE, a European initiative, is a framework of open source platform components you can use to access and manage heterogeneous context information by way of open APIs. (For more on FIWARE, see the "FIWARE" sidebar in this chapter.)

Open & Agile Smart Cities (OASC) (https://oascities.org) is a nonprofit, international smart city network of over 140 smart cities that are participating in the creation of open APIs. Their goal is to increase the speed of urban innovation and development while decreasing cost and inefficiency. The OASC supports the digital transformation of cities.

REMEMBER

When you begin to think about the advantages of sharing data and functionality efficiently across a city's systems, it becomes clear that APIs make cities smarter. To whet your appetite, check out https://dataportals.org/, which lists a number of cities with open APIs.

Chapter **9**

Unleashing the Power of City Data

D ata plays an important role in running any organization, including cities. More than ever, data is an essential ingredient in increasing the effectiveness of city operations. The role of data in a city context, however, continues to be undeveloped. This chapter makes the case for the improved utilization of data and provides important insights on how to develop and execute a city data strategy. In addition, you discover the value of open data and understand why specialized data science skills and leadership are required in order to be successful.

Becoming City-Data-Savvy

Technology creates a lot of data. Cities with technology create a lot of data. With more systems and devices coming online every day, the volume of data produced, collected, and stored is growing rapidly. It's not just information such as your Facebook posts, Instagram photos, Google searches, and online forms you fill out — it's also all the data produced by the myriad of processes taking place behind the scenes. For example, just one self-driving car generates over 4,000 gigabytes of data for each hour of driving. Now multiply that by the millions of autonomous vehicles that will come online in the next few years and it's clear that just this one type of urban activity will create a colossal amount of data. This colossal amount of data is called *data exhaust.* Though that's an appropriate term for vehicles, it applies to all the data that spins off electronic transactions.

Between this data exhaust and the growing number of interactions that people have with all their devices, data growth is headed off the charts. In fact, right now it's over 2.5 quintillion bytes of data every day. The technical phrase for that scale is, "Dude, that's a lot!" While I'm at it, here's another mind-blowing fact. Considering all the data that's been produced since people started using computers many decades ago, remarkably, 90 percent of all data ever created has happened in just the past two years. (See Figure 9-1.) Technologists have come up with an appropriate term for this scale of data: *big data.* That isn't exactly an inspired choice, I suppose, but at least it's accurate.

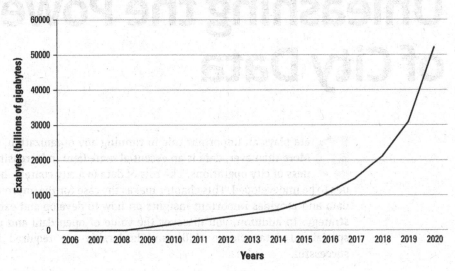

FIGURE 9-1:
The growth of data being created and stored worldwide.

Every type of organization is now producing, collecting, and storing big data. The clever ones are using it to run their businesses better, to more deeply understand their customers, and to build new products and services. When organizations use data in a way that improves operations, increases their bottom lines, and helps them to outperform their competitors, they're called *data-savvy.* This term indicates that they have recognized the value of data, developed the relevant skills to manage that data, and implemented a strategy to use data as a core instrument of organizational success. Kudos to them.

The popular role of data today has created a marketplace with a broad range of software tools that help with analysis and decision-making. It has also created a high demand for data-related skills and has even helped establish a new branch of study and expertise, called *data science.*

The private sector has recognized the value of data and data-savviness; rejecting the value of data is hardly conceivable in a for-profit organization. Other sectors of the economy have been slower to fully embrace their data love. Government has been a laggard, but those days are coming to an end. Today, government agencies — and cities, in particular — are jumping head-first into the realm of data science. In a field where everything is scarce, governments have an abundance of data.

Governments create, collect, and store a wide variety of datasets that include ingredients such as crime reports, permits, library lending information, demographics, pavement conditions, geospatial features, tax information, project status, and so much more. With the addition of digital sensors across a city landscape, the amount and variety of data is set to explode in the years ahead.

Using this government data to improve operations, make better decisions, build trust and transparency, and enable innovation solutions has the power to build better and smarter cities.

REMEMBER

The smart use of data is a fundamental aspect of a smart city.

Enabling data-driven decision-making

When you learn to fly a single-engine plane, part of the training process requires you to rely on the instruments regardless of what your brain might tell you to do. You wear a special cap that prevents you from looking outside. The instructor puts the plane into an usual configuration — let's say a climb with low power — in order to create the conditions for an emergency situation. The instructor then tells you to use only the instruments to recover the flight orientation to a safe flying configuration. What happens is that your brain receives signals from the body, such as information about balance, that tell you to take actions that are wrong. But if you rely on what the instruments are saying, you make the correct maneuvers. The first few times you do this exercise, you have to fight your brain. In other words, you have to trust what the instruments are telling you versus what your brain wants you to believe.

This example is analogous to how you must treat data. Good data tells the truth. Even though you might often want to believe something else based on how you believe something should be or on instinct relative to experience, you need to become comfortable with using data to make organizational decisions.

REMEMBER

Data will provide important insight, but it won't necessarily tell you what action to take. That part still largely remains a human function. You will need to consider context, politics, and economics, amongst many other factors.

There's room for tacit knowledge, intuition, and experience, but they should be used sparingly and likely only in combination with what story the data tells. In fact, you must become hungry for exceptionally good data. The more you have and the richer it is, the higher the likelihood of a more informed data-driven decision.

REMEMBER

Data leads to information that then becomes knowledge. This knowledge provides essential insights. It's not uncommon now for leaders to feel constrained by not being presented with sufficient information to make an informed decision. A smart city cannot exist without the smart use of data.

Managing data

It's hard to think of an organization today that doesn't use data in some capacity. But, the existence of data within an organization doesn't equate to any evidence that it's being properly managed.

Making a city smarter by using data as the rich, valuable asset it is requires the deliberate use of specialized tools, talent, and processes. Data has a life cycle, from creation to retirement, and to glean its optimum value, this life cycle must be managed — a process known as *data management*.

Data management typically includes these activities:

>> Having the ability to collect, create, update, and remove data across disparate systems

>> Possessing the capability to retain data in various formats across different types of storage systems

>> Ensuring the high availability of data to authorized users

>> Maintaining disaster recovery options consistent with organizational needs

>> Supporting data's utilization across different types of systems and solutions

>> Managing data privacy and security

>> Being able to archive and destroy data according to policy and compliance requirements

REMEMBER

These minimum data activities must be addressed in your data strategy. You find out how to develop a data strategy in the next section.

You can easily test whether data is being well managed in a city. Consider the following basic questions:

>> Does every data set have an owner?

>> Can authorized people access the right data when they need it?

>> If a disaster — such as a cyberattack, a fire that destroys systems, or an accidental loss or deletion of files — occurs, is service restored quickly and without a headache?

>> Can data move securely between people and systems in order to best leverage its value?

>> Is talent readily available to produce reports, identify insights, and perform research with data?

If the answer to these questions is generally yes, you're in a better position than most. On the other hand, if any of these questions can't be answered with high confidence, there's a good chance you don't have a data management strategy, or the existing strategy needs to be reworked.

Many larger cities have already embraced data management, but many still need to elevate this competency to the mature level it deserves. Smaller cities, while recognizing its value, struggle with this topic because of challenges with insufficient budgets to afford data scientists and specialized tools. My advice is for all city agencies to create a data strategy that rightsizes it against needs and the available budget. For example, for a large city, hire a chief data officer (CDO), and for the smaller ones, find staff that are interested in the topic who can carry out data roles as part of their other responsibilities.

TIP

To find out more about hiring a chief data officer, see the "Hiring a city chief data officer" section, later in this chapter.

Developing a data strategy

Cities must have a data strategy if they want to have operational excellence, increased quality of life, and better performance results. The purpose of any strategy is to have a plan designed to achieve some desired outcomes.

Recognizing that data is your friend and that it can provide enormous value in every aspect of building and operating a smart city means that you have to create a deliberate set of actions to achieve results.

REMEMBER

A data strategy is an agreed-on plan that all appropriate stakeholders sign off on.

A mistake that many organizations make after developing a strategy is to blindly follow it, even as circumstances change. The right way to deal with a strategy is to regularly confirm with stakeholders that the desired outcomes are still relevant and, if appropriate, modify the actions periodically. After all, nothing stays the same. Organizational agility is a valued 21st century characteristic.

The worst type of strategy is one that's created and never acted on. Creating a strategic plan isn't the goal — achieving your outcomes is. Many excellent strategic plans are sitting on the shelves of executives, simply gathering dust.

TIP

A data strategy must include, at minimum:

>> A description of the roles and responsibilities that various leaders and staff play in the management of data

>> The capabilities desired from the supporting systems

>> Any policy, legal, or regulatory requirements

>> An articulation of how data value will be derived

Creating any strategy usually follows a sequence similar to this one:

1. **Agree on the vision.**

    Document and agree on the desired results (the *vision*) of the plan. It's defining what you want the future to look like. Often, this is the hardest step. You might be surprised to discover the degree to which stakeholders aren't on the same page when this exercise first begins. However, after all the arm wrestling and debating end, it's gratifying when everyone does finally agree on the vision.

2. **Perform a gap analysis.**

    A what? A *gap analysis* is the result of identifying the difference between where the organization's current performance is and where you want it to be. For example, you might look at business metrics and determine where you are versus where you want to be. Only by completing a gap analysis can you take the next step and identify and define your objectives.

3. **Identify the objectives.**

    To reach your desired outcomes, often called goals, means that you need to have actions to get there. These are the plan's *objectives*. They should be SMART: *specific, measurable, attainable, realistic,* and *time-bound*. My guess is that you've heard this acronym before (over in Chapter 5), so I hope that it's a good reminder.

4. **Define how the plan and the outcomes will be measured.**

    Okay, here's another truism: What gets measured gets managed. In my career, this one has served me well. Without metrics, how do you know whether you're winning? Define those targets. Don't overlook this essential part of the strategy.

5. **Get the right people to sign off on the strategy.**

This step is important. Without the right people putting their signatures on the plan, you'll experience issues later on. It's much harder for a leader to argue that they didn't support or agree with a plan if there's evidence that they have endorsed it. Making the final sign-off less difficult can be achieved by engaging those leaders throughout the strategy creation process.

6. **Execute the strategy and evolve as necessary.**

Yup, do the work. During this essential phase you'll be obtaining funding, identifying project resources, running projects, and training or recruiting the right talent to manage the outcome.

REMEMBER

Though this set of steps is applicable to creating a data strategy, it can be applied to any strategy. Use it every time you identify a goal and need to come up with a plan. A more detailed treatment of strategy development is covered in Chapter 5.

Implementing data governance

Data management is concerned with how you use data to run your organizations and make good decisions. Equally important is that you also need to ensure that agreed-on data policies and processes, accountabilities, decision structures, and enforcement rules are in place. The implementation of these qualities is called *data governance*: It's the difference between poor data management and excellent data management. Many organizations manage data —well, maybe all do —but far fewer manage it well.

REMEMBER

Data governance is the science of managing data well. If it doesn't already exist, data governance must be part of the city's data strategy.

Focus areas of data governance

Data governance is a large, complex, and important topic; a whole book is required in order to fully appreciate how to successfully implement it. To quickly understand its scope, these four areas address the major themes of data governance:

>> **Policy:** With policy, you're creating guidelines for particular data situations that everyone must follow. An example is backup and retention, which may in fact be required by law (see the compliance section below). A policy might state that certain types of data must be backed up every day and that it'll be stored for at least three years. A policy typically describes how such guidelines will be enforced as well.

>> **Quality:** In data governance, quality refers to the degree of confidence you have in the data to help with a particular objective. If you're basing important

decisions on data, you had better be confident that it's at least accurate and complete. In data governance, you want to have processes and practices that can support the integrity of the data you've collected.

>> **Compliance:** Compliance ensures that data is handled in a way that meets not only organizational policies and rules but also industry and governmental policies, rules, and laws. In particular, many governments have specific laws governing data use and management. For example, if a community member requests access to some city data, a formal process might have to be followed — including the time allowed to respond and the rights that the requestor has to view and use the data.

>> **Business intelligence:** Business intelligence is one of the hot terms in data these days. You could say that business intelligence is another term for data management, or an umbrella term for all the things an organization does to glean value from data. Both are acceptable.

REMEMBER

In a city context, business intelligence is about the strategies and technologies used for analyzing data. Applying data governance to business intelligence means ensuring that the right people have access to the right data at the right time. It's also about the rights people have regarding each dataset.

Data ownership

A central requirement of data governance is having an identified owner for every major dataset in an organization. It might seem intuitive, but it continues to be rare.

Organizations have no problem taking at face value the fact that the human resources department is responsible for the hiring process or that the facilities manager is responsible for taking care of issues with buildings. However, when it comes to data, seldom does anyone know who is responsible. A *data owner* is the person who will worry each day that the data is backed up, kept current, and secured from unauthorized users, and who will — perhaps most importantly — be the expert when it comes to determining what the data is and how it might be used.

REMEMBER

If there's only one thing you do regarding data governance, I suggest identifying data owners and providing them with specific responsibilities.

The data governance board (DGB)

Okay, so you've created a data governance strategy as part of your overall city data strategy. Congrats! You now need a team of people who meet regularly to provide oversight for data governance and who will continue to evolve the policies and rules for the organization. They also need to capture metrics to monitor progress and report on data value. This team is known as the *data governance board.*

The members and the responsibilities of this board are determined by each organization. It makes sense for this board to consist of at least

>> A few data owners and staff who are passionate about data

>> Data analysts from different departments

>> The chief data officer or equivalent

>> The chief information officer or equivalent or subordinate

>> A member of the city clerk's office

>> Someone from the city manager's or administrator's office

>> Possibly one or two members of the public who possess data skills

REMEMBER

The board must be given appropriate authority by leadership. A team with documented responsibilities helps ensure better-quality data and better outcomes with data use.

It might feel like there's some level of redundancy here between data management, data strategy, and data governance. In truth, you'll see overlap — see Figure 9-2 — but all are ultimately separate and important aspects of developing a mature approach to handling and optimizing the data of a city. Each one is also highly complementary.

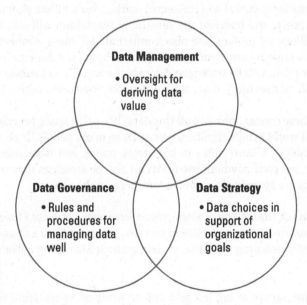

Data Management
• Oversight for deriving data value

Data Governance
• Rules and procedures for managing data well

Data Strategy
• Data choices in support of organizational goals

FIGURE 9-2:
Blended data leadership activities ensure optimum success.

TIP If you like the topic of data governance, a little research will quickly show you that it actually encompasses much more than just the items I've introduced here. Check out the Data Governance Institute (www.datagovernance.com) for more on the topic.

Working with City Data

In most city agencies, scarcity dominates. As examples, there's never enough money or time to address every problem and never sufficient staffing for all the needs that arise. However, in one area — data —there's an abundance. Cities by nature create, use, manage, and store a lot of it.

Having this abundance doesn't mean that the benefits are being realized proportionally with the data's potential value. Neither does it mean that the data is being managed well or being secured appropriately. In this section, I take a look at some ways you can work better with all that lovely, abundant data to make your city smarter.

Securing data

The first few decades of the 21st century have seen a continuation and acceleration of an increasingly digital and connected world. Over 4 billion people are connected to the Internet, and many of the remaining few billion will join in the next few years. Billions of devices are also connected. All these connected people and devices are creating large volumes of data. In 2020, it's anticipated that over 200 exabytes of data will be transferred across the world's networks. To gain a sense of the scale of that much data, it's 1,000 to the power of 6 bytes. That's a lot.

With all these connections and all this data, it's a ripe space for criminals. Though the digital world brings significant benefits to many people, it also creates plenty of vulnerabilities. Sure, you can buy items online and have them delivered the same day, but your payment methods can also be stolen as they travel across the Internet or are stored on a server somewhere on the planet.

In 2018, in the United States alone, there were over 1,200 data breaches, resulting in the exposure of over 446 million records. You can't have a discussion about the benefits of unleashing the value of data without also being sober about the risks of data.

Without the luxury of big budgets and an army of information security professionals, cities are frequent targets of cyberattacks. For a long time, cities have avoided major cybersecurity attacks. No longer. For this reason, data security plans and actions must be central to a data strategy. In addition, with every new system that goes online, a security strategy must be developed and executed.

REMEMBER

In recent years, many cities have been the victim of a particularly nefarious form of cyberattack software called *ransomware*. This software is deployed by criminals in order to cut off access to city systems and files. Restored access will only be granted by the criminals upon payment by the city of a ransom. If system backups don't exist, a city has almost no other option than to pay the criminals. American cities such as New Orleans and Atlanta have been attacked. The cost of a ransomware attack on the city of Baltimore in 2019 is estimated to have cost the city around $18 million.

WARNING

Don't let cybersecurity be an afterthought. Cities must consider it a new, required competency. I discuss cybersecurity in more detail — including understanding the threats and the steps a city can take to improve security — in Chapter 10.

Opening data

In most cases, the data a city government manages belongs to the community. Intuitively, this means that most of it should be readily available for any community member to access it. Reality, though, lies far from this rosy picture. In many cities, accessing data from city hall can be a bureaucratic trek.

However, over the past decade, a positive global trend has emerged: Cities and other government agencies are proactively creating easier ways for those seeking nonprotected data to gain easy access to it. Cities are opening their data in such a way that it can be accessed seamlessly online.

Data that's electronically accessible without restriction and in a format that can be processed by other computer applications is called *open data*. Open data is producing more results than just making data available. Easy access to the same data that government staff have access to can increase transparency and trust. Let's be honest about this: All too often, there's too little trust between government and the people it serves, and anything that can be done to build better bridges is a good thing.

TIP

Open data enables better decision-making because it enables a broader group of stakeholders to analyze data and bring ideas and insights to a public discussion.

Creating solutions using open data has become popular over the past ten years. It's empowering. Rather than wait for a city to produce a solution, a motivated individual or organization can access the data and have it power a community solution. (For some examples of how open data can inspire solutions, see Appendix D.)

Open data is part of a broader phenomenon called open government. *Open government* is a movement that believes citizens have the right to access government data and to be informed about proceedings. It includes the ability for citizens to have many ways — including electronic ways — to participate in, and collaborate with, government.

Though open government and open data are pursued in many countries around the world, use and access is uneven and results aren't yet definitive. In places where implementation is mature and adoption is high, one can already see the benefits that come from transparency, trust, and collaboration. To understand how open data in different countries contributes towards economic and social benefits, see some research at www.opendata500.com/.

Examining the principles of open data

To better understand what constitutes a dataset as open data, the following characteristics must be met. Anything less can't be considered open data:

>> **Complete:** A data set provided via open data should be available in its entirety.

>> **Primary:** Data must be from the original source and not in aggregate or modified form.

>> **Timely:** As soon as some data is created, it must be posted online. Current data has high value to it.

>> **Accessible:** Data must be available to everyone online and for almost any use without restrictions.

>> **Machine-processable:** Data must be in at least one common format, such as comma-separated values (CSV), that can be easily consumed by another computer application.

>> **Nondiscriminatory:** Access to data must not require any special access rights, such as a username or password.

>> **Nonproprietary:** There must be no special requirements, such as the need to purchase a specialized piece of software, in order to open, view, and process the data.

>> **License-free:** Data must not require permission for use or be subject to any copyright, patent, trademark, or trade secret regulation.

Creating an open data portal

In my opinion, every city should make open data a default offering. In addition to increasing transparency and trust, it can reduce the administrative cost and time to the city by eliminating the need to research, collect, and deliver each data request.

To make open data meet the eight principles for use (see the previous section), the data has to be posted in a location that's accessible and user friendly. The preferred approach by most cities now is to create an open data portal that's a branch of its existing website.

REMEMBER

An *open data portal* is an online, one-stop shop to search for and retrieve city datasets. Typically, datasets are stored in categories such as public safety, budget, or transportation. Sophisticated open portals include deeper explanations of the data and perhaps a few examples of how it's being used. I've included a long list of international open data portal examples in Appendix C. In addition, this website has a comprehensive catalog of open data portals: www.dataportals.org/.

Data can typically be viewed, queried, and manipulated online. In addition, most portals provide a variety of ways to download the data. It's not uncommon to have these file formats supported:

>> **CSV** (comma-separated values)

>> **XLS** (file format for Microsoft Excel)

>> **XML** (extended markup language)

It's also popular to offer an *application programming interface (API)*, which enables another software program to directly access the data on the open data portal. An API can enable an independent solution to provide capabilities that require direct access to a city's data. For example, a third-party solution used for permitting might provide historical permitting data within the application. The user would never be aware that it was being retrieved in real-time from the city's open data portal. I discuss APIs in greater depth in Chapter 8.

TIP

Open data portals can provide the data needed to power community hackathons and challenges that help to solve problems. These topics are discussed in detail in Chapter 7.

Finally, over 100 governments and organizations from around the world have collaborated together to form the Open Data Charter (ODC). Its goal is to open up data based on a shared set of principles, not unlike those I share earlier in this section. In addition, the ODC is tasked with pushing policies and practices to enable governments to collect, share, and use well-governed data. They view open data as another mechanism to help respond to social, economic, and environmental challenges. You can learn more here: https://opendatacharter.net/.

Making sense of data through analytics

Data is created, collected, and stored as a product of running an organization — but it should not stop there. When you have access to an abundance of data, additional value can be gleaned from inspecting it to discover insights and to help support decision-making. This is the role of data analytics.

Data analytics includes the processes, techniques, and tools for exploring, extracting, categorizing, visualizing, and analyzing data and its patterns. Okay, that's a mouthful. Basically, it's about looking at a dataset and figuring out what it can tell you.

For a city, there's no end to the list of information that mayors, city managers, community members, and other stakeholders want to know. The dynamic nature of cities means that there's always something new to explore and discover. The kinds of insights a city focuses on are reflective of the needs of every community. They're reminders that it's almost impossible to generalize the notion of a smart city, because every city has unique demands and challenges. The data analytics that are important to the city of Moscow, Russia, are different from those that are important to Moscow, Idaho.

Data visualization

Data in its raw form is boring and unintuitive. Without background knowledge and perhaps some training, it can be nearly impossible to make sense of it. Today, you can find tools and skills that enable data to be presented in ways that quickly convey a story.

Data visualization has emerged as a powerful way to communicate complex information and to make sense of it quickly. Combining visualization with storytelling can maximize comprehension and lead to better, more informed decisions. For a quality example of data storytelling, check out Our World in Data, a site managed by a team at the University of Oxford: https://ourworldindata.org.

Combining visuals with a story results in

>> Enhancing comprehension of complex issues

>> Reducing the time it takes to interpret the data

>> Increasing the memorability of the message

>> Improving the likelihood of action

>> Increasing the number of people who can understand and act on the data

Five concepts of data visualization

It's not enough to simply take some data and make it look pretty by using graphical metaphors. To win an audience requires that data visualization follow some basic concepts. Here are five to get you started:

>> **Integrity:** A visualization must be an accurate reflection of the underlying data. In the process of creating an elaborate visualization, there's always the risk of misleading the audience. It might be unintended, so validate it with trusted colleagues before sharing broadly.

>> **Meaningful:** The manner and types of visualizations used must resonate with the audience. For example, if you're trying to communicate in the domain of budgets and finance, the imagery used should be consistent with factors such as money and accounting. Choosing the right metaphors is essential, too. If you make it too abstract, you lose the audience.

>> **Simplicity:** Remember to keep it simple, stupid (KISS). The last thing you want to do is take a complex topic and create a complex visualization. Don't communicate too much. If your visualization is growing overly complex, it probably means that you need more than one visualization.

>> **Relevant:** Although there's always a temptation, avoid the use of metaphors and imagery that aren't directly aligned with what's being communicated in the visualization. For example, if you're communicating a story about tax revenues collected and the state of the economy, it's probably not necessary to capture and illustrate the methods of payment used.

>> **Beautiful:** Visualizations should look great. They're pieces of art. Well, sometimes. (I've seen some real beasts over the years.) Use boldness and color. Great visualizations require training and specific skills. The difference between an okay visualization and a great visualization is a chasm. They can also be interactive when available online; some great examples can be found here:

```
www.datapine.com/blog/best-data-visualizations
```

A data visualization on its own is created for others to interpret and make decisions. However, when data visualization is presented with a narrative in order to communicate a point, it's known as an *infographic*. Infographics typically use multiple data visualizations, and, just like data visualizations, they can be interactive.

Figure 9-3 illustrates the use of data visualization to tell a story by using an infographic.

"Infographics | Data Visualization," by Amy Weiss, is licensed under CC BY-NC-ND 4.0

FIGURE 9-3: An example of data visualization to tell a story by way of an infographic format.

Using geographic information systems (GIS)

A geographic information system (GIS) is a system that captures, analyzes, manipulates, presents, manages, and stores geographic features and boundaries on Earth. Examples of features include borders, rivers, roads, bridges, buildings, signposts, and electrical lines. In addition to location and orientation, many more object details are stored, such as type, age, size, altitude, and much more.

A common use of a GIS is to create a specialized map. For example, a request may come in for a map that illustrates all the city's traffic signals and how they're connected to the network controlling them. A GIS system can use its geospatial database to promptly spin up such a request.

Now, you might not always think of it this way, but a GIS is, in effect, a city data system. It's an essential and important one, too. I'd argue that the best and most common way to represent a city is, in fact, by using a GIS. It's also the tool used across many city departments to help run their various operations, such as in these examples:

>> Police using it for documenting the locations of incidents

>> Public works using it for road construction

>> Planning departments using it for approving building permits relative to land use rules

>> Emergency operations centers (EOCs) using it to prepare for, mitigate, and respond to disasters

>> All manner of decision-makers using it when their decisions rely on geospatial information

City GIS information can also be used in combination with third-party solutions. For example, Google Maps can include local information in the app.

REMEMBER

Used correctly, a GIS is an essential decision-making tool, because it provides business intelligence in the form of location intelligence. (Figure 9-4, for example, shows New York City's evacuation zones during Hurricane Sandy.) When considering a smart city project or any sort of innovation that would require geospatial data, a high-quality GIS has to be part of the mix.

FIGURE 9-4:
An example of
GIS in action.

*Creation commons license details: "Open Data and online mapping for Hurricane Sandy Cleanup"
by @gletham GIS, Social, Mobile Tech Images is licensed under CC BY 2.0*

SOLVING URBAN TRAFFIC CHALLENGES WITH GEOSPATIAL ANALYTICS

Metro Cebu, the second most populous metropolitan area in the Philippines at approximately 3 million residents, serves as the economic and transportation hub of central Philippines. In 2014, the Philippine Department of Transportation and Communication awarded the construction and maintenance of a new international terminal at Mactan Cebu International Airport. Completed in July 2018, the new terminal increased annual passenger traffic from 4.5 million to 12.5 million.

While a boon for economic and tourist activity, both in metropolitan Cebu and across the central and southern Philippines, the additional passenger load was a factor putting considerable strain on traffic infrastructure and natural resources across the region. In October 2019, the provincial board of Cebu approved a resolution declaring a traffic emergency, asking President Duterte to "help us find a solution."

Because historical data around traffic was lacking, a novel approach to quantify traffic and land conversion trends was initiated by the geospatial analytics firm, Orbital Insight. Using high-resolution satellite imagery dating back to 2014, Orbital Insight deployed computer vision algorithms to identify and count all visible cars in imagery across the region. This fully automated process identified millions of cars, showing an increase in traffic consistent with construction milestones at the airport. Further analytical techniques deployed show the spatial expansion of high-traffic clusters across the city, indicating congestion spread outward from main commercial districts and infrastructure choke points to engulf much of the urban area. (See the image below.)

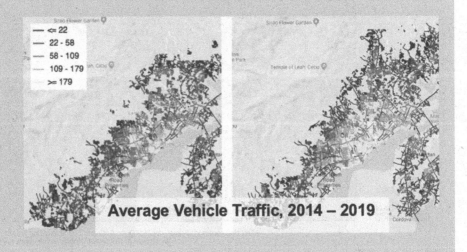

Average Vehicle Traffic, 2014 – 2019

A second series of algorithms were deployed, identifying each pixel of the satellite image as a building, road, forest, agricultural, or "other" class. By creating a series of land use maps showing urban extent, Orbital Insight was able to quantify conversion of forest and agricultural land to built-up areas and pinpoint exact locations where that occurred. The image below shows numerous tiles, approximately 500 by 500 meters in size, where the surface area of new buildings doubled or more than tripled from 2015 to 2019.

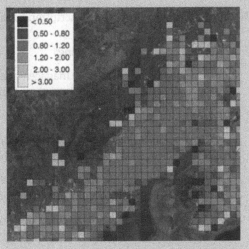

Case study contributed courtesy of Orbital Insight.

Hiring a city chief data officer

Building and operating a smart city means having the right talent. From creating the smart city vision through to the implementation and maintenance of that vision, this might mean hiring vendors and contractors, retraining existing staff, and bringing on new staff. Without the right blend of experienced support, achieving your desired outcomes is much harder.

In this chapter, the case has been made for the essential role of data in a smart city. Unleashing the value of data requires staff with skills and experiences in this domain. For a city of a certain size and complexity, I recommend considering a senior executive to provide leadership and oversight for the successful implementation and operation of the data strategy.

Determining whether a city requires a full-time, senior role is at the discretion of every city. Today, it's becoming more common for cities with a population over 1 million to have someone designated to serve in the data leadership role. However, even a small city with big smart city ambitions and a generous budget might consider it as well.

Data leadership should be, at minimum, a part of some city executive's portfolio of responsibilities.

Here's an example of the role description for a city's chief data officer (CDO):

>> **Reports to any of the following:**

- City manager, assistant city manager, chief operations officer, chief financial officer, or chief information officer

>> **Core objectives:**

- To develop, lead, and execute the data strategy of the city by partnering with colleagues within the city and stakeholders in the community

- To lead data governance and support the creation of policies and procedures that drive the creation of value from city data

- To provide best practices and oversight for the creation, collection, organization, storage, and analysis of city data assets while ensuring that security, privacy, and compliance requirements are met

- Improving the use of data through systems, behaviors, reporting, and innovation while working with teams across the city

>> **Desired background:**

- An understanding of both private and public sector organizational operating practices

- A minimum of a bachelor's degree in information technology, data science, or a related field

- Five to ten years of related experience and senior-level leadership

- Expert-level project management experience

- An analytical mindset

- A passion for data management

4

Planning for an Urban Future

Chapter 10

Building a Secure Foundation

"This City is what it is because our citizens are what they are."

—PLATO

C ities reflect the times and conditions in which people live. Today, technology is playing a central role in almost every aspect of the human experience. Municipalities are becoming more technology-enabled not only because of efficiencies and better outcomes but also because people have come to expect that cities will use and deploy solutions that mirror experiences in other areas of life. If you can fill in some basic information and then click a button to snag a table reservation at your favorite restaurant, you will probably eventually expect to do the same when requesting a building permit. If you can visit your doctor via telemedicine, you'll likely expect to be able to attend a public meeting over your smartphone as well.

Your community wants a smarter city. To meet these expectations, local governments are becoming more digital and integrating technology across city departments.

The increased adoption of connected and digital technologies brings considerable benefits, but it also elevates the potential for security risks. More technology means a larger canvas for vulnerabilities, such as cybercrime, and a bigger risk to your privacy.

But security in your city isn't limited to the technologies you deploy. Security also means protecting your community from a wide range of risks. A responsibility of every local government is to enable a safe environment for its constituents. Threats to that safe environment can include crime or terrorism or an inability to withstand the dangers of a natural disaster.

A strategy for securing your community must be foundational to any smart city effort. After all, when people don't feel safe, every aspect of life is impacted.

Securing Your Smart City

The increased incidence and impact of cybercrimes and disasters that have beset so many of the world's cities in recent years is a reminder that security must be a priority. The rapid spread of technology, as well as the impact of climate change and its related extreme weather events, are creating new risks for communities. Fortunately, new technologies and a growing number of best practices are helping cities be smarter and more secure in how they deploy protections. Just remember that, as important as it is to put in place methods of prevention and mitigation, it's also vital to be able to bounce back if the worst does occur.

In this section, I discuss the foundational areas of securing your smart city. Even if you're not ready to implement your smart city strategy, I strongly recommend these security technologies and suggestions for every city.

Urban resilience

Cities have succeeded in so many positive ways, from lifting billions of people out of extreme poverty to becoming the driving force of economic prosperity in the world. But for all their remarkable accomplishments, cities still face enormous challenges and threats. As many cities grow larger and more complex in the 21st century, the challenges that confront them are magnified as well. The major threats that urban environments face include the effects of climate change, cyber-attacks, pandemics, decaying infrastructure, natural disasters, and terrorism.

As an example, across the planet, 616 cities — home to 1.7 billion people — are at risk of flooding (shown in Figure 10-1), which endangers more city residents than any other natural disaster. The scientific consensus is that climate change will continue to cause sea-level rise and more extreme weather events, which will result in a higher frequency of major urban flooding. Earthquakes and storms follow as the second and third natural disaster risks, respectively.

FIGURE 10-1:
Street flooding is now a frequent occurrence even in the most sophisticated urban environments. (New Orleans, after being struck by Hurricane Katrina.)

What distinguishes a city that can adapt and prosper despite these challenges from those that verge on the brink of collapse when confronted with major disruption?

Those cities that bounce back quicker are those that embrace, plan, and execute resiliency strategies. *Urban resiliency* is defined as the capacity of a city to survive and grow despite chronic stresses and acute shocks. A *chronic stress* can be thought of as a slow-moving disaster, such as high unemployment or deteriorating transportation systems. An *acute shock* is a sudden event, such as an earthquake, a terrorist attack, or a disease outbreak.

The United Nations' 2030 Agenda for Sustainable Development recognizes and reaffirms the urgent need to reduce the risk of disasters. The core deliverable of this agenda, the Sustainable Development Goals (SDGs), as discussed in Chapter 2, makes urban resiliency a goal: "Goal 11: Make cities and human settlements inclusive, safe, resilient, and sustainable." The specific target is here:

By 2030, significantly reduce the number of deaths and the number of people affected and substantially decrease the direct economic losses relative to global gross domestic product caused by disasters, including water-related disasters, with a focus on protecting the poor and people in vulnerable situations. This is measured by (a) the number of deaths, missing persons, and persons affected by disaster per 100,000 people and, (b) Direct disaster economic loss in relation to global GDP, including disaster damage to critical infrastructure and disruption of basic services.

WARNING

Urban resiliency is never finished. Cities must plan for an ongoing process.

Resilient cities are positioned well to help protect people lives, secure development gains, and foster an investible cityscape. Building this urban resiliency requires understanding the city in-depth and the interdependencies and risks that may exist. It's only by recognizing the potential stresses and shocks a city may encounter that a resiliency plan can be constructed. Any plan must reflect the risk profile of the community. For example, if a city is built directly above a fault line, considerable focus will be placed on earthquake preparedness and resilience. The same goes for waterfront communities and the risk of flooding and for housing on hillsides at risk of mudslides.

To lead efforts, many cities are hiring a chief resiliency officer (CRO). This executive-level leader reports to the mayor or city manager. The main responsibility of the person in this role is to bring stakeholders together in order to leverage resources and experts in the development and execution of a resilience strategy.

TIP

Resilient cities are smarter cities. Urban projects, where it makes logical sense, should be executed with resiliency in mind. The positive outcomes of doing this are known as the *resilience dividend* — the economic, social, and physical benefits garnered when projects are designed in an integrated, risk-aware, and inclusive manner.

Characteristics of resilient systems

In addition to the drivers of urban resiliency, the CRF (see sidebar) integrated many years of research to identify these seven characteristics that city resiliency systems require:

>> **Reflective:** Uses the past to inform the future

>> **Resourceful:** Explores alternative ways to use resources

>> **Inclusive:** Engages a broad group of stakeholders in decision-making

>> **Integrated:** Assimilates different systems and organizations

>> **Robust:** Deploys well-designed and -built solutions

>> **Redundant:** Ensures that additional capacity is available to accommodate risks

>> **Flexible:** Remains open to evolving strategies in response to changing circumstances

CITY RESILIENCE FRAMEWORK (CRF)

Together, the Rockefeller Foundation and the professional services firm Arup developed the City Resilience Framework (CRF) in consultation with cities across the world. Its purpose is to serve as a planning and decision-making tool to help guide city leaders in making investments to strengthen their response to stresses and shocks. The tool can be used to identify areas for improvement, systemic weaknesses, and opportunities for mitigating risk.

The framework identifies 12 universal factors and drivers that contribute to urban resiliency. The 12 factors are categorized into these four dimensions:

- **Leadership and strategy**
  - Effective leadership and management
  - Empowered stakeholders
  - Integrated development planning
- **Health and well-being**
  - Minimal human vulnerability
  - Diverse livelihoods and employment
  - Effective safeguards to human health and life
- **Economy and society**
  - Sustainable economy
  - Comprehensive security and rule of law
  - Collective identity and community support

- **Infrastructure and environment**
  - Reduced exposure and fragility
  - Effective provision of critical services
  - Reliable mobility and communications

For more on the CRF, check out this link:

www.rockefellerfoundation.org/report/city-resilience-framework

Examples of resiliency solutions

Though actually stopping urban disasters from happening may not be possible (think of natural disasters, such as earthquakes and tornadoes), informing people in advance can have real benefits. Storm tracking satellites and weather prediction modeling have made dramatic advances in the past few years. Early warning systems can shut down the flow of natural gas in pipelines to reduce the likelihood of fires. Advance notice of earthquakes would make it possible to instruct elevators to stop at the nearest floor and let people out so that they'd avoid being trapped. Many of these systems are now being powered by low-cost Internet of Things (IoT) sensors (discussed in Chapter 8) that are being deployed across cities.

With the widespread popularity of smartphones and mobile phones, agencies are using the digital channels to communicate to community members on their devices. In addition to the common social media sites, such as Facebook and Twitter, agencies make specific disaster management apps available to constituents. Important real-time updates can be communicated, and the dialogue can be two-way between the city and the resident. Information on evacuation routes, when power will be restored, where to shelter, and other actions that can be taken can result in reduced risk and injury.

Open data platforms (discussed in Chapter 9) are being used to publish and distribute data on resilience-related items. Communities can learn about issues and monitor the performance of their government. Open data is also a way to encourage community engagement on resilience decision-making as well as in developing solutions.

The increasing frequency of cyberattacks on cities has resulted in a greater focus — but still not nearly enough — on cybersecurity (discussed later in this chapter, in the section "Cybersecurity"). The smartest cities are deploying system redundancies and intrusion detection solutions, keeping software current, backing up all data, and training and testing their staff in *cyberhygiene* (good information security practices). When these cities are attacked, they're able to continue operations or, at worst, recover quickly.

Finally, the risk of periodic disease epidemics, and even pandemics, are all too real. Just in the past few decades, countries and cities have dealt with a number of deadly challenges, including HIV, Ebola, SARS, MERS, bird flu, and now COVID-19. With cities having a concentration of people and many with notable population densities, they're particularly vulnerable to a contagion. Resilience efforts have included reading the temperatures of passengers arriving at city airports, reporting certain symptoms to health authorities when returning ill from a trip, and launching large-scale educational campaigns.

In early 2020, the world was thrown into turmoil by the arrival of the aforementioned COVID-19, a new and highly contagious coronavirus. The last event of this scale was the Spanish flu, in 1918. Caught largely by surprise, cities had no resilience strategy for such a crisis. With no plan, no medicine, and no vaccine, the only recourse for most cities was to temporarily make their residents stay at home, except for essential workers.

As this book was being completed, this crisis was still unfolding. New, innovative solutions were emerging for tracking the virus and apps were being deployed in cities for helping with virus contact tracing and symptom management. Cities such as London, New York, and Mexico City were beginning to convert road lanes exclusively for bicycles. With public transportation still not a safe option, many constituents were turning to bikes. Restaurant and grocery delivery services were skyrocketing in popularity as people were being asked to stay at home. Sadly, the economic picture was also deteriorating quickly, with unemployment rising and sales plummeting. The economic toll on city revenues will be severe and could very likely impact many planned and in-progress smart city efforts.

One lesson was already clear: The absence of a pandemic resilience strategy was imposing a heavy price on almost every city across the world.

Public safety

Common characteristics of an urban environment are the sounds and visuals of wailing sirens and flashing lights of ambulances, police cars, and fire trucks. Few provisions are more fundamental in a modern city today than public safety. It's a fundamental role of local government. Feeling protected and safe is central to enjoying a good quality of life.

Local public safety organizations include fire departments, emergency medical services, and law enforcement. The typical urban issues that law enforcement in particular deals with include burglary, noise, narcotics use, trespassing, harassment, inebriation, accidents, cybercrime, and other quality-of-life issues. Public safety is concerned with the prevention of, and protection from, events — such as injury, property damage, crimes, and disasters — that can impact the safety of the community.

Despite public safety being a priority and the work required becoming more sophisticated, the tools and processes to deliver services have remained stagnant over the years and haven't kept up with progress. For example, emergency services have remained relatively unchanged for around 50 years. Certainly, there are improvements, such as better navigation systems, which have improved response times, but the basic process of receiving a call, dispatching a vehicle, and attending to the issue remains the same. This state of affairs continues while community expectations have greatly increased. Today, constituents want public safety organizations to do more than react to situations in progress. They want a proactive approach to managing operations, events, and emergency situations.

Bringing innovation to public safety departments and making them smarter has faced considerable challenges. Issues include poor funding, public resistance to controversial technologies such as *predictive policing* (using data to anticipate a crime — go here to learn more: nij.ojp.gov/topics/articles/overview-predictive-policing), a lack of technical expertise, infrastructure difficulties such as poor connectivity, as well as privacy and security concerns. These challenges are being addressed, but progress has been difficult. I provide some recommendations at the end of this section on how best to move the ball forward.

Public safety technology innovation is making progress, and many organizations have been able to embrace it, but they remain a small minority. Advances have included the increased use of closed circuit TV (or CCTV, as shown in Figure 10-2), body-worn cameras, integrated command centers, improved wireless communications, broader adoption of software solutions, social media safety alerts, and predictive data analysis.

FIGURE 10-2:
Closed circuit TV for public safety is a common and controversial part of urban life.

From 2016 to 2021, public safety agencies across the world will spend $246.17 billion to protect cities, with investments in communication networks and devices, command and control, video surveillance, and other equipment.

REMEMBER

Innovating public safety is central to the creation of smarter cities. After all, if the intent of smart cities is to improve the quality of life, feeling safe and being protected are inherent characteristics of life quality.

In a smart city, public safety can address these three areas, at minimum:

>> Improve the protection of people, assets, and facilities.

>> Increase operational efficiency.

>> Enhance insights and data-driven decision-making.

Let's explore how these areas can be made smarter using innovative technologies:

>> **Integrated command centers:** Build a central physical or virtual facility that provides public safety digital tools and incorporates information on the safety environment and activities.

>> **Unified security management:** Deploy a collaborative system that incorporates enhanced situational awareness and presents a complete operating picture.

>> **Response coordination:** Use information systems to correlate and interpret disparate information feeds and engage multiple teams in timely actions. Leverage the explosive growth of public safety data.

>> **Collaborative investigation management:** Adopt a platform that integrates and enables the work of multiple entities in researching, recording, documenting, and building reports and recommendations.

>> **Intelligent incident management:** Implement a collaborative decision management system to define response and contingency strategies that can result in predefined manual and automatic actions.

>> **Mobile digital tools:** Provide connected devices to mobile public safety staff that provide, for example, timely access to information, geospatial content, cameras for recording activities, and image recognition software that can be used for multiple purposes — looking up a license plate number, for example.

>> **Records management systems:** Deploy a system that stores and analyzes new, *rich-media* — video, images, and audio — and integrates multiple sources. Make the information easily accessible on any device dependent on the role of the public safety professional.

>> **Sensors:** Use a wide range of innovations that can consume and process information in the physical world, such as video surveillance, the IoT, and drones. You can learn more about these approaches in Chapter 8.

WARNING

Surveillance, recording, and image recognition technologies should be carefully evaluated in consultation with your community. In addition, local and national laws may impose limitations. Proceed with caution and with a focus on privacy considerations. It's a good idea to develop local regulations in the use of these technologies should the decision be made to deploy them.

When it comes to increasing innovation and building smarter public safety solutions, follow these steps:

1. **Invest in digital infrastructure.**

   This is the foundational requirement for enabling high-quality information technology services in a city, region, and country. Though the upfront costs may be high, they're quickly recovered by way of improved community productivity, competitiveness, and innovation. Public safety is one of many city services and community functions that will benefit. With both stationary and mobile needs, dependent on the situation, public safety needs access to a range of wired and wireless capabilities. They also need to be able to handle the large volume of data that has accompanied the digital revolution. In addition, as public safety gains productivity efficiencies, formerly consumed funds may become available to invest in more innovative public safety tools.

2. **Engage the community.**

   By default, delivering public safety services requires help from the community — by helping to solve crimes and prevent disruptive behavior, for example. However, for a variety of reasons, in many communities the relationship between, say, police and residents can be less than trusting. By proactively working to change this dynamic, police can build rapport and confidence. With increased support from community members, public safety may gain advocates for their budget requests and innovation efforts. Additionally, public safety can take advantage of collaboration platforms and social media to interact with the community. These tools can be used to elicit feedback and ideas, ask questions, conduct surveys, and garner written support. Finally, public safety organizations must focus on improved privacy and security, not just because they have a responsibility to do so, but rather to demonstrate their commitment to the community. Given the public's sensitivity in these areas, particularly privacy, efforts can go a long way. Confidence in security and privacy build confidence with constituents.

3. **Publish open data.**

   In Chapter 9, I discuss open data in detail. Public safety teams need to strongly consider actively participating in your city's open data strategy. By doing this, public safety departments can promote transparency and accountability, which can lead to gains in trust and confidence. In addition, by publishing public safety data, external stakeholders can perform analyses that can help efforts, and entrepreneurs and creative residents can build innovation solutions.

4. **Integrate existing and new systems.**

   Public safety organizations use a number of information systems. Many, such as dispatch systems and incident management, are considered fairly commonplace today. Typically, each public safety department has its own system, and each one is provided by different vendors without any integration. To yield the benefits of consolidation and improve innovation, you should explore opportunities to integrate disparate systems. Done well, more timely information can be used for faster outcomes, and process efficiencies can be realized. In addition, work to integrate people and ideas. Public safety can't be successful in a digital world on its own. It requires the collaboration of many departments and stakeholders.

5. Deliver learning and education.

The next few years will bring leaps in new digital innovation to public safety organizations. Personnel will be asked to use more technology tools and data analytics to perform their work. More of the repetitive aspects of their jobs will be automated, and the remaining work will require enhanced skills. Do not assume that your public safety teams will be ready for all the changes that are coming. Those who will succeed are the teams who are trained and confident in digital skills and in the use of the attendant technologies. In a recent Accenture survey, 72 percent of police professionals said that learning-and-development opportunities are important to the future of their organization.

FirstNet

During the attacks on New York City on September 11, 2001, and in the days that followed, serious weaknesses were discovered in the city's available communication networks. With land and mobile phone line usage overwhelmed, many calls could not be completed. This was frustrating for the residents of the city, but it was particularly problematic to public safety. In trying to deliver essential first responder services, police, fire, and paramedics could not communicate effectively. The existing networks were inadequate, and it was clear that public safety shouldn't be competing with non-essential consumer calling. City leaders and others quickly realized that something had to be done to eliminate this challenge in the future, not only for New York City but also for cities all over the United States.

In 2004, the 9/11 Commission Report identified serious gaps in emergency communications and recommended a dedicated nationwide network for public safety communications.

In February 2012, after several years of discussion, development, and campaigning, the First Responder Network Authority was created by an act passed into federal law. The law allocated 20 megahertz of the broadband spectrum and $7 billion to establish a network dedicated to the nation's first responders.

(continued)

(continued)

The First Responder Network Authority was then required to engage in a competitive procurement process to identify a vendor that could build and manage the network. In March 2017, AT&T was awarded a 25-year contract.

The new network was named FirstNet, and accountability was assigned to the National Telecommunications and Information Administration (NTIA), which is part of the US Department of Commerce.

FirstNet (at https://firstnet.gov) was launched in 2018 under the leadership of the First Responder Network Authority (FirstNet Authority), whose mission is now to manage the partnership with AT&T and to improve the offering over time.

These are the six priority objectives of FirstNet:

- **Network core:** Essential architecture, infrastructure, and technology for the network to function
- **Coverage and capacity:** Support for broad and reliable access to the network
- **Situational awareness:** Ability to provide real-time access, collection, and distribution of information
- **Voice communications:** Provision of high-quality, reliable voice communications
- **Secure information exchange:** Accessing, exchanging, and managing data securely
- **User experience:** Designed to meet the specific needs of public safety users

Addressing Digital Security and Privacy

The third industrial revolution — the one that began around the late 1950s and ushered in the era of electronics and information technology — has largely been a boon for society. It's hard to imagine a world today without the Internet and all its connected devices and systems that support and power our modern lifestyles. The capabilities of a smartphone, for example, are close to magical, at least in my view.

But humans are just teasing at the possibilities, and the technologies of tomorrow will leave those of today in the dust. The most powerful smartphones of today will seem quaint within ten years. The world will almost certainly be hyperconnected in many more ways than before. People and machines will be integrated to an extent unimaginable today, and technologies will have pervaded every aspect of the human experience, including our cities.

Though humans will continue to enjoy many of the benefits of the digital transformation, mitigating the security risks and privacy challenges may impose a high price. This section discusses these risks and challenges and suggests possible ways to tackle them as you build your smart city.

Cybersecurity

The world's information systems store and move vast amounts of data around the globe every second. These systems control critical aspects of the modern world, including large domains such as energy, transportation, water, financial services, hospitals, military, and the global supply chain. With billions of connections and their supporting infrastructure, security vulnerabilities are abundant and provide a healthy feast for criminal opportunities. These risks have been around since the dawn of computers, but the accelerated nature of the connected and digital world has made these hazards not only greater in scale but also more frequent and dangerous.

To put the price of information security breaches in perspective, the annual cost worldwide will surpass $5 trillion by 2024. Currently, the yearly costs are around $3 trillion, which means an annual growth rate of 11 percent.

In the 1980s, with the beginning of the widespread use of networked computers, *hackers* (individuals trying to gain unauthorized access to systems) became commonplace. Other threats, such as *worms* (software that replicates across networks and can enable system intrusion) began to emerge.

The term *cybersecurity* was coined to define the protection of data, systems, and networks.

In the 1990s, with connectivity and computer use skyrocketing (particularly with the arrival of the Internet for broad adoption), cybersecurity breaches rose exponentially. Firewalls for preventing unauthorized access and antivirus software became prevalent. An information security industry blossomed that is worth over $100 billion annually today.

By the 2000s, governments around the world were passing tough legislation to punish criminals and create deterrents.

Today, threats are changing and growing more sophisticated and complex. Fortunately, cybersecurity innovation is also evolving quickly. New approaches include behavioral analytics, improved encryption, artificial intelligence, and quantum cryptography. Yet, despite significant progress in defense systems, cybercrimes continue to grow year after year.

Cities, characterized as they are by connected and dependent software and hardware systems, are particularly vulnerable. Though even the private sector has struggled to defend itself from cybercriminals, the public sector, with its lack of resources, has lagged considerably in the investment and talent needed to protect urban systems. In recent years, cities have been the target of significant attacks. Several high-profile cities in the United States were the victims of ransomware that resulted in major systems being offline for days and huge costs to recover.

Some of the reasons that cities have been laggards in cybersecurity are the high costs involved in information security, insufficient prioritization by city leadership, and the state of legacy systems. Reducing vulnerabilities means keeping systems up-to-date with the latest versions of software. The many priorities, distractions, and budget constraints of city information technology (IT) departments has resulted in too many systems falling behind in necessary maintenance. Cloud-based systems such as software as a service (SaaS) have been gaining in popularity for government because the maintenance of software is handled by the vendor.

WARNING

The creators of a smart city strategy — one that will invariably increase the use of technologies across the urban landscape — cannot waver in their commitment to information security; doing so would greatly increase the risk posed by cybercriminals. Cybersecurity must be a top priority for every city — and even more so as the smart city work gets underway.

You can reduce the cybersecurity risks in your smart city strategy by following these tips. The list isn't definitive, by any means, but it's a good start:

>> **Hire a chief information security officer or equivalent to lead your cybersecurity efforts.** It can be rightsized for the city size. This person may or may not need a team.

>> **Create a cybersecurity strategy.** Information security must not be a piecemeal afterthought. It must be comprehensive — it requires the full endorsement of city leadership and elected officials.

>> **Establish cybersecurity standards.** This broad area can be defined relative to your city size and needs. An example of a standard may be the minimum required security software on a laptop that is used by city staff.

>> **Develop and deploy cybersecurity policies and procedures.** This is part of the execution of the strategy. These policies should include staff, vendor, and community security responsibilities. (What security standards must a vendor meet before it can bid on a project, for example?)

>> **Employ good cyberhygiene.** Cyber-what? Yup, cyberhygiene is all about good security practices when handling systems and data. For example, keeping

antivirus and antimalware up-to-date, changing passwords often, remembering to never give out your password, and using a virtual private network (VPN) when outside the office.

>> **Ensure that comprehensive backups of data are completed often.** This includes all data in the cloud, in your on-premises data center, and on devices such as desktops and laptops. Seems like an obvious recommendation, but, sadly, it's often neglected and poorly implemented.

>> **Define a risk-based approach.** Not every piece of data and every system has the same value. For example, determine a rating scale that identifies your high-, medium-, and low-priority solutions. Then implement cybersecurity measures that are appropriate for each category. You'll invest more energy and money in the high priority, and less in the others. This also helps with managing the cybersecurity budget.

>> **Ensure that the security of the IoT devices you deploy have been thoroughly evaluated.** Such devices — sensors, for example — will likely proliferate around your smart city. Additional software and hardware may be required to reach your minimum-security requirements.

REMEMBER

Make sure that your smart city is also a cybersecure city.

Privacy

In October 2017, to much fanfare, Canadian prime minister Justin Trudeau stood on Toronto's 12-acre abandoned waterfront Quayside district with Alphabet's (Google's parent company) executive chairman Eric Schmidt and announced the intention to build a smart neighborhood.

The project would be designed and delivered by Sidewalk Labs, a sister company of Google. It proposed a future-ready urban area with all the latest sustainable smart city technology, including an advanced smart power grid, a host of friendly digital services, and a highly efficient waste management system. The promise of a beautiful, modern, and efficient neighborhood for Torontonians that could work as a model for future cities was compelling. (You can learn more about the project at www.sidewalktoronto.ca.)

In the two years that followed the grand vision for the smart development, the project was beset with criticism and controversy. Given Sidewalk Labs' potential for unconstrained access to the details of the built environment and the people who would live there, the community of Toronto and privacy advocates determined it was a step too far. The outcry was loud and clear, and it put the project in jeopardy, with resignations, firings, civic resistance, and legal action. In an unexpected twist, while concessions were made that did eventually meet many of the demands of the broader Toronto community, the economic fallout from the COVID-19 global pandemic resulted in the project being shelved.

City leaders and vendors from all over the world now view the proposed Sidewalk smart community project and its challenges as a substantial learning opportunity.

The debate around the use of data and personal information (PI) in smart cities and urban innovation is a priority topic in communities around the globe. It's a serious and important issue and requires everyone's attention. At its core is the question of how a city's performance and quality of life can benefit from data-enabled technologies without compromising privacy.

REMEMBER

A basic assumption that everyone should hold is that privacy is a human right.

Privacy is one of those human expectations that is often hard to define precisely, and its interpretation and perspective are frequently dependent on specific cultures. Broadly defined, *privacy* is about having your life be free from unwanted intrusion and unauthorized disclosure of your personal data.

Cities are built and operated on data, much of it personal in nature. Consider the information that cities may store about you: your address, birthdate, medical history, income, criminal background, voter registration, permit requests, driving record, fines, education, and more.

REMEMBER

The one thing that cities have in abundance is data, and much of that data is about people. Collecting, storing, and using this data is required in order to deliver expected services. Even though the city may collect and use the data, the majority of it belongs to the community. It's not owned by the city.

In Chapters 7 and 9, I explore in some depth the role of data in being an engine of urban innovation. As smart cities develop, the need to capture data will accelerate. Consider for a moment a smart streetlight (discussed in detail in Chapter 8), replete with sensors for collecting information. Here are just a few of the uses:

>> **Automated license plate recognition (ALPR):** Parking ticket and public safety uses

>> **Light sensor:** Activated when there's movement for energy-saving and public safety uses

>> **Closed circuit TV (CCTV):** Recording activities in surrounding areas, perhaps for public safety uses

>> **Traffic counter:** Multiple uses that include intersection redesign

>> **Environmental sensor:** Detecting and reporting on air pollution, for example

>> **Gunshot detection:** For gunshot detection (in case you were wondering)

With a smart streetlight, you're just scratching the surface of the new technologies that will eventually be deployed in smart cities. It's clear in this list that each of these collection devices has value. But the privacy implications for any one of them is significant.

TIP

Measures must be deployed to ensure data privacy both to meet those required by law and in consultation with the community. For an example of law, see the later sidebar, "General Data Protection Regulations (GDPR)." Of course, ensuring compliance with the law is essential, but I recommend that any data collection devices that you intend to deploy should gain approval for use from your community.

REMEMBER

One of the most important actions any agency can take to reduce the risk of privacy issues is to de-identify data (also known as *anonymization*). This means that data is stripped either at the point of collection of any personal information (PI) or when data is accessed by those with permission only to view it in aggregate.

The privacy of data in your smart city requires, at minimum:

>> Regulation

>> Governance

>> Tools

>> Enforcement

There's no doubt that privacy in smart cities is concerning to many people and will need to be addressed if smart cities are to succeed. Be open and empathetic to the privacy concerns of your constituents.

GENERAL DATA PROTECTION REGULATION (GDPR)

The General Data Protection Regulation (GDPR) is the toughest privacy and security law in the world. (It's at https://gdpr.eu.) Though it was drafted and passed by the European Union (EU), it imposes obligations on organizations anywhere, as long as they target or collect data related to people in the EU. The regulation was put into effect on May 25, 2018. The GDPR levies harsh fines against those who violate its privacy-and-security standards, with penalties reaching into the tens of millions of euros.

(continued)

(continued)

It's a large and complex law. However, in summary, here are the seven data protection principles; note that a *data subject* is legalese for anyone who uses the Internet:

- **Lawfulness, fairness, and transparency:** Processing must be lawful, fair, and transparent to the data subject.

- **Purpose limitation:** You must process data for the legitimate purposes specified explicitly to the data subject when you collected it.

- **Data minimization:** You should collect and process only as much data as absolutely necessary for the purposes specified.

- **Accuracy:** You must keep personal data accurate and up-to-date.

- **Storage limitation:** You may store personally identifying data only for as long as necessary for the specified purpose.

- **Integrity and confidentiality:** Processing must be done in such a way as to ensure appropriate security, integrity, and confidentiality (by using encryption, for example).

- **Accountability:** The person ultimately responsible for data management in an organization must be able to demonstrate GDPR compliance with all these principles.

Additionally, data subjects (you and I) are entitled to certain data privacy rights:

- The right to be informed

- The right of access

- The right to have data corrected

- The right to erasure

- The right to restrict processing

- The right to move your data from one system to another

- The right to object to how your data is being collected and managed

- Rights in relation to automated decision-making and profiling

Chapter 11

Imagining the City of the Future

Thinking about and imagining the future of cities is a necessary activity for many leaders, including national and city officials, academics, solution providers, and community stakeholders. The greatest challenge here is to ensure that you think big and think creatively. Whether it's the intractable and frustrating challenges of urban transportation or the existential risk of the climate emergency, these types of issues won't be solved by making small, incremental changes. The evidence suggests that some of the innovation necessary to build smart, sustainable, and resilient cities has yet to be invented and will require considerable research and investment.

In this chapter, I share why I believe that there's reason to be optimistic, despite the extent of the urban problems yet to be solved. I help you explore city strategies that are potential game-changers, including those focusing on making communities greener and healthier. Finally, I use transportation — a high-priority smart city topic — as the basis to share how some innovators are thinking about mobility solutions. Flying cars may not be available yet at your local vehicle dealership, and it sure does feel like an audacious bet, but plenty of people are working on making it happen soon (although flying cars are likely to be on-demand service rather than a purchase option). That's the kind of thinking and action that future cities will require.

Recognizing That the Best Is Yet to Come

Cities have come a long way in the past century. They have become centers of productivity and prosperity for billions of people, yet the spectrum of city experiences — from good to bad — ranges greatly, and massive problems continue to exist.

The trajectory, with a few exceptions, is nevertheless trending toward an improved quality of life for many more people. Better governance, greater wealth, new technologies, increased respect for the environment (albeit a slow and inconsistent process), and bold new ideas for delivering services have all contributed toward a brighter future for cities. Yes, I'm an optimist, but I'm also sober and realistic about urban challenges such as poverty, homelessness, environmental degradation, inequality, lack of inclusiveness, crime, depletion of natural resources, and much more.

REMEMBER

Don't allow the tough nature of the challenges to deter you from the important work of focusing on solving them.

The 21st century is the century of cities. Urban centers are well positioned for further improvements and even game-changing transformations. Cities will be smarter, but what the word *smart* means will evolve in the years ahead. In this chapter, I help you explore an expanded definition of what it means to deliver a smarter city. It's about moving beyond technology and exploring the need to have healthier, more sustainable, and more inclusive communities. I also share the growing concept of regenerative cities that are created and operated to exist in harmony with the natural world. I hope that, for you, it becomes increasingly clear that without these loftier goals, cities will never truly be smart.

I also touch on some big ideas whose time may be coming. For example, are we humans destined to have our cities congested by cars, or can that become a problem of the past? I look at a few other ideas to help open your mind and consider the possibilities. It's not an exhaustive review — you can think of it more as a chance to provoke you into thinking big and imagining what might lie ahead for cities.

REMEMBER

If humans are going to have a higher quality of life and solve the challenges of today, they're going to have to do a lot of things differently. This isn't a list of nice-to-have options — this is essential work. The future of the world's cities depends on it. I really do believe that the best is yet to come. I hope you do, too.

Green cities

The patterns of development in which cities have grown differ widely from city to city. Some urban areas have been constrained by geographic boundaries, such as mountains and oceans; some are designed to be compact and dense with growth upward rather than outward; and many more — particularly, beginning in the 20th century — have been defined by significant urban sprawl and the emergence of suburbia. Some were developed off of a master-plan; others, not so much. Growth has often been planned as a response to population changes, not as an anticipatory effort.

What remains now is a wide spectrum of urban effectiveness, from cities that function relatively well (a minority) to those that struggle in various areas every day. In the category of challenges that now face every city on this spectrum is the question of sustainability. Historically, this area hasn't been a priority. Acknowledging a human future that will be almost entirely urban, and recognizing that cities are the biggest contributor toward the climate crisis, means that the subject of sustainability is now a top priority.

What do I mean by sustainability in this context? Here, it's the ability of humans to exist in harmony with nature while ensuring that today's human behaviors don't deprive future generations of what they require for healthy and prosperous lives. Adopting environmentally sustainable actions has become a moral and imperative obligation for city dwellers.

Sustainability can be extended to include social and economic measures as well. Together with the environment, accounting for and reporting on the impact of these three dimensions (social, economic, and environmental) by cities and organizations is known as the *triple-bottom line.*

The history of humans, particularly since the advent of the industrial revolutions, has been a history of our limitless exploitation of nature's resources. Humans have treated the planet as if it were an infinite provider and as an ecosystem immune from harm. Oh, boy — have we been wrong! The urban world has come at the cost of depleted natural resources and a planet in distress. Sustainability recognizes that this situation cannot continue and that every citizen of the planet must take proactive steps to bend the curve to ensure a greener future.

REMEMBER

If humans are going to make a huge difference in working toward carefully managing natural resources and healing the planet, it's going to happen primarily in cities. (Rural areas don't get a pass, but the issues are different there.)

REMEMBER

Creating more sustainable urban environments means creating and retrofitting cities with green efforts. Cities must become green cities.

Cities with green initiatives are a part of what is often seen as a movement. It's been happening for many years, but with projections for the climate crisis growing more dire every year, and with more community awareness of air and water quality, for example, the adoption of sustainability initiatives has kicked up a notch.

The green cities movement is now made up of thousands of cities around the world that are working hard to decrease the human impact on the environment by engaging in these (and thousands of other) creative initiatives, for example:

>> Reducing waste

>> Expanding recycling

>> Increasing housing density

>> Expanding green spaces such as parks

>> Decreasing carbon emissions

>> Supporting urban farming

>> Encouraging ecofriendly local businesses

>> Increasing public transportation

>> Making travel by foot or bicycle more accessible

>> Reducing vehicle congestion via tolls and prohibited areas

>> Supporting green buildings (as described in Chapter 3)

>> Planting more trees (urban forests, for example)

As the third decade of the 21st century begins, cities are focusing more on their green efforts. Communities are demanding it. Many cities now have green teams, including a senior executive to lead efforts such as a chief sustainability officer (CSO), and such teams have often come up with multiyear green strategies with a range of different types of projects.

City leaders are creating regulations, policies, and other governance structures to ensure that sustainability is embedded into city operations. They're also passing laws to enforce environmentally friendly behaviors. For example, the elimination of plastic bags used in retail has been widely adopted by cities around the world.

Many cities have also adopted carbon reduction goals, which are sometimes mandated at a regional or national level as well. Some communities have opted to be more aggressive than even those mandates suggest. These goals can include targets for moving toward more electric vehicles and reductions in the use of coal, gas, and oil for energy production.

URBAN FORESTS INCREASE QUALITY OF LIFE

The idea of planting trees in cities is as old as cities themselves. All cities have some number of trees, but many, such as Tampa, Florida, are covered by 30 percent or more of green canopy. Rio de Janeiro's Tijuca Forest, planted back in 1844 in order to recover areas previously cleared for sugar and coffee, is considered to be the largest urban forest. Green infrastructure is implemented at multiple scales from the neighborhood to the city to the regional level.

Urban forests come in many different forms, including:

- Parks
- Street trees
- Landscaped boulevards
- Gardens
- River and coastal promenades
- Greenways
- Nature preserves
- Industrial sites

Though trees have always had value in beautification efforts, cities have now recognized that urban forests offer many more benefits. Urban forests are dynamic ecosystems that provide important functions for people and animals. Trees improve quality of life by filtering air pollution, reducing smog, supporting wildlife, and sheltering buildings from heat and cold. (Trees can reduce the energy needed to manage building temperature by 10 percent.) Urban forests continue to add beauty, form, and structure to urban design. They reduce noise and, by providing places to recreate, urban forests strengthen social connections, encourage community revitalization, and add economic value to cities. In recent years, a focus on climate change mitigation has made urban forestry a new priority for city leaders and constituents.

Urban forests can moderate local climate, slow wind and stormwater, and filter sunlight. Many cities suffer from the *urban heat island* (UHI) effect — an urban area that is significantly hotter than its surrounding rural areas due to human activities. Fortunately, urban forests can help to mitigate the effects of UHI and reduce the unhealthy consequences that impact cities in summer months.

(continued)

(continued)

Trees lower temperatures not only by shading but by the *urban breeze cycle*. This cycle is created by the variation in temperatures of two nearby areas with different amounts of trees. As a result of different temperature in each of the areas, the atmospheric pressure is altered between them and this creates wind. This breeze helps to cool the air and lower the temperature in the city.

The leaders of countries and cities have recognized the high value of urban forests. For example, India has pledged to keep one-third of its land area under a green canopy. In one effort in August 2019, Indians planted 220 million trees in one day.

There are many urban forestry organizations around the world including a high likelihood of one in your city. As a starting point, you can take a look at the California Urban Forest Council at https://caufc.org/.

ANNUAL EARTH DAY

In 1970, the first Earth Day was held to bring attention to, and drive action designed to protect, the global environment. Twenty million Americans —10 percent of the population at the time — showed up in cities across the country to demand an agenda for a better environment. In the 50 years since that first Earth Day, the movement has grown to become the world's largest recruiter to the environmental movement, now working year-round with more than 75,000 partners in over 190 countries. Areas of focus include climate change, education, restoration, plastics, and pollution. The work is global and is supported from regional offices across the world.

Earth Day is held with a different theme each year on April 22. Recognizing that cities are on the frontline of climate change and therefore have a responsibility to protect the environment, Earth Day places particular emphasis on engaging local government in leading action. City leaders are encouraged to make Earth Day a citywide event that brings together all types of community stakeholders. The day is presented as an opportunity to launch environmental initiatives and to support civic engagement and action. Participation can engage all aspects of society and can result in meaningful change. Efforts focus on promoting action, education, and volunteerism.

Earth Day campaigns are entirely aligned with supporting the efforts and intent of green cities. The focus on the future of the planet through mobilizing the efforts of thousands of cities acts as a catalyst for year-round efforts.

You can learn more about the Earth Day movement at www.earthday.org.

Perhaps everyone should behave as though every day is Earth Day.

The United Nations' Sustainable Development Goals (SDGs), which are 17 bold-but-achievable major target areas for improving the lives of people all over the world, has several areas that are addressed via greener cities. I discuss the SDGs in more detail in Chapter 2.

REMEMBER

A green city is a smart city.

Inclusive cities

The emergence of cities over the past few hundred years has been the leading driver of better living. In developed nations, cities have the best chance to provide superior healthcare, education, job opportunities, and overall quality of life to the most amount of people. In developing nations, cities are quickly bringing millions of people out of poverty and are ultimately providing many of the same benefits as developed cities. With over half of the planet now living in cities, this means around 4 billion more humans have the potential for a better life.

However, as is all too clear, access to opportunities and a higher quality of life isn't evenly distributed. Though the rising tide typically lifts all ships, too many people in cities today aren't experiencing many of the benefits afforded to others.

Cities continue to exclude far too many people from enjoying urban advantages by creating adverse conditions such as

>> Economic inequality

>> Social alienation

>> Poor education

>> Housing unaffordability

>> Insufficient access to services such as public transport

>> Poor support for people with disabilities

>> Lack of access to technology (Internet access, for example)

>> Challenging environmental factors

Cities need to become more inclusive. Urban inequality is a human rights issue.

REMEMBER

An *inclusive* city is one that, in the process of its development and daily operations, acknowledges that a focused and concerted effort must be made to expand opportunities and prosperity to all constituents.

Categories of community members that are disproportionately excluded from equal opportunities include, but are not limited to, people in lower income brackets, elderly populations, single mothers, minority groups, and people with physical and mental disabilities.

TIP

Ensuring that cities are more inclusive means taking proactive steps, but the process starts with your acknowledgment of the issues. Work must be done to research and measure the extent of the challenges facing those who are excluded. With that task complete, you can then develop a strategy to deal with the issues.

Smart city strategies can be one of the right places to design, develop, and embed initiatives to tackle issues of inclusion. You will be well served by aligning your smart city work with the goals of inclusiveness.

Here are a few examples:

>> Developing innovation districts, which provide incentives and low barriers of entry for more people to start businesses. (I discuss innovation districts in Chapter 7.)

>> Using data to improve the understanding of the community, leading to better data-informed decision-making. (I discuss urban data in Chapter 7.)

>> Providing for expanded, low-cost (or free) Internet access so that residents can access information around education, health, and jobs as well as carry out jobs that can be performed online. Those online services must also be accessible to people with disabilities, such as those with impaired eyesight or hearing.

>> Allowing for physical accommodations that enable all people to access all areas and services, such as buildings and transportation.

>> Providing economic education as a public service.

>> Providing low cost (or free) public transportation to support greater access to employment centers.

>> Addressing crime with new technologies, such as motion-activated streetlights.

>> Proving your identity. In some cities, simply proving your identity can be a challenge, which can hinder the ability to have something as fundamental as a bank account. Technology can help with this issue.

Many cities in the world struggle when it comes to fostering inclusiveness. If you strive for a more peaceful and fair future for all people, inclusiveness concerns have to be acted on. In fact, it's number 11 in the SDGs (which are discussed in Chapter 2). The goal states: "Make cities and human settlements inclusive, safe, resilient, and sustainable."

REMEMBER

It's hard to imagine a city being smart if it doesn't act to be inclusive.

Healthy cities

You have much to consider as you strive to increase the quality of life for as many people as possible in cities. Supporting the future of cities isn't a one-dimensional challenge. The positive urban aspirations of humans — the journey to smarter communities — must accommodate the totality of the human experience. Consider that city dwellers are exposed every single day to varying degrees of

>> Noise

>> Air and water pollution

>> Crowding

>> Public safety concerns

>> Lack of open spaces

>> Mental and physical challenges

>> Disease factors

>> Issues of equality and equity

>> Poor sanitation measures

Too many cities, and their rapid urban development, are imposing a burden on the well-being of communities.

REMEMBER

You cannot separate the city lifestyle and environment from humans' state of health. Quality of life is greatly impacted by whether cities are healthy places to live.

In recognition of the role that cities play in the health of communities, another layer of strategy is required — it's a component of the multidimensional nature of smart cities. Thousands of cities around the world are now pursuing healthy city activities.

These cities are working to create and improve their physical and social environments to enable their constituents to live and experience all the fullness of life.

This is the idea behind healthy cities.

Unsurprisingly, the World Health Organization (WHO), based in Geneva, Switzerland, has played an important role in defining and supporting the concept of healthy cities. Taken directly from its website (`www.who.int/healthy_settings/types/cities/en`), WHO maintains that the aim of a healthy city is to

>> Create a health-supportive environment

>> Achieve a good quality of life

>> Accommodate basic sanitation and hygiene needs

>> Supply access to healthcare

All cities have the capacity to become healthy cities. It begins — similarly to smart, sustainable, and inclusive city efforts — with a recognition of the need and then a commitment to act. At their core, healthy cities are about incorporating health considerations into urban development and management.

According to the Alliance for Healthy Cities (`www.alliance-healthycities.com/index.html`), a strategy for a healthy city should include these ingredients:

>> Political commitment

>> Community participation

>> Development of a city health profile

>> Local action plan

>> Periodic monitoring and evaluation

>> Research and analysis

>> Information sharing

>> Linkage to community and human development

>> National and international networking

Aligning with the theme that a smart city is never completed, a healthy city is also defined by the continuation of efforts rather than by a defined final outcome. It isn't measured by achieving a particular health status. Moreover, it makes health a priority and attempts to improve the health of everyone. What's fundamentally required is a commitment to health and a structure and process to address the challenges that may arise.

TIP

Healthy cities place well-being high on the political and social agendas and recognize that success can be achieved only by the collaboration of public, private, voluntary, and community organizations.

Healthy cities are smart cities.

THE TEN KEY COMPONENTS OF CREATING HEALTHY, EQUITABLE COMMUNITIES

The County of San Mateo, a large region in northern California (USA), has created the following list of components for a healthy community (check out www.gethealthysmc.org), based on analyzing local heath data and research and on gathering extensive community feedback:

- **Healthy, stable, and affordable housing:** Socially integrated, stable, and affordable housing, housing near transit, energy-efficient housing, housing for all income and age levels, healthy indoor air quality, and free of pests, mold, tobacco, and similar negative conditions

- **Complete neighborhoods and communities:** People-centered design with housing, businesses, services, schools, jobs, recreation, and public transit in close proximity; easy access to open spaces, affordable healthy foods, and thriving small businesses; high-quality infrastructure and street design with good lighting and landscaping to support public transit and walkability

- **High-quality education system:** Strong programs from K–12 to college-level and trade schools, universal childhood and enrichment programs, affordable after-school programs and childcare, youth career and skill development, and adult education

- **Thriving and inclusive economy:** Diverse local small businesses, economic opportunities with family-supportive wages and benefits, fair labor practices, job skills trainings, and community support of new and current businesses

- **Healthy food access:** Affordable, fresh, local, and culturally appropriate foods at grocery stores and farmers markets, space and resources to grow food in schools and neighborhoods, accessible clean drinking water, and access to school gardens and garden-based education for children

- **Active transportation options:** Affordable and accessible transportation for all ages, such as walking, biking, and public transit; innovative, easy-to-use, fast, well-connected, and efficient transit located near jobs, housing, and retail; and quality bike and pedestrian infrastructure

(continued)

(continued)

- **Safe and diverse public places, parks, and open spaces:** Public places (plazas and miniparks, for example) in convenient locations across neighborhoods for people to be active, relax, socialize, and host community events, as well as age and culturally appropriate programs and amenities such as benches and community gardens

- **Sense of community, where everyone feels that they belong and are safe:** Safe and socially cohesive neighborhoods, opportunities for the community to connect, local leadership that is representative of community demographics, and empowered residents who are involved in decision-making as well as social and civic engagement

- **Clean environment:** Clean air, soil, water, and natural systems, plentiful green space, ample permeable land that can be used to filter water and reduce flooding, healthy trees, and affordable, sustainable energy and drinking water supplies

- **Community-based public services and infrastructure for all people:** Affordable childcare, high-value healthcare, access to mental health and substance use prevention and treatment where the right care is provided at the right time and place, age-in-place opportunities, culturally and linguistically supportive services, and accessible libraries, recreation facilities, and patient-centered medical centers

Regenerative cities

Cities are enormous consumers of resources. Food, water, energy, and vast amounts of goods travel into cities — sometimes, from great distances. These items are processed by the city and its inhabitants and then discarded in the form of waste and pollution to the environment. In addition, activities such as transportation, energy production, and factory work consume fossil fuels and produce greenhouse gases that science now confirms are responsible for climate change.

As many cities grow, their appetites follow, meaning more resources are needed to meet demand. Sure, the urban world is often prosperous, but it doesn't come free. The price to the planet is exceptionally high.

WARNING

If urbanization is going to be viable in the long term, excessive resource consumption must change.

Green and sustainable cities are about ensuring that today's cities can meet their own needs without compromising future generations from being able to meet *their* needs. This important notion is finding a welcome reception in many cities around the world. However, with cities rapidly growing and resource consumption exceeding what the planet can provide, the initial goal of many cities, for a green and sustainable future, may not be sufficient over the long term.

A bolder ambition comes in the form of a relatively new concept called the regenerative city. *Regenerative* urban development is based on the recognition that, in order for the earth to continue to provide in abundance, a city must work to ensure the health of the environment. More specifically, regenerative cities aim to put in place efforts to reduce resource consumption, particularly when the ability to replenish those resources has been exceeded. The goal is to reverse natural resource depletion by actively improving the capacity of natural ecosystems.

Okay, what might a regenerative city look like in practice? At its core, a regenerative city must rethink its traditional role away from *linear consumption* — a process predicated on the notion that a city exists to process resources and produce and dispose of waste. (See Figure 11-1.) Instead, a city must find ways to replicate the circular systems found in nature, where waste becomes input for new growth. As examples, used freshwater can be treated and then reintroduced into other urban water needs, waste can be used to produce energy, and nutrients in waste and sewage can be applied to urban agriculture.

FIGURE 11-1: The tragedy of city prosperity is the volume of waste that's created and the depletion of the planet's natural resources.

Regenerative cities are also about self-sufficiency. Rather than rely on importing all needs, a regenerative city can look for ways to produce its own energy, food, and other goods from within its own boundaries. If everything cannot be produced locally, city leaders and providers should attempt to reach out just a little further beyond their own borders to elicit needs. The idea here is to acquire resource needs as close to its geographic location as possible. Connecting a city to its own land and resources creates a special relationship for communities that elevates the value of resources and can build a higher appreciation of the cost of consumption.

CIRCULAR ECONOMY IN CITIES

The concept of the circular economy is gaining popularity as a regenerative system that aims to reduce consumption, waste, emissions, and energy in an urban context. The journey to a circular economy requires decoupling economic activity from the consumption of finite resources.

Circular cities upend traditional ways of thinking about product use and disposal. They work to extend the lifetime of materials and products, which may mean bringing items back into use instead of creating waste from them. It also includes determining whether something can be rented instead of being purchased. In an ideal scenario, community members discard few items and engage in sharing.

The transition to a circular economy can be achieved by committing to strategies that include

- Recycling

- Creating longer-lasting products

- Improving maintenance

- Focusing on repairs

- Reusing products

- Refurbishing

The concept of the circular economy in cities is gaining particular interest in Europe. Cities such as Amsterdam, Rotterdam, and Glasgow are all in the early stages of implementing circular city strategies.

For information and resources on the circular economy in cities, check out this link:

    www.ellenmacarthurfoundation.org/our-work/activities/circular-economy-
        in-cities

REMEMBER

The aspirations of the regenerative city are ambitious. They require a deep cultural, emotional, and behavioral shift in the relationship communities have with their city. It means seeing a city as a living ecosystem that must be treated with sensitivity and care. A constituent can no longer see the city as an unlimited provider of resources. That person must understand their relationship relative to the sustainability and health of their city and then make completely new choices based on that understanding.

A small number of cities around the world have committed themselves to becoming regenerative cities — Wittenberg, in Germany, for example — while others incorporate aspects of the concept in their sustainability efforts.

ReGen Villages (www.regenvillages.com/) is an organization that partners with landowners and architects to develop resilient neighborhoods that power and feed self-reliant families. Their approach to regenerative resiliency includes the use of artificial intelligence to enable communities to thrive through surplus energy, clean water, and high-yield organic food.

The idea of regenerative cities is bold and will be difficult to pursue for many communities. For those who have the nerve to take the journey, it won't be quick, either.

Though significant challenges must be overcome, the regenerative city may be a big idea whose time has come. It's a smart city strategy.

Envisioning Big Ideas

Solving the big urban challenges heading this way will require bold leadership and ambitious new ideas. More often than not, it won't be sufficient to use 20th century solutions to solve 21st century problems. The scale and complexity of the city issues that touch every aspect of the human experience, from health to the climate to economics and beyond, require humans to think and act differently. This new century necessitates public leaders who are prepared to take greater risks, embrace emerging technologies, build coalitions of advocates who support disruptive innovation, and can communicate a vision with passion and conviction that not everyone will buy into at first.

When reviewing the urban innovation landscape, this approach is clearly beginning to resonate with many leaders. They are taking action. Whether they call it a smart city strategy or use another name (the term matters much less than the positive impact of the work), they're creating and executing on a new vision for their communities. Ideas that would have been previously shunned are now moving forward, sometimes in an experimental manner, and often deploying at scale.

Examples are vast and varied and include embracing digitalization and cloud technologies, implementing sensor networks, radically reducing carbon emissions, improving waste management, moving to renewables, building innovation districts, expanding Internet access (including jumping head-first into 5G, the next phase of high-speed wireless connectivity), and much more. This list only touches the surface of the bold and creative work being pursued across the world. It's one of the reasons I love the smart city space — it's so remarkably broad, and every area is important and impactful.

To appreciate what having bold ideas really means, you only have to take a look at the transportation space. The manner and impact of moving people and goods in urban settings is so significant that it can now be thought of as a defining quality. No matter the city, people have to travel from one place to another.

Transportation is a complex and layered component of every community. Just think about even the basic infrastructure of sidewalks, roads, bridges, tunnels, bicycle lanes, trains, buses, cars, trucks, signal systems, and parking. In many urban areas, a city's real estate can be consumed by up to 60 percent in support of transportation. Yes, it's a Very Big Deal.

To bring focus to what it means to envision big ideas, I've selected examples of thinking boldly and ambitiously about transportation. In the following sections, I discuss just a few ideas that can help you put big ideas into perspective: Hyperloops, flying cars, and cities without cars. Each of these ideas is in varying stages of exploration and development.

Think about the challenges that each of these ideas faces. Also consider how you might go about communicating the benefits of exploring these ideas to a skeptical community.

Okay, let's take a look at each of these big ideas.

Hyperloop

A vital function of a city is to support the movement of people and goods from place to place. That may be between points in a city or a way to travel to and from other areas outside the metropolitan area. You only have to look at any city center to observe the wide variety of mechanisms that have been created for this job.

The size of many cities now means that walking as a means to get where you want to go is somewhat limited. Bicycles and e-bikes fill a large need, particularly in municipalities that have made the investment to support them. Ironically, bikes, which have been around for a long time, are one of the great new city ideas whose time has finally come. They are carbon-free and wonderful for human health.

However, today it's the gas-powered vehicle that has the dominant role in moving people around. The streets and highways are congested with cars, buses, and trucks. No doubt these vehicles have had a good run, but between the carbon they spew into the air, the perpetual traffic jams they create, the increasing costs their owners incur, and the high number of accidents involving them, they present urgent challenges. (I discuss a potentially better, alternative future of autonomous vehicles in Chapter 8.)

All manner of trains service cities, and these are markedly better ways to move people and goods. From light rail to bullet trains, they're often fast, low-carbon emitters that do the job safer and at a lower cost — everything that a car isn't, in other words. But they too have their limitations. Many are not that fast, they are expensive to build, and connections can be limited. The opportunities for new, transformational means of transport are wide open.

One example of a big, new, futuristic idea for transporting people and goods is Hyperloop. *Hyperloop* (which is an idea from Elon Musk, the CEO of Tesla and SpaceX) is a form of belowground and aboveground transportation that can move at a speed of 700 miles (1127 km) per hour in floating pods. These pods, shown in Figure 11-2, travel within low-pressure tubes on air skis to reduce friction. Reducing air friction enables the pods to travel at the speed of airlines but without leaving the ground.

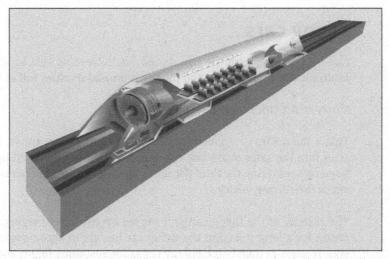

FIGURE 11-2:
Conceptual art for a Hyperloop pod.

The power for the system can be derived from solar panels along the tube route. When all costs are considered, Hyperloop is supposed to be much cheaper to build and operate than traditional rail. It should also be much faster to build than a new train network. An intricate system of connections and frequent departures can enable people to travel to more locations without having to transfer to another pod.

Hyperloop is still in the experimental and early development phases. The idea has been adopted by a handful of organizations, each with its own, particular flavor of system. Projects are in various stages in the US, India, Saudi Arabia, Europe, and the UAE.

If successful (and it's still a big *if*), Hyperloop networks might make travel between major cities such as Melbourne and Sydney in Australia fast, convenient, and greener. It would offer a compelling alternative to air travel. Hyperloop might enable people to live farther away from work (perhaps in lower-cost areas), further increase trade, and lower the cost of travel.

REMEMBER

People traveling at 700 mph in pods within tubes may sound like science fiction, but it's this kind of bold, visionary thinking that will help build a better, smarter tomorrow.

To learn more, check out this video showing an implementation being developed from Virgin, called Hyperloop One:

```
https://hyperloop-one.com
```

Flying cars

And here we are, with the real reason you're reading this book. A multitude of futuristic cartoons, novels, and movies promised us cities full of flying cars.

Surely smart cities must have cars that fly?

That's the dream — convenient, fast, and uncongested travel. But alas, as you stare into the skies above any city today, there are no cars to be seen. How can humans be entering the third decade of the 21st century and not be hopping in and out of their flying vehicles?

The absence of the flying car isn't caused by any lack of trying — it has been a dream for a long time. But the flying car has yet to become widely available for such reasons as high costs, energy needs for sustained flight, and the availability of necessary technology and materials. Sure, there have been commercial flying cars, but only a limited number of buyers. Until recently, the flying car has been a niche market.

REMEMBER

But the times are changing. Among the reasons are the availability of new technologies and materials, significant risk-taking investments, improved batteries, smarter software, and the potential for a larger market, given the significant increase in affluent urbanites in many major cities.

It looks a bit like a race now to see who can gain early entry into the urban flying car market. A large number of carmakers, airplane manufacturers, and a growing list of start-ups are rushing to produce the first viable, consumer-focused flying cars and air taxis. Among the known players now making rapid progress are Boeing, Porsche, Uber, Airbus, and Ehang.

There's a wide range of design concepts, with many of them adopting the technology and inspiration of drones but at a scale to carry passengers. The success of drones in many domains has contributed greatly toward new innovation in the air transport field. (I discuss drone use in the urban space in Chapter 8.)

A popular vision for flying car design is vertical take-off and landing, or VTOL. As its name suggests, this vehicle would depart its destination by rising upward and then land at the destination by descending vertically. This system avoids the need for any type of runway — an impractical requirement in a dense urban environment. To this end, urban planners imagine flying cars departing and landing on special elevated surfaces, perhaps at the top of buildings. Other designs imagine cars driving normally on roads and then using VTOL to fly as desired.

Though the promise of flying cars and air taxis is tantalizingly close — the projection is widespread adoption beginning in the late 2020s — major challenges still exist, including

>> **Batteries:** Most people believe that flying cars will be electric, to enable better movement management, eliminate carbon emissions, simplify design, and provide reliability. The power requirements to get lift and maintain flight — particularly with the weight of humans — is significantly more than that of a ground-based vehicle. Though the battery technology exists to power a flying car for minutes, to be viable it will need to power longer rides, including the capacity for backup in case of a main battery failure.

>> **Legislation:** Every country will need to develop and pass laws and regulations for this new form of transport. New form factors will require completely new certifications. Everyone knows that governments don't move quickly — particularly in complex areas such as this one. The industry is working hard already to get the ball rolling.

>> **Acceptance and use:** It isn't clear yet whether the public is ready for flying cars. Will people be comfortable riding around in autonomous passenger drones? Can safety expectations be met for both passengers and those on the ground? Is the market big enough to make the product viable? City residents may not tolerate the noise of these vehicles unless new technology can find a way to muffle the cars' sounds.

>> **Cost:** You can secure a helicopter ride within an urban area, but it's cost restrictive. This concept is largely limited to executives from wealthy enterprises that can afford it. The cost of flying cars — whether to rent, buy, or pay per ride — will need to be at a level that enables a viable market. In addition, the cost of building and maintaining the vehicles will need to be similarly priced right. Mass-producing lightweight, aircraft-class cars has never been done. For those vying to get into this market, cost is a paramount concern.

We humans will soon know whether flying cars take to the skies of our cities. If they do, they will usher in a radical phase of urban change.

Take a look at Uber's vision for air taxis:

```
www.uber.com/us/en/elevate/uberair
```

Cities without cars

Without a doubt, the arrival of the automobile and other gas-powered vehicles has had major effects on cities — both good and bad. For all their remarkable conveniences, efficiencies, and economic clout, cars have levied a hefty price on urban centers and all who live there.

Upon the introduction and widespread adoption of the car, communities that existed before its invention have had to create massive accommodations for it and all its requirements, such as widening streets (which often led to the destruction of historical artifacts), installing land-consuming parking spaces, and building networks of gas stations. The car transformed these towns in ways that have had significant detrimental effects, creating painful congestion, taking space away from other needs, causing dangerous conditions for pedestrians, and polluting the air. Visit Venice, Italy (when it's not too crowded with wandering tourists), and you can experience the brief wonder and joy of a metropolis with no motorized vehicles on the streets.

Later on, when cities were built after the arrival of the car, they were purposely designed to be automobile-friendly — in fact, at the cost of people-friendliness. Contemporary city centers may manage large volumes of traffic, but they've struggled to create a sense of place or community. On average, between 50 and 60 percent of city center real estate is dedicated to vehicles. For all the many remarkable benefits that cars have brought to cities, in the long run they've created enormous challenges.

Is there the possibility of an alternative future — one where cars can be removed from the city center, resulting in an enhanced quality of life, reduced pollution, and the creation of a new model for human-centered urban living?

Reducing and eliminating cars from city centers is happening in communities across the world. Sometimes, the cars are simply banned. At other times, high tolls — a congestion charge — are implemented to deter traffic. As one Norwegian mayor put it, "The objective is to give the streets back to the people."

City centers are becoming places where people meet, diners eat at outdoor restaurants, kids play safely, art is exhibited, and performances are played. Benches are added, trees and plants create a rich tapestry, pollution and crime levels drop, and bicycles safely traverse town squares. Centers now mimic the characteristics of small parks and all their attendant social and environmental benefits.

Eliminating the huge areas set aside for cars is also enabling denser urban housing to be built. This is much needed in centers that have a limited housing supply and where subsequently costs have skyrocketed.

REMEMBER

Pedestrian and bicycle-only areas enable *placemaking* — the deliberate creation of public spaces that support the health, happiness, and well-being of communities.

Madrid (Spain), Oslo (Norway), Hamburg (Germany), Ghent (Belgium), Chengdu (China), and Mexico City (Mexico) are among the top cities already banning cars in their city centers. (See Figure 11-3.) Many more have plans to do so in the works. Some cities that want to experiment and gradually implement such bans — such as Paris, France — specify a weekday when cars aren't allowed on specific roads.

Carless city centers won't work for every city, and there are trade-offs and costs. In addition to some expected community opposition, removing cars can mean a huge hit to the economy — and it certainly limits the options for large numbers of people getting where they need to go. Accommodations and alternatives have to be provided such as expanded public transportation. Modifications are required in order to shift from road to park, for example. Bridges and bike paths may need to be built.

Other factors come into play here. In most developed nations, car ownership is declining. (This is, sadly, not the case in developing nations, where car ownership is generally growing as wealth increases.) The developed world has gone beyond what is known as *peak car* — the high point of car ownership — and ever since, the number of cars being sold has been declining. Generationally, millennials are also turning away from buying cars. The use of on-demand vehicles, such as Uber,

Grab, and DiDi, is also changing car use dynamics. For example, parking spaces are less important when you're dropped off at your location. It's also anticipated that on-demand autonomous vehicles (AVs) will be potentially better at optimizing traffic flow and congestion on reduced road networks. The debate is still wide open on the potential true impact of AVs.

FIGURE 11-3:
Pedestrian areas are quieter and safer, have less pollution, and support placemaking.

TIP

Given some clear advantages, many cities are starting to look at whether banning cars in certain areas makes sense — you need to determine whether you have the community support for it and the vision to make it happen, and whether it's the *smart* thing for the city to do.

Chapter **12**

Engaging in Your City's Future

I t's a fact now that most people's destiny lies in cities. This includes your children and your grandchildren and their children too. With this in mind, this chapter looks at ways that you can play a part in shaping the future of your community. Assuming that a city's residents have interest and motivation, they now have more ways than ever to have a voice and to contribute to the function and success of their community. In this chapter, I'm especially interested in sharing ways to become an urban innovator, including discussing the increasing popularity of the role of the citizen scientist.

The work of cities and the role of civic engagement is to improve conditions for the community — including elevating the quality of life and the standard of living for as many people as possible. But achieving each of these goals requires different approaches. In this chapter, the distinction between them is explained, which may help you to better focus your efforts, depending on the desired outcomes. The chapter concludes with advice on specific actions you can take tomorrow to help your city.

Embracing an Urban Future

Parag Khanna, in his book *Connectography: Mapping the Future of Global Civilization*, wrote that "cities are mankind's most enduring and stable mode of social organization, outlasting all empires and nations over which they have presided." Impressive, right?

Cities have been called humanity's greatest invention. They are highly productive and interdependent entities that strive and often succeed in providing for every human need (but not necessarily accessible to every human yet). Today, cities generate 80 percent of gross domestic product (GDP); their continued success is easily reflected in their rapid population and geographic growth in almost every region of the world (Figure 12-1 illustrates the rapid population growth of cities while rural areas begin to decline). Across the planet, humans have built around 75,000 cities, and each week they grow, by 3 million new migrants from rural settings. Cities consume 3 percent of Earth's land surface and over half of all humans now convene in these urban areas. City land use is projected to grow to almost 10 percent by 2030. This represents a vast shift in a short amount of time. It's the equivalent of 20,000 football fields being paved over every day.

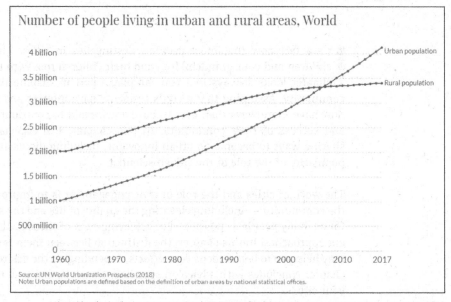

FIGURE 12-1: The data is clear: Our future belongs to cities.

Despite the odds, many cities are doing a commendable job when it comes to delivering human needs such as food, medicine, education, water, sanitation, jobs, entertainment, and other services to several billion people. However, humans are finally acknowledging the many, often hidden, costs for this success — cities providing the illusion of abundance while overconsuming a rapidly depleting natural world, for example.

WARNING

Cities are energy intensive, consuming 80 percent of the global supply — and they have a growing appetite. Science now firmly provides evidence that the resource consumption and operating behaviors of cities are large contributors to the planetary climate crisis. Cities now produce 67 percent of greenhouse gas emissions, which will increase to 74 percent by 2030. The interdependence of urbanization means that no city can solve the climate crisis alone and that, without solutions, no city will escape its consequences.

Cities often provide well for the majority of their residents, but far too many people are still disenfranchised from the promise of urbanization. People continue to struggle with persistent challenges that include issues of poverty, hunger, uneven economic opportunity, homelessness, crime, healthcare access, and societal inclusivity. Even today, in the first decades of the 21st century, one in three city dwellers lives in a slum, which means they lack access to one or more service: clean water, adequate sanitation, sufficient living space, or durability of housing.

Fortunately, the data suggests continuously marked improvement. For those suffering, however, such data is irrelevant. The United Nation Sustainability Development Goals (SDGs), which I discuss in Chapter 2, makes reducing and eliminating many of these issues a priority by keeping national and city leaders focused and accountable.

REMEMBER

Creatively solving persistent urban challenges and building on the successes of cities is what being smart is all about. Smart cities have a bias for bold solutions. Another way to consider what becoming a smart city means is to consider it a form of optimism. If city leaders commit to being more innovative, to experimenting with new ways of overcoming issues, and to investing in riskier and more ambitious ideas, they're demonstrating that they believe in a better tomorrow. They believe that current challenges can be solved and that the future will be better than today.

The future is urban. It's been a bumpy ride getting there, but now people have to deal with the certainty that, for most humans, the quality of cities equates to quality of life. Better cities will make for a better life for more people. We must never ignore our rural brothers and sisters, and appropriate focus must remain there; however, that's a subject for another book. To improve the quality of life for the highest number of people, we must recognize and embrace positive strategies for our urban future.

It might seem that embracing our urban future is primarily the job of governments, nongovernmental organizations (NGOs), and the private sector. There's no doubt they will all play leading roles. However, there's now, more than ever, an entry point and a role for everyone who would choose to engage with their communities. Our urban future is reliant on creative partnerships between disparate stakeholders. In this chapter, I explore a few ways that you and your community can participate in making your city smarter.

REMEMBER

The future must not be about excluding anyone from helping to define it. Moreover, it must be about being as inclusive as possible.

An increase in civic engagement

Civic engagement is a broad term that describes the way in which community members can get involved in the community and political activities of their city. It's a form of a public-private partnership (PPP).

Civic engagement enables social connections, interactions, participation, and involvement that are designed to support some form of targeted outcome that benefits an individual, an organization, or the city — or perhaps all three.

You can engage with your community and support change in several traditional ways, such as serving on a committee that's open to the public. Central to democratic methods is the act of voting. A vote is a voice in the decision-making process. By my own observations, some local issues are decided when the vote majority is in the low double digits. It's a reminder that every vote counts.

Some popular methods are used for gleaning insight and recommendations from community members that can be presented to government leaders to help inform them of issues. Depending on the community, these can range from a permanent entity, such as an architectural review board (ARB) that replaces members every few years, to a temporary one, such as a committee designed to support consequential projects until they're completed.

Another engagement process involves showing up at an official public meeting to speak in favor of or against an issue. Letters, phone calls, emails, and Facebook posts are all important engagement options, but few statements are clearer than contributing your time and energy to be in-person at a debate when you could be doing a million other things with your time.

Finally, a liberal interpretation of traditional civic engagement can also include a wide variety of volunteer activities that range from coaching a sports team to helping clean up a beach or park.

REMEMBER

Having a voice, providing your opinion, making suggestions, and engaging in other forms of discussion-based civic engagement are enormously important. These actions provide a modicum of resident empowerment. However, community members now have the potential for many more options, including the ability to participate in positive, action-oriented activities.

Frustrated no more, people have greater opportunities to lead and participate in doing the work of positive change. It has moved beyond dialogue and Saturday morning volunteerism. In the age of smart cities, civic engagement is being redefined.

Equipped with online tools and software, residents can engage and deliver solutions in completely new ways. Similarly, city government can elicit engagement using these tools as well. Suppose that a decision needs to be made on the placement of a public art piece. The city has decided to solicit plenty of input via its community engagement channels, both traditional and contemporary. When it adopts technology solutions, the opportunity for a larger volume of input and a more diverse set of views grows considerably. Community members gain the convenience of participating in the decision via the channel of their choice. If they want to show up at public meetings on a Wednesday night, they have that option. But if they prefer to express their views on a website or an app, they now have this convenience too.

WARNING

Just because more options exist doesn't mean that you can take greater civic engagement for granted. When a new tool is introduced, there's always an uptick in participation, but if you really want a sizable increase in input, you need to make the effort to market the new channels and to make the case for participation. Let me be honest: Civic engagement isn't necessarily high on the agenda for a large proportion of people in cities. For many, life is already complicated enough and full of other priorities.

The difficult challenges facing cities requires a lot of voices at the table. These voices are needed to not only communicate different perspectives on an issue and ensure inclusivity of opinion but also bring diverse, fresh, and innovative ideas forward for consideration. New tools are extending participation from essential dialogue to action-oriented efforts. Smart city strategies demand civic engagement. Fortunately, technology is supporting more ways to do just that.

The next two sections take a look at two roles that are changing the game when it comes to community engagement.

Urban innovators

In the 21st century, the best new ideas that get implemented are no longer the sole domain of large private corporations with deep pockets and political power (though they're still largely the dominant players). Equipped with as little as a laptop and an Internet connection, game-changing ideas can emerge from just about anywhere and by anyone — and can often then be implemented quickly at scale. It's a disruptive and powerful phenomenon, and though we've been at it for a few years, it's far too soon to know the long-term implications. It has helped to increase the democratization of the marketplace, enabling more entrants and driving greater velocity in the spread of innovation.

Now, a new generation of innovators is embracing this power to build solutions that are directed at improving the urban world. Dare I say it? It's to help support smarter cities. They're *urban innovators*. You could say they're the entrepreneurs of the urban world.

These innovators are often your neighbors and friends, but they can also be businesspeople who see an opportunity to build a government technology business. It's a relatively new category of business, known as *govtech* or *urbantech*.

An individual may use their technology talents in a range of ways through civic engagement. For example, someone might write an application that supports a committee, or they might gather and analyze data to support decision-making. Individuals and teams can participate in hackathons and challenges that try to solve specific community issues. (I discuss hackathons and challenges in detail in Chapter 7.) The fact that urban innovators face no insurmountable barriers when it comes to entering the marketplace of ideas is highly empowering. These new tools are enabling a more action-oriented approach to civic engagement.

REMEMBER

In a world driven by software, those with programming skills offer powerful capabilities to those outside of government as well as those within.

Urban innovators also build businesses that solve community problems and help make cities better. They see an opportunity and, rather than wait for others to solve the problem and monetize the solution, they pursue it themselves. Sometimes they approach the market like any other business; at other times, they're launched out of hackathons and other civic challenges. (Check out the work of NewCities and its use of urban innovation challenges as an example of such an approach at https://newcities.org.) In just the past few years, a growing ecosystem of govtech businesses has emerged as a way of solving problems across the spectrum of urban challenges. With low entry barriers and pressing needs, the urban innovator looks like a promising addition to the partnerships required to build smarter communities.

That said, it's not a slam-dunk. Govtech is still maturing, and selling into government remains complicated. Of course, the buyer may be the community, and that also has its challenges. But the signs are good. Urban innovators are having success all over the world, with new products being introduced regularly and data to support increasing revenue opportunities in the years ahead. After all, cities have lots of problems to solve.

Citizen scientists

City governments can be successful only by collaborating with other entities. The days of an agency taking on everything itself are over. (I'm not sure they were ever really successful on their own.) Because city challenges these days are generally too complex to solve without outside help — budgets are stretched and insufficient talent exists for diverse tasks — eliciting assistance from diverse sources is a necessary and encouraged approach. Some cities are better at this than others. Civic engagement should take many forms. It's great for both the government and the resident. It turns out that civic-minded community members often want to help. They just need to be asked.

REMEMBER

Smart and engaged citizens help to make smart cities.

Over the past few years, a new role and source of value has emerged from within communities: the citizen scientist, an amateur scientist who conducts scientific research under the direction of a professional. The term has been popular for a long time when referring to a nonprofessional person who does work for a scientific institution or another type of private entity, but more recently the person in this role has been helping cities with essential research activities as well as the creation and sharing of knowledge. The technological focus of smart cities, in particular, has elevated the concept. The term *civic scientist* is sometimes used for the specific research done to support urban and public policy.

The citizen scientist can perform a diverse range of tasks. A basic activity may be to collect data in the community — counting how many people are riding a bicycle on a certain street during specific times, for example. In this way, the person filling this role is acting like a human sensor. To acquire sufficient sample sizes, multiple citizen scientists collecting data become a form of crowdsourcing. In a more developed role, the person can help interpret data by using a variety of analytical tools. Finally, depending on skill and experience levels, the citizen scientist can be engaged in the definition of the problem, the collection of data, the data analysis, and any subsequent recommendations. The level of participation depends on the individual's skills and the needs of the project.

REMEMBER

Citizen science is a learning opportunity, elevating an appreciation for science at a community level. For all age groups, engagement in this type of work forces the person to delve more deeply into a topic and to truly appreciate it in an enlightened way. It's easy to criticize others at a distance for not solving a problem, but it's a little more sobering when you get up close to an issue and recognize the nature of the challenge.

Here are a few examples of citizen science projects:

» Collecting water quality data to improve the health of water bodies

» Observing wildfire smoke and its health effects to increase understanding about smoke exposures and how they impact communities

» Identifying specific physical elements across a city landscape for input into a geographic information system (GIS), as explained in Chapter 9

» Recording city noise at various locations and times in order to inform policy development on noise pollution

» Collecting air quality samples using cyclists wearing portable air sensors, where data is mapped and available in real-time for anyone to observe

For more on the work of citizen scientists, check out the Citizen Science Association website at www.citizenscience.org.

Continuous improvement in urban quality of life

During the first industrial revolution, which witnessed the beginning of a multi-century mass migration of people from rural areas to urban areas, cities were pretty miserable places. Sure, they offered opportunity, education, and more social services, but city life came with some notable trade-offs. Disease was common, crime was epidemic, air and water quality were poor, housing was cramped, and sanitation was primitive. (I'd argue that dumping human sewage on the street was never a good idea.)

Despite these often horrendous conditions, cities continued their popularity, and populations skyrocketed. Even with poor conditions, many of the new city immigrants concluded that cities offered a better quality of life over the harsh reality of rural poverty. Over time, particularly in the more developed nations, cities gradually evolved in a positive direction. Rather than deteriorate further as populations and demands increased, cities improved. These dense urban areas generated wealth by way of high levels of commercial and industrial activity, and this provided the funds for improved infrastructure and services. Better governance, positive economic trends, increasing community expectations, new innovation, and a healthy dose of social activism all contributed to a continuous uptick in the quality of life and standard of living.

Of course, for many cities, progress hasn't been a straight line. The significant consequences of war, economic downturns, natural disasters, and social unrest are among the many setbacks that have disrupted steady upward progress. That said, many of the leading cities of the world have thrived in the long run despite these events. Take a look at New York, London, Berlin, Paris, Tokyo, Manila, St. Petersburg, Hiroshima, and similar cities that all suffered severely during bad times. What you see today, on balance, are success stories. Each one certainly has its own major challenges, but all are testaments to the endurance of urban inventions.

REMEMBER

Cities have succeeded despite some remarkable setbacks, and they continue to improve to this day. The smart city movement reflects human optimism about the future and doubles down on the bet that cities will continue to improve. The most difficult urban challenges, such as the impact of a changing climate and eliminating poverty, may still lie ahead of us, but we've demonstrated the human capacity to overcome seemingly intractable challenges in the past.

All things being equal, you should expect increasing quality of life and standards of living for even more people in the urban future — assuming that city leaders and community members make a number of good choices and attract a little bit of luck.

The difference between quality of life and standard of living

I refer to the term *quality of life* often in this book. After all, the intent of building smarter cities is to increase the quality of life for the highest number of people. But another quantitative term is often used to describe the status of a community: *standard of living*. You might assume that these two terms mean relatively the same thing, but in fact they don't. As you look out into an urban future and think about your smart city goals and objectives and how they are measured and described, I believe it's important to understand the difference in these terms.

Standard of living

The *standard of living* is a quantitative way of comparing the conditions of people in two or more different geographic areas. It includes diverse metrics such as wealth and income (the primary measure), availability of services and goods, employment opportunities, incidence of disease, life expectancy, and number of vacation days. It can be used, say, to compare Melbourne and Sydney or Athens and Tel Aviv. In your city, it can be used to even compare neighborhoods.

Identifying the right metrics, and tracking them over time, can help you understand your communities' challenges and also measure the progress of work aimed at standard-of-living improvements and better equity.

Though the standard of living is often measured in terms of income, studies have shown that greater wealth doesn't equate to greater happiness. Quality of life is a better measure of happiness.

You can measure and track global standards of living in many ways. Governments, NGOs, academia, and others all offer up a variety of approaches. The United Nations created the Human Development Index (HDI) to compare, measure, and rank the social and economic development of all countries. The index has these four main areas of interest:

>> Average years of schooling

>> Expected years a student will attend schooling

>> Life expectancy at birth

>> Gross national income per capita

The emphasis is on individuals and measures the opportunities they have for achieving satisfying work and fulfilling lives. The HDI is used to supplement other development measurements, such as the popular gross domestic product (GDP). The index can also be used to evaluate the policy choices of countries.

Quality of life

Quality of life (QoL), unlike the standard of living, is somewhat more subjective. A definition that everyone agrees with, and a set of metrics for that definition, continue to be elusive. However, the ultimate goal of QoL is to measure happiness. It can be influenced by personal lifestyle choices and personal preferences, and it has a focus on emotional, physical, material, and social well-being. The degree to which these types of needs are met support some level of life satisfaction.

Metrics considered in QoL include the environment in which a person lives, their physical and mental health, available leisure time, education, and social belonging. But given the subjective nature of QoL, many interpretations exist. For example, the United Nations' Universal Declaration of Human Rights, adopted in 1948, provides this list of factors that can be considered in evaluating QoL:

>> Equal protection under the law

>> Freedom from discrimination

- » Freedom of movement

- » The right to be treated equally without regard to gender, race, language, religion, political beliefs, nationality, socioeconomic status, and more

- » The right to privacy

- » Freedom of thought

- » Free choice of employment

- » The right to rest and to leisure

- » The right to an education

- » The right to human dignity

There's a tight connection between well-delivered urban services and a community's health, sense of well-being, and feeling of comfort. The better these factors are, the more the community is said to be livable.

REMEMBER

Smart cities are synonymous with the goals of livable cities. Livability has a focus on areas such as sustainability, cleanliness, air and water quality, and the reduction of noise pollution.

One approach to reporting on global QoL is the annual World Happiness Report. This report, developed by a group of independent experts, ranks 156 countries by their happiness level. (See Figure 12-2.) The report reflects a global interest in using happiness as an indicator of the quality of the human experience. It enables governments, communities, and other types of organizations to use the data to inform public policy. It uses data such as GDP per capita, life expectancy, having someone to count on, freedom to make life choices, freedom from corruption, and generosity levels to develop the score and ranking.

Finally, a 2018 report studying 50 cities, by global consulting firm McKinsey, found that smart city initiatives can improve QoL indicators by 10 to 30 percent. Highlights of the report suggest that smart technologies can improve conditions in these areas:

- » **Public safety:** Reduce urban fatalities by 8 to 10 percent.

- » **Transportation:** Cut commuting times by 15 to 20 percent.

- » **Health:** Reduce the disease burden (healthy life lost due to disability or death, in other words) by 8 to 15 percent.

- » **Environment:** Reduce harmful emissions by 10 to 15 percent and the negative effects from air pollution by 8 to 15 percent.

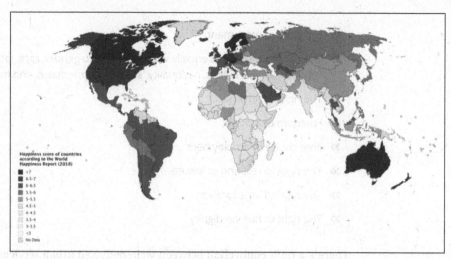

FIGURE 12-2:
Map showing happiness of countries by their score from the 2018 World Happiness Report.

The full report, *Smart Cities – Digital Solutions for a More Livable Future*, can be found here: www.mckinsey.com/~/media/.

TIP

Surprisingly, the smart city initiatives that were studied had only a modest impact on jobs and GDP. The report suggested that smart city strategies should not be pursued solely for the purpose of economic development.

Making a Better Tomorrow

Humans are an optimistic bunch. Despite so many setbacks and challenges in our short history, most people believe that tomorrow will be better than today. In the past 200 years alone, humans together have completely reinvented the human experience. Though life was once short and miserable, today billions of people have a chance to live a long, fulfilling life.

Despite approaching 8 billion people, Planet Earth has more abundance, more opportunity, and much less poverty than ever before. In just the past 70 years, extreme poverty — for those living on less than $2 per day — has dropped from almost 50 percent to less than 10 percent.

Major challenges, including hunger, child labor, cost of food, violent crime and homicides, as well as child mortality, are all way down and falling further. At the same time, areas such as leisure time, life expectancy, democracies, literacy, and access to the Internet are all increasing.

Wars between states — by far the most destructive of all conflicts — are all but obsolete. Without a doubt, massive challenges exist, but on many accounts, now may be the best time to be alive for the highest number of people. Social and traditional media may provide a different narrative, but the macro data and trendlines can be trusted. Today is better than yesterday, and tomorrow will most likely be better than today.

The best days ahead will be in the cities. In the decades ahead, that's where humanity will be hanging out. This is our human destiny. When it comes to that destiny, some communities are more prepared than others. Fortunately, a global movement is underway: a smarter city movement. Many people have a passion to make the cities of tomorrow better places to live, work, and play. All types of people through the strata of society, from elected officials to schoolchildren, are finding ways to make their communities smarter, more sustainable, and more resilient. They have the motivation, energy, vision, and the tools to be agents of change. Existing and emerging technologies are lowering barriers and opening up opportunities for participation and action.

The early results are in. Done right, leading cities are demonstrating what is possible. From Dubai to Dublin, from Barcelona to Berlin, and from Singapore to Shanghai, smart approaches are yielding success in improved energy use, transportation options, waste management, economic opportunity, health management, cleaner air and water, sustainability, Internet connectivity, building management, digital city services, and more. These cities are engaged in the art of the possible. Their work is building confidence in the 75,000 or so other global cities that will need to have their own plans to prepare for a better tomorrow.

REMEMBER

The smart city movement isn't some type of temporary trend that will be forgotten in a few years. It's the future for almost every person on the planet. It might be called something else down the road, but the intent will remain the same. With this destiny, that of future generations, and the planet aligned to the fate of cities, everyone has a responsibility to drive positive change.

I actually have good news: It's never been easier to get engaged with your community and make a difference. Making a better tomorrow can't be about pointing to someone else and assuming that it's their job. Today and tomorrow, making cities and their communities better requires me, you, and most of our colleagues, friends, and family to be involved. It's all hands on deck.

If you're a city leader or just a concerned resident, now is the time to build a better tomorrow. Anyone can be part of the smart city movement.

It's your community — get involved

In her book *The Death and Life of Great American Cities*, the urban theorist Jane Jacobs wrote, "Cities have the capability of providing something for everybody, only because, and only when, they are created by everybody."

A local government's investment in technology is essential to driving the smart city agenda, but there is significant momentum and value generated by empowered and engaged community members in co-creating their own city.

If you are a motivated community member and are prepared to volunteer your time, there's never been a better time to be part of helping to create the future of your city. The diversity of needs means that all types of talent and input have value. It's easy to think that you need to be a technologist to be involved in smart city work, but that's really just one entry point. Cities need all types of volunteer talent. Beyond technology roles, some of the opportunities might include these:

>> Writer

>> Analyst

>> Legal expert

>> Communicator

>> Advocate

>> Educator

>> Engineer

>> Citizen scientists

>> Subject matter expert

>> Inventor

>> Accountant

Local agencies often advertise their needs on the official city website, including jobs, contract work, proposal solicitations, and volunteer opportunities. If information you're looking for isn't listed there, make an appointment with a senior city official to discuss opportunities. Unlike other government agencies — at the regional and federal level, for example — it can be a lot easier to meet with decision-makers of a city. Local government is closest to the resident, given the immediacy of how decisions made at city hall impact people. This intimacy often provides the context for easier access to people in positions of power. You will likely be welcomed. Hearing directly from community members is essential to running a city and is typically embraced by city leaders. Importantly, most leaders will be delighted by your interest in helping.

Don't look at your city government as some unapproachable and closed entity. After all, the people who work there are made up of community members just like you. Those who do reach out to their government leaders are often surprised by how open they are to listen to your ideas and even find a way for you to help.

Of course, as with everything else, there are exceptions. You might find it hard to find the right person to talk to, or perhaps you won't get a response. It happens. But don't be disheartened. Try someone else. You'll eventually find someone in local government who will help you.

Now, it's possible that, for any number of reasons, your local government has no role for you or no way to integrate your skills into the smart city strategy. Frankly, you might get disappointed and not get any response from city hall.

What then? I recommend the following:

>> **Look for allies.** See whether a non-city entity that is providing a service might be an entry point for you. For example, an organization involved in sustainability efforts might be privately funded and need volunteers. Cities always have a lot of volunteer organizations that provide some valuable civic service. Another option is to see who in the private sector is providing services to city hall and the community. Approach a relevant provider and see what role you can play. I know they'll love to hear from you.

>> **Start something yourself.** This is probably the hardest route, but it might also be the most impactful. You can do a variety of things ranging from starting your own business in the smart city space to hosting an educational meet-up or leading a volunteer effort. What will make sense is to align your interests — both skills and area-wise — with the most relevant part of city operations. For example, if you're interested in transportation issues, find out what the big pain points are and focus on them.

The bottom line is that you can become involved in your community in plenty of ways, from the simple to the complex. You choose. Your city is waiting.

Five things you can do tomorrow

Here are five ideas for things you can do to help your city become smarter, beginning tomorrow:

>> **Find out who's leading the smart city strategy at your city and make an appointment to meet with them.** Discuss your interest and ask how you can help. Of course, this advice assumes that your city has a smart city

strategy. If it doesn't, meet with the mayor, head of technology, planning director, the city manager, or similar and discuss your ideas with them. Again, ask how you can help.

>> **Determine which committees are available and whether they have any openings for new members.** Almost every city has a city-appointed group of residents who meet, confer, and advise city officials on various topics. Perhaps you'll uncover committees on transportation, Internet access, planning, smart city efforts, or technology.

>> **Find out whether your community hosts urban-related hackathons, as discussed in Chapter 7.** If it does, sign up and attend. No matter what your skills are, the organizers will find a role for you. You'll have fun, network with new people, and maybe even add good value to the event. You should also consider attending smart city events locally or out-of-town. (Travel may not be necessary, as many events are now being held online. Many are free to attend.) Perform an online search and sign up for one or more.

>> **Track down and sign up for volunteer opportunities.** There's always a lot to do in a city. Volunteer activities can range from clean-up efforts — say, on a beach, in a river, or in a park — to citizen science research work. You may be able to help with climate-related activities or a beautification project. Volunteering for your city is often highly rewarding work.

>> **Determine whether you have opportunities to be an educator.** It's a sure bet that you have knowledge that others would find useful. You may be able to give a talk at a city office, library, or school. Smart cities need smart, engaged people. Educators are essential to the work. In fact, multiple studies have suggested that investing in human capital — teaching — can be as great as, or even more important than, technology in creating economically vibrant cities.

Of course, you have so many other ways to make a difference in your community. Check out your city's official website. Do an Internet search. In the 21st century, there have never been more ways for you to have a voice and to be an agent of change in your community. More than ever, the pursuit of smarter communities will require greater civic participation and engagement. Opportunities abound.

Step up and perhaps *you* will change the world.

5
The Part of Tens

IN THIS PART . . .

Understand potential risks of a smart city strategy.

Explore how cities will shape the future.

Chapter **13**

Ten Smart City Pitfalls to Avoid

B eginning the journey to create a smart city is a bold and courageous first step. The risks and costs are high, and positive outcomes aren't guaranteed. Most cities that haven't yet committed to a strategy may be able to detect an element of inevitability that the day will soon come. Evolving needs and community expectations will demand it. The promise of new technology in solving urban issues and delivering better results is simply too compelling — and in some cases too urgent — to ignore.

But you do need to recognize pragmatic hesitancy. Those risks and costs are concerning. Reputations are at stake. The work is difficult and complex. However, the day will eventually come when a vision and a plan for a smart city (or whatever other term is used) are demanded and when work will need to begin. Cities won't be able to sit this one out. Action will be required.

When the decision is made to move forward with a smart city strategy, it's time to evaluate the risks and come up with steps to lessen the danger. That means an ongoing risk management strategy must be part of the work as well. Consider establishing a *risk register* — a tool for documenting risks and the actions taken to address each risk. Fortunately, many case studies are available for review from cities of all sizes all over the world. Learn from them.

In this chapter, I identify ten smart city pitfalls to avoid. If you avoid these pitfalls, you will certainly reduce risk throughout your smart city program. But this is only one short list: Do your homework and identify issues that may be specific to particular initiatives — for example, around energy, transportation, health, or drone usage.

I guess it's smart to be smart about smart city risks.

Making Your Smart City Project a Tech Program and Putting IT in Charge

With the focus of smart city work revolving around the use of technology, it seems intuitive to consider it a technology program. Following that logic, it would seem to make sense for many cities to assign the work to their information technology (IT) team. Both assumptions seem reasonable but may be mistakes. Certainly, smart city technology is a core requirement; however, this program is about people. Keep in mind that technology adoption is an enabler, not the outcome. You must always return to fundamentals. Smart cities are about improving the quality of life for communities. Use this core belief to drive the work, and remind stakeholders frequently.

The risk of making a smart city strategy a technology program and assigning it to the IT team is high, for the reasons described in this list:

>> **Placing the focus on technology can alienate many stakeholders.** They may feel that they cannot contribute because they have insufficient knowledge or prerequisite skills. The fact is, smart city programs have greater success when all parts of an agency and the community have high levels of engagement.

>> **Your IT leader and team, despite their brilliance, may not be qualified to take ownership of this multidisciplinary program.** It's a leap to assume that knowledge of technology equates to competence in running projects that span across city domains. Sure, your IT leader may be a superstar who has the capability and knowledge to lead a smart city strategy. In that case, embrace this approach. In most cases though, it's unlikely.

>> **Placing the emphasis on technology may result in a program that receives less priority and attention than it deserves.** The smart city program has the potential to be seen as simply another set of technology projects. The reality is that smart city work needs leadership at the highest level of the organization and that the focus at all times must remain on benefits to people.

REMEMBER

Despite any caveats I might give, your IT leader and team must be essential and valued program partners. There's little doubt that their contributions will be critical to the success of the smart city program.

Garnering Insufficient Support and Engagement from Stakeholders

On any given day, a government agency is managing numerous projects. Big cities may even have hundreds of projects running, which is what consumes a good deal of city staff capacity. For this reason, the processes for identifying projects, getting them budgeted, and then executing them is fairly routine. More often than not, a project is managed and delivered by a single department. Sometimes, more than one department is involved, but an all-departments program remains quite rare. You should consider the smart city program an all-department effort. As a result of continuing routine practices, departments may be inclined to move forward with smart city projects with insufficient engagement. Sure, they'll embrace their normal network of involved participants, but they may not extend across other city departments and deep into the community. It's not deliberate — it's just that everyone defaults to their own routine.

REMEMBER

After a smart city program is approved — the emphasis *must be* on stakeholder engagement. Spend some time determining who should be considered a stakeholder. Be liberal in your inclusion of people you may not typically consider.

The work to create a smarter and more sustainable city is a long-term effort. Engaging stakeholders and advocating for success early is a valuable approach. After stakeholders are identified, you must work with them to include them in discussions related to defining the vision, agreeing on goals and objectives, identifying projects and vendors, and more. Engagement at this level builds trust among participants. It may create a heavier administrative burden, and it can slow the process, but the dividend makes it worthwhile. Certainly, a lack of support and engagement always guarantees bigger and more frustrating challenges.

TIP

To be inclusive, use a variety of platforms that include everything from traditional in-person meetings to online collaboration tools.

Limiting Efforts to Your City Boundaries

Suppose that the mayor proposes that your city work on becoming a smart city. It sounds like you need to build a vision and a strategy for your community. That's reasonable. But wait — might there be an opportunity to engage participants outside the city limits? All too often, the natural inclination is to focus solely on a single city. It makes sense on many levels. However, is it possible to be completely successful if the broader world isn't considered?

The term *broader world* may refer to adjoining cities or to the local region. It may also mean engaging with federal organizations. Cities don't exist in a vacuum. They are entirely dependent on their interdependence with other communities and external organizations. Here are some examples:

>> **Public transportation:** A public transportation system that serves a region can't be considered only in the context of a single city or a few cities. If your smart city work impacts public transport, you need to engage with regional transport providers.

>> **Public safety:** Your city might invest heavily in new technology to combat crime, but if you limit that work to your city's borders and fail to engage surrounding communities, you might be restricting the effectiveness of your efforts.

>> **Environment:** One of the most obvious suggestions for engaging participants beyond your own city is any effort related to the environment and climate change. Most people acknowledge that humans won't solve air, water, and climate issues, for example, by doing work in a silo. These areas don't respect borders. The best outcomes will be achieved when collaboration exists at the regional and national levels, where appropriate.

Finally, smart city leaders can explore regional efforts if it means sharing cost. It's highly possible that the work you're doing would be of interest to cities nearby. Go ahead and have that conversation with them. A smart city effort executed by several cities will reduce costs and may even be more successful due to regional collaboration. Even if it's more difficult, the effort may well be worth it. You won't know unless you explore it.

Paying Insufficient Attention to Inclusiveness Issues

Most everyone enjoys using new technologies. I know I do. But there's always a risk that deploying a new smart city technology and process may have a positive impact on one part of the community while overlooking, or even limiting, others. That is *unacceptable*. Cities belong to everyone. Cities must serve everyone. Private organizations may have the right to choose their customers, but cities do not and should not. For example, even when a city digitizes a simple analog process, such as putting a form online, it must retain alternatives for those who lack the technological savvy or access to the necessary technology. It's a unique city characteristic and responsibility.

Because smart city efforts can range in their impact on a community, careful consideration must be given to inclusiveness. Urban innovation has the real potential to create and increase social inequity. Specifically, in the design of a new service, teams must assess whether everyone who may be impacted by the change continues to be served with equal access, respect, and attention. Ensuring analog options for online services may be relatively straightforward, but many smart city projects involve both the digital and physical worlds. For example, services that use audio and visual cues must be accessible by those who have limitations in those sensory areas. Inclusive smart cities require broad community engagement and collaboration — and a commitment to human-centered urban design.

REMEMBER

To date, the lack of a focus on inclusiveness in smart city programs has been an area of notable criticism. It's time to make inclusiveness a priority and a mandatory part of the work. Improving the quality of life in cities must not be an experience for only a subset of a community — it's a goal that must benefit everyone.

Moving Forward with Inadequate Governance

For many people, the term *governance* may not be familiar, but the purpose is typically well understood. Simply defined, *governance* involves the structures put in place by organizations and teams to achieve measurable results toward achieving their goals. These goals can include the strategy of an entire organization, a project, or a program. The structures of governance can include these tasks:

>> Identifying leadership and staffing positions

>> Defining reporting relationships to be put in place

>> Determining how decisions on funding are made

>> Choosing how issues are escalated

>> Selecting which processes are adopted

To launch a smart city program without agreement on a rigorous governance structure (also called a *framework*) is a recipe for possible failure. I acknowledge that the skills in putting together a governance framework may not be present in many cities. This is why I encourage you to explore assistance from an external party. Good governance can produce good results. It's worth the time and expense needed to produce an agreeable approach. (I discuss and provide guidance on implementing governance in Chapter 6.)

REMEMBER

You'll know whether your city has good governance in place if qualities such as clear accountability, process documentation and transparency, specific role definitions, reporting structures, goals, objectives, program and project alignment with strategy, and metrics are all defined and agreed on. Consider these and more as the pillars of governance success.

Working with No Clear Vision for the Program

Let me be honest: Running a small handful of technology-related city projects does not a smart city make. That's just a handful of technology projects. The work to create a smarter community will likely be a multiyear effort with clear, bold, and ambitious goals. A meaningful shift must take place in terms of how services are delivered and operations are conducted. Quality of life should be measurably improved and experienced. This kind of game-changing work requires a *vision* — preferably, one articulated by way of a vision statement that includes a short description of what the organization wants to become. The vision, which is a signpost of where the enterprise is headed, guides all stakeholders in their decision-making and their actions.

A smart city vision should be aligned with the city's broader strategy and approved by the community. In fact, determining a vision for your smart city work is an important way to engage constituents. Don't stop at the vision, either: It's the starting point that gets converted to goals, objectives, and then projects. Deep engagement with city staff and community members helps to ensure that the right priorities are identified and there's agreement on the work to be done. Bring lots of data to these decision-making activities.

REMEMBER

A great vision is a great start to your smart city work. Without this vision, you have no signpost. Later, you may find that this lack is a guarantee of facing program challenges further down the road. Make the creation of a smart city vision one of the first things your team does. Chapter 4 has a focus on vision creation.

Downplaying the Essential Roles of Security and Privacy

A trade-off will continue to exist between the benefits that technology and data bring to the world and the attendant risks that come with them. As people acquire and deploy more digitally based solutions in their homes, businesses, and cities — and even on themselves — everyone clearly recognizes the many advantages that each new innovation brings. Emerging technologies are rapidly changing the world in surprising ways. What isn't clear is the extent of any risks that each one may present. Part of the challenge is that the nature of the risks continues to evolve. Cybersecurity is a particularly dynamic space: The bad guys are generally outpacing anyone's ability to fully protect software and hardware security vulnerabilities. Leaps in cybersecurity are being made, but a long road lies ahead if we humans are ever to have the upper hand in completely protecting our systems.

One of the core by-products of city government services is the collection, management, and storage of data. It's the one asset that every government has in abundance. Just consider all the services that need system and data support. The amount of data collected in forms alone is humungous for most agencies. Now cities are deploying an array of different sensors that capture details such as video, air and water quality, traffic information, and much more. All these devices collect and produce data. Though protecting city data has always been important, the volume, velocity, and variety of it now has significantly elevated the risks to it.

As remarkable as it may sound, the responsibility and degree to which protections are put in place in many cities around the world is at each city's discretion. That said, many efforts are taking place, ranging from new industry standards to new regulations and laws that are being applied. For example, the European Union's General Data Protection Regulation (GDPR) is a law that's being enforced across member nations to protect the personal data of EU citizens. In California, the California Consumer Privacy Act (CCPA) is a similar law, albeit less restrictive, that attempts to protect the personal information of Californians.

Not making cybersecurity and privacy a priority in all city operations today is a mistake. The financial costs, loss of organizational credibility, damage to brand, severe disruption of services, potential downstream crimes, and pain to individuals it may cause make the stakes simply too high. Your smart city strategy will increase these cybersecurity and privacy risks. As one public sector cybersecurity professional once advised me, "We shouldn't be creating smart cities — we should be creating *safe and secure* smart cities."

City cybersecurity and privacy is discussed in detail in Chapter 10.

Sharing Successes and Failures Too Narrowly

Government workers often take the brunt of stereotyping that characterizes them as lazy and unproductive. A few of those might exist, but isn't that true in every industry? The truth in my experience is quite different. I've worked in city government for many years, and I've also interacted with many of them all over the world. In that capacity, I've often encountered the most passionate, selfless, and hard-working people I've ever met. Some of the work can be thankless, but still, so many do the necessary, routine work of ensuring that their government services can function.

What also strikes me is the volume of important work that gets done that nobody notices and is never publicized. Few cities have marketing departments, in the private sector sense. Sure, they have communications teams who do vital work — such work may even include creating campaigns to attract businesses and tourists — but the everyday achievements of most cities are lightly reported on municipal websites and, at best, in local newspapers. In other words, cities can do a much better job of telling their stories.

Given the broad interest in smart cities, this work has received more attention than many of the programs that cities work on. The scale and transformational potential of the work is attractive for journalists and analysts, and so a decent amount of new content is being produced on this topic. So much of it, though, is being led by third parties, not by the city itself. Managing the narrative may be limited to infrequent press releases. (Check out Chapter 8 for a discussion on several contemporary communication techniques.)

Cities need to tell their smart city stories. They need to do this as not only a marketing tool but also a way to keep their communities apprised and engaged. They also need to do it to help other cities. Of course, they'd love to share only the good stories and best practices, but enormous value lies in sharing the failures as well. Of course, no city leader wants to expose the bad things that happen, so this strategy won't be wholeheartedly embraced. However, the value in sharing those failures not only demonstrates transparency and honesty but can also be helpful in communicating the complexity and difficulty of the work for the benefit of other communities.

TIP

Embrace and share your smart city strategy strengths and weaknesses. More communities will reap the rewards of this approach and, as a result, many more may prosper. Wouldn't that be a good thing?

Sticking Stubbornly to the Old Ways of Doing Things

Most people love predictability. They enjoy their routines. It's a lovely experience to visit a favorite restaurant after a long absence and find that the dish you love is still on the menu and tastes *exactly* how you remember it. But predictability and routine in a work context — particularly, as humans traverse the fourth industrial revolution — may not be that desirable. I'm not talking about the comfort of a paycheck or the reliable trust of a colleague. I'm referring to the need for organizations to change — often quickly — to respond to a world in transition.

The biggest risk to organizations today is the lack of relevancy. If you're doing the same thing while everything around you (including your customers) is changing, you're not demonstrating your relevancy and you're likely on a trajectory toward failure. Continuous modifications of products and services, and even operations, is becoming a characteristic of the times. The ability to evolve and reinvent at a moment's notice appears to be emerging as a competitive advantage.

In city government, change often happens slowly, and for plenty of good reasons, such as not having the budget to change or not wanting to upset a community by introducing a new process or having little appetite for even a modest amount of risk. Each of these is a legitimate concern and must be respected. But can the slow pace of city government innovation and a conservative mindset be sustained and acceptable when the world is rapidly changing?

With city complexity and community expectations increasing, and with a growing number of intractable issues emerging, business-as-usual for a city appears to be under pressure. Because a smart city strategy is often a response to these challenges, this means that the capacity to embrace change must also expand. Sticking to the old ways of doing things while simultaneously pursuing a smart city program would appear to be incompatible. Leaders who are more flexible, ready to change, and prepared to take more risks may drive more success in their efforts than those who cling to the predictability of the ways things have always been done.

Thinking Too Short-Term

Depending on the political system of a city agency, projects may be tied to the term of leadership. In the United States, terms typically last four years, so many initiatives are targeted to kick off and be completed in that period. Though getting the right things done well is the purpose of leadership, it's reasonable to also say that there may be additional motivations too. For example, if the initiative is a success in a single term, an official may take credit for the change and also increase their chance of being reelected or appointed to another term. Sometimes the reason for the timing is that the budget exists and the need is now greatest. There are a whole lot of reasons why, and when, work is done in a city. Many are specific to the particular city.

It's fair to say that many smart city projects can be completed in a reasonably short period (at least in a city context). For example, it's possible to create and deploy apps that can be quite useful to a community well within a four-year time period. That said, the complexity and reach of an entire smart city program will likely stretch over much longer periods. A smart city strategy typically has bold and ambitious goals. It requires a lot of individual projects, many of which are interdependent and require new, complex software, hardware, and process requirements.

You can easily fall into the short-term trap, where the team is looking just a few years into the future. Like everyone, they're impatient to realize successful outcomes. A more pragmatic approach to the smart city work is to see it on the short-, medium-, and long-term horizons. As Steven Covey, educator and author of *The 7 Habits of Highly Effective People,* has famously said, "Begin with the end in mind." A smart city strategy requires a long-term mindset, but with a focus on delivering value along the way. Too much short-term thinking may result in these errors:

>> Incorrectly setting expectations for the organization and community

>> Underspecifying the overall smart city architecture

>> Poorly communicating the long-term budgeting requirements

>> Sprinting at the start when everyone should be preparing for a marathon

REMEMBER

A smart city strategy is a long-term effort. Plan for it.

Chapter **14**

Ten Ways Cities Will Define Our Human Future

With the vast majority of people destined to live in cities by the middle of the 21st century, the future of humans is inextricably interwoven with the future of cities. Every aspect of life will be shaped by the urban world — that includes living conditions, health, safety, work and careers, and recreation.

People have shaped cities, and, in turn, cities have shaped people. People will become what they design and build. They will enjoy or suffer the consequences of their city decisions. No doubt continuing the trend of the past few hundred years, cities will evolve and be molded by human needs and desires as well as by innovation, cultures, and the changing environment.

In this chapter, I explore ten ways that cities will define the human future. Of course, it's not an exhaustive list; my idea here is to concentrate on areas that are echoed throughout this book and are characteristic of current smart city trends. I cover major areas such as digitalization, sustainability, data, diversity, transportation, and healthcare. I'm confident that many of the projections I make will come to pass. I'm equally confident that I'll get many things wrong. After all, there's no proven way to predict the future with absolute accuracy. The only things that humans can ever predict is that things will change and that they'll often be surprised by what happens. The best that humans can do is use the knowledge they have today, explore and leverage their understanding of events and trends of the past, and make a good guess at where everyone is headed in the future. It's an important thing to do.

Most People Will Live, Work, and Play Their Entire Lives in Cities

It is estimated by the United Nations that, around the year 2008, the world changed from being majority rural to majority urban. As recently as the 1950s, only 30 percent of the world lived in cities. From 2008 onward, cities have been growing rapidly, and rural areas have continued to see population decline. The United Nations maintains that around 3 million people move into cities every week. At this rate, within a couple of decades, including natural population growth, the urban population could grow by 3 billion.

Assuming that this trend continues, it's a fair assumption that the future of humanity will belong to cities. This future is a profoundly different world from the entire history as *homo sapiens* to date. Within a few decades, most humans will know a life only in an urban context. The countryside will be somewhere that you visit, not a place where you live. Life will continue in rural areas, and some people will move from cities to be part of that life. But those will be a minority.

Rural parts of the world will still be vitally important for agriculture, tourism, for those that live there, preserving culture and habitat, and more. Humanity's destiny in an urban future should not come at the price of rural heritage and value. In fact, it should increase the importance of the natural world because of its importance to a sustainable urban ecosystem.

By 2050, an urban future for 70 percent of humans will mean that the way they work, play, and live will all reflect this reality. Unless they mess it up, smarter cities have the potential to provide more career opportunities, better education and healthcare, and a safer and more prosperous environment. Of course, as you look out from today, there are many unknowns that humans will need to understand and confront, such as the impact of climate change, automation, and other natural and manmade threats. Our human responses to each will also define and shape our life in cities. Remember that cities have already shaped human behavior and destiny — they'll just become a lot more important and complex in the years ahead.

REMEMBER

Recognizing that the future is urban should reinforce the urgency to prepare and act in building smarter cities for not only communities today but also all communities to come.

The Increasing Demands of Sustainability Will Shape Human Behavior

Sustainability is generally defined as the manner in which humans can meet their needs today without compromising the ability of future generations to meet their needs. Sustainability is typically evaluated by way of the dimensions of people, profit, and planet. Stated another way, each dimension equates to social, economic, and environment factors. Being sustainable and having sustainable development doesn't mean curtailing progress. In fact, humans have to maintain sustainability while innovating and increasing the quality of life for communities.

Each sustainable dimension of people, profit, and planet requires continual behavioral changes as the world moves forward. As the increasingly dominant infrastructure of human life, cities may have the greatest levers to influence these three areas.

With the *people* (social) dimension, I am referring to the degree that cities support areas such as equality, inclusion, health, and happiness. With *profit* (economics), I'm referring to areas such as living wages, low-impact supply chains, and job opportunities. Finally, the *planet* (environmental) aspect may be the most familiar to you. This term refers to areas such as reducing carbon emissions, improving waste and resource management, and eliminating toxins in the air, water, plants, and soil.

The nature of dynamic city operations and activities drives changes in people, profit, and planet. Cities are responsible for 80 percent of gross domestic product (GDP) — as well as 70 percent of carbon emissions. Intuitively, with more of humanity now living in urban areas, the challenges of equality, inclusion, and other critical, people-centered concerns continue to dominate city development. Cities have always defined how people behave, including which lifestyle options are available and adopted, the management of consumption and waste, and economic decisions that impact opportunities and safety nets.

Without a doubt, the dimensions of sustainability — people, profit, and planet — will be further defined by the world's developing cities and, in turn, human behavior.

City Interactions Will Increasingly Be Digital

The third industrial revolution began in the 1950s. During this time, the world saw the emergence of electronics and computers. Consistent with a revolution, the world has never been the same since. And, by the way, its impact is *still* to be felt in many parts of the world. For example, the Internet is still unavailable to 40 percent of the world (although this number is improving rapidly). Wait until that 40 percent catches up with everyone else!

The world is also in a third wave of the Internet, and you can anticipate many more waves to come. The third wave includes the Internet as a platform for facilitation, such as ride-hailing (Uber, for example) and for connecting devices in an Internet of Things (being able to see who's at the front door using an Internet-connected device and a remote camera, for example).

The most visible aspect of the third industrial revolution for many people has been the move from analog to digital services. You've seen digitalization change the way people interact, consume, and deliver services in every industry. It started with websites, and now smartphones, smartwatches, and smart assistants are some of the ways everyone experiences digital.

As the third decade of the 21st century begins, almost 80 percent of organizations are engaging in some form of digital transformation. They're either undergoing a process of digitalization of their analog services, or they're completely reinventing their businesses using the tools of the digital world.

As you can imagine, cities are also at various stages of a digital transformation. Some are considering the work ahead, and others are well into their efforts. Digital transformations are often considered a subset of a smart city strategy.

Just like the private sector, the public sector is embracing digital to enable better community experiences, lower costs through automation, add more value by integrating services, and meet the growing expectations of constituents.

Though city governments will need to offer a variety of channels for their communities to interact for some time to come — after all, you can't assume that everyone has a computer or smartphone or even knows how to use them — they will increasingly build and support digital experiences. Already, many services can be accessed via a website, and lots of cities are beginning to offer apps on smartphones. For example, the city of Dubai offers the Dubai Now app, which supports 85 services directly on a smartphone, at

www.smartdubai.ae/apps-services/details/dubai-now

REMEMBER

Given the global momentum and all the benefits arising from digitalization, it is clear that, over time, the way you interact with your local city government will be progressively more digital.

City Data Will Drive Community Decision-Making

Data has been called "the oil of the 21st century." That's because data has tremendous value for an organization. For example, with the right tools and expertise, a business can use data to target the marketing of its product or service at only individuals who have a high likelihood of becoming buyers. Data can help companies make informed decisions that range from optimizing fuel usage on aircraft to determining where to build a retail presence for maximum market reach. Data runs the digital economy — an economy that's gradually proving its dominance.

Fortunately, data is the one element that most cities have in abundance. Though urban data has largely been a product of city activities, particularly as information technology has played a bigger role in city operations, it hasn't historically been used in a derivative role. By this, I mean that cities haven't been leveraging data for uses beyond its primary purpose. For example, a city may collect and store data on issues reported, such as vandalism or abandoned trash. But might it not be valuable to analyze the data and use it to determine behavioral trends, their origins, and potential solutions? (For more on how urban data is being used to solve problems and create new solutions, see Chapter 7.)

A breakthrough with city data began around 15 years ago, when cities started making their data sets freely available online. Communities could, for the first time, perform all sorts of actions on this data, called *open data*, including analysis, repurposing, application development, and more. Open data, and data in general, is the core of smart city work. (I cover open data in more detail in Chapter 9.)

Today, data finally plays a more important role in cities. As cities bring on the right talent and acquire the tools, they are leveraging the value of data for all types of benefits. This includes decision-making at city hall and decision-making in the community. And although they're playing catch-up, cities are also putting more effort into securing the data and protecting privacy. City stakeholders are recognizing the value of this rich asset. Cities have finally discovered the new oil.

People Will Have Expanded Opportunities to Co-Create and Collaborate on Urban Solutions

It wasn't that long ago that communities had to rely entirely on their local governments to provide city services. The assumption was that people paid taxes and the municipality in return had the responsibility to provide solutions. Yes, this is still generally the arrangement and expectation. However, it has become clear that the scale and complexity of many contemporary urban environments means that government-provided services are often a delicate balancing act of priority management. In other words, there's only a limited amount of money, talent, and time at city hall to deliver against all the needs of a community. These constraints create enormous frustration, by both constituents and city staff who just want to do the right thing.

Fortunately, public-private partnerships (PPPs) that bring together talent and resources from both sectors are often used to tackle issues and create more capacity. PPPs are widely adopted today, and barely a large project is not approached in this way.

In addition, technology is enabling more nongovernmental players to participate in creating and delivering urban services. It can answer an important question: If a local government can't prioritize a solution to be created and delivered, can another entity step up and do it?

Today, private enterprise and community members are participating in the delivery of urban services in a variety of ways. In addition to collaborating via PPPs, these private stakeholders can use entrepreneurship, technology, and open data to create all manner of services. City halls all over the world are embracing private engagement in solution building and encouraging collaboration from across city departments with outside partners. City management, recognizing their own limitations and also the benefits of leveraging private participation, are encouraging co-creation and collaboration. Urban innovation is becoming a team sport. In many instances today, getting urban solutions created and deployed won't rely solely on the frustration of waiting for a local government to prioritize and deliver the need, and I expect this collaborative approach to become even more common.

Crime May Be Reduced Significantly

It may seem implausible that, in many cities around the world, and particularly in the United States, crime has dropped and continues to decline. A hyperconnected world where people are consuming news in higher volume by way of more media channels than ever before may give you the impression that cities are more dangerous and violent than in the past. The data just doesn't support it. In fact, overall, the world is more peaceful, and more people than ever live in safer environments. In western Europe in the 1300s, there were around 70 murders for every 100,000 people. Today, it's 1.

Certainly, there's much work still to do. Far too many people continue to be the victims of urban crime, and the benefits that many cities are experiencing in reduced lawbreaking isn't evenly distributed.

Though humans have had a fairly violent past, to say the least, beginning around the 1990s, many cities began to see sharp declines in many types of crime, some with drops as big as 50 percent. The phenomenon was most pronounced in the United States, which had seen increasing violent urban crime from the 1950s through the end of the 1980s. But other violent cities around the world saw decreases as well. São Paulo, Brazil, once one of the world's most dangerous cities, saw crime dramatically drop beginning around 1999. Between 1990 and 2015, homicides declined in Europe by 56 percent and in Asia by 38 percent. Something changed, and cities began to get safer.

Safer cities also resulted in urban renewal. Abandoned and run-down areas began to be transformed into livable, prosperous areas. Schoolkids no longer consumed by the fear of crime could focus more on learning. The drop in urban crime has had, and continues to have, many positive outcomes.

So, what happened? The reasons that cities are becoming safer isn't yet well understood, though plenty of research has been conducted and conclusions formed. Explanations range from aging populations, better law enforcement and innovation, reduced male unemployment, local community mobilization, more cultural diversity, and improved economic conditions.

REMEMBER

Having a clear understanding of the reasons for the sharp decline in crime would be important for other cities because they would be able to adopt the successful efforts of others.

When cities are safe, people are freer. This freedom enables more innovation, better education, cleaner and healthier environments, and greater prosperity. Unless an unanticipated change occurs, all signals suggest that smarter cities will be even safer in the future. I think everyone can agree that this is a good thing and an important enabler of an improved quality of life.

More Diversity Will Show Up in What Humans Do and How They Work

The nature of work has changed radically over several hundred years. Before the mid-1700s, most people worked off the land or ran small businesses. With the advent of the first industrial revolution, factories emerged that attracted labor from rural areas into urban areas. This immigration from the countryside was the catalyst for many towns to grow into cities.

In the 1800s, the second industrial revolution saw a massive expansion of factories and city work. It offered people predictable labor, increased incomes, and the possibility of a better quality of life (though conditions remained poor for too many people for a long period). The labor union movement expanded greatly in the 19th and 20th centuries, which helped to improve city-and-factory working conditions.

During the third industrial revolution, which began around the 1950s, electronics and computers provided new tools, opportunities, and careers. Computers significantly increased productivity and changed the way millions of workers performed their work.

Now, in the 21st century, the world is entering a fourth industrial revolution, and work is evolving again. In addition, as the main source of global economic power and the location where most people now live, cities today have proven themselves to be inextricably linked to work.

Most striking is the variety of ways in which work is changing. For example, historically most people have worked for an organization, but now greater numbers are working as freelancers. In particular, the United States has seen a major shift in this direction. More than 53 million individuals — 34 percent of the American workforce — now work independently. Many of the jobs are part of the sharing economy that primarily serves the urban environment, such as ride hailing, deliveries, and household services.

Another influence on the evolution of work is the impact of automation and artificial intelligence. A recent study suggested that by 2030, up to 800 million global workers could be displaced by robotics. That's 20 percent of the world's workforce. Some argue that automation may be a boon to workers, augmenting their work rather than replacing it. In fact, some research maintains that new technologies may create more meaningful and higher-paying opportunities.

As a driver of economic progress, smarter cities will need to support and incentivize new opportunities and businesses, reduce barriers to entrepreneurship, provision workforce retooling and education options, and deploy programs to unlock talent. They'll also need to support less-skilled workers, the most likely group to be negatively impacted by new technologies and the increasing demand for highly skilled staff and the creative class. Smarter cities can also create and support an ecosystem of innovation that embraces change and progress rather than fights it.

Cities that ignore these employment shifts and don't take action run the risk of growing inequality, unemployment and all that comes with it, and economic decline.

But the intersection of the future of cities and that of people's changing work will have many upsides. Notably, more workers will have flexibility in where and how they work. This means more time in their city homes or at coffee shops and co-working spaces. This increased freedom will continue to produce new urban support services, such as on-demand dog walking services, and recreational options, such as new food experiences, for workers who have more control over their time.

Cities and their communities have the opportunity to participate in defining the future of work. For example, this will involve choices around policy and education. Done right, cities have the possibility of continued and increasing prosperity, and urban workers will have many more options to consider when it comes to employment, including where and how they work.

The Way People and Goods Move Will Continue to Evolve

One of the most visible ways that cities are changing in front of your eyes is the number of new forms of transportation that are suddenly shuttling around people and goods. The roads and sidewalks of the urban world were already replete with a variety of transportation modes. From motorized tuk-tuks to pulled rickshaws, from horses to rollerblades, and from convertibles to light rail, humans have found a multitude of ways to get around. Culture, cost, and geography in each city play a big role in shaping the options offered.

It seems that we're far from done. Automobiles, now dominating the city landscape, are themselves in a period of change. Increased interest in sustainability is literally driving the growth of electric-powered vehicles. Still a niche, but rapidly expanding, electric cars may dominate in the second half of the 21st century. Hydrogen as a fuel is also gaining interest and buyers, but it's too early to know whether it will have long-term traction. The emergence of self-driving vehicles or fully autonomous vehicles (AVs) is gathering speed, and all car manufacturers are betting on a vast AV future.

REMEMBER

It would be too narrow to consider AVs only from the perspective of self-driving. They have the potential to change everything, from reduced congestion and accidents to insurance disruption and reinvented city design. (I discuss AVs in more detail in Chapter 8.)

The other area of mobility that has seen remarkable growth is in *personal transportation*. These are devices built primarily for one person. Though bicycles have long been popular, use continues to increase in many cities around the world with the introduction of bikes available for rental in free-standing racks or just parked alone on the sidewalk. Gaining particular popularity is the e-bike — a bicycle with a small motor that helps with propulsion and ease at climbing hills. Other personal transportation includes an eclectic mix of scooters (and e-scooters), electric unicycles, the Segway, self-balancing wheels, hoverboards, hovercycles, monowheel scooters, and electric mopeds. I have no doubt that by the time this book goes to print, even more will be on the market.

Cities where adoption is high for these contraptions, such as San Francisco, are making for a colorful streetscape. It's also creating safety hazards that range from collisions with larger motorized vehicles to people tripping over abandoned devices on the sidewalk. In some cities, rental bikes being thrown into canals or hung in trees and other odd places have become forms of vandalism and creativity, respectively.

With multiple modes of transportation available, people have many ways of getting from one place to another. It means that a trip might involve a variety of modalities. Using an app to optimize a trip so that, for example, the lowest carbon footprint is utilized is now possible. It might mean walking a certain distance, and then pedaling an e-bike, and then riding light rail, and, finally, taking a short walk. These apps consider mobility as a service, or MaaS. This may mean that the app determines a cost for the entire trip and distributes the funds to the various modalities used. The world's urban environments are optimized for MaaS, and adoption of this approach appears to be gaining popularity in cities across the world. For MaaS to function in a city, it's almost certain that both the public and private sectors have to partner to optimize it. The data gleaned from MaaS is also helping all partners develop better solutions and is informing city leaders about transportation patterns and needs.

REMEMBER

The most fundamental form of transport is walking. That's why communities are demanding that their cities plan for, develop, and promote walk-friendly neighborhoods and for their urban cores to be more accessible, convenient, and safe for walking. Walking is good for one's health, the environment, and the economy.

The notion of a walk score has gained popularity as a way to measure the degree that neighborhoods have good walkability. (For more information on walk scores, check out www.walkscore.com.)

The emergence of cars in the past century created vast planetary change, both in physical appearance and in enabling new human enterprise. But, as the century came to a close, it became clear that cars have created many challenges, including congestion, accidents, high transport costs, damage to the environment, and an often ugly urban and suburban architecture. Continuing to manufacture and deploy more cars in volume to global urban centers is unsustainable. In the 21st century, these mounting challenges have created a momentum for mobility innovation.

From automobiles to public transport and personal mobility, you can expect transportation to evolve rapidly in the decades ahead. These changes will modify the very shape of the world's cities as well as our own human behavior, just as it has for the past few hundred years.

The Delivery of Healthcare Will Be Transformed

In Chapter 11, I discuss the global movement to enable healthy cities. Healthy cities are about incorporating health considerations into urban development and management. It's a concept unsurprisingly endorsed by the World Health Organization (WHO) and organizations such as the Alliance for Healthy Cities. The main principles include creating a health-supportive environment, improving quality of life, providing basic sanitation, and making access to healthcare available. These principles have obvious intersections with smart city goals, because they require innovation and technology at a community scale.

Similar to almost all city efforts, there is a role in community healthcare for the government and a role for other stakeholders, such as the private sector. In some cities, the provision of healthcare services is a core responsibility, though in others the city plays a supporting role. Many government healthcare systems around the world are run by region, county, state, or nation. In addition, the private sector is a major provider in many societies.

Healthcare systems are deeply integrated into every economy and they are expensive and complex to run. Modern medicine is often a miracle, but it comes with a hefty price tag. It's not just the pure monetary aspect, but the necessary overhead of infrastructure, services, supplies, talent, and systems that are required to make it function. It's also quite evident that most healthcare systems are designed to support communities that are operating at a steady state each day. In the event of a major incident, a nature disaster, or even a disease epidemic or pandemic, many systems can quickly fail under the duress of the demands being placed on it.

Together with a number of recent scientific and medical breakthroughs, improved use of healthcare data, and a willing entrepreneurial spirit, a new era of healthcare innovation has begun. In addition, a greater awareness of personal responsibility in health outcomes and a multigenerational desire to make better lifestyle choices to avoid disease and extend life are also contributing to the growth in healthcare solutions.

Health networks are intertwined with urban systems. For example, city hospital systems rely on elaborate communications systems, public safety personnel and services, transport infrastructure that includes municipal vehicles, and city policies and regulations. As health networks evolve, so do the supporting urban systems, and vice versa.

Two developments in particular are driving changes in how healthcare is being considered and delivered in cities. The first is *telemedicine* — the remote diagnosis and treatment of patients using telecommunications technology. This transformation brings many benefits that include lower cost, more convenience, greater timeliness, increased access to more resources (because distance is no longer a limitation, a patient can access specialists in distant locations, in other words), and the ability to serve more people. But it also means a higher degree of reliance on good urban telecommunications. It might also force the consolidation of facilities, resulting in some medical facilities closing down or downsizing in certain communities.

The second change comes in the form of behavioral shifts. Communities are becoming much more engaged in the care of their physical and mental needs. People are demanding clean air and water. They want to live in a state of peace and not have to worry about their safety. Urban noise pollution is acknowledged as a stressor, and more emphasis is being placed on reducing and eliminating it. Community members are educating themselves and adopting a wide range of new activities, such as outdoor activities that range from walking, jogging, yoga, tai chi, parkour, and cycling to finding quiet places to meditate within the urban environment. Various forms of outdoor *mindfulness* are being practiced — this is a therapeutic technique for inducing an improved mental state by focusing awareness on the present moment while acknowledging and accepting thoughts, feelings, and bodily sensations. Clean air and low noise are some of the conducive environmental qualities that lend themselves toward successful mindfulness.

In the years ahead, every city will want to be a healthy city. The public and private sectors will innovate in completely new ways that take advantage of medical breakthroughs and the changing behavior of the communities they serve. A few decades from now, the way city healthcare is delivered and consumed may be barely recognizable.

Everything Will Be Delivered

In 1965, while an undergraduate at Yale University, Frederick Smith wrote a term paper proposing a system designed for faster delivery by moving packages by air at night, when airports weren't congested. After he graduated, Frederick pursued his idea and started operations in 1973. By July 1975, he had a popular and profitable business. It was called Federal Express. Later, the name was shortened to what everyone knows today as FedEx.

For the past few decades, urban delivery services have continued to rapidly evolve and innovate. Being able to send a letter or package across the world and have it delivered in two days was magical. But, in a society bent on faster gratification and hypercompetition, two days would quickly become unacceptable. Soon, overnight delivery arrived, and that was quickly followed by same-day delivery. Today, some products can be delivered in a city within two hours. This immediacy is changing the nature of consumption. No longer limited to time-sensitive or business-related items for commercial entities, everyone can now order a dozen eggs or a ream of copier paper and have them hand-delivered to their front door.

In just the past few years, residential deliveries have surged. Consumers are spending more time buying online instead of visiting physical stores. Purchasing behaviors are quickly changing. Malls and retail stores are in decline and being displaced by consumers acquiring smaller amounts of products in greater frequency online. Food delivery in particular has exploded, creating an entire economy around services that pick up and deliver. The data is inconclusive as to whether the greater numbers of delivery trips are being offset by fewer people traveling to stores and restaurants. With stay-at-home orders during the Covid-19 pandemic, urban delivery services, and in particular those for restaurant food, have exploded. While this period may represent an outlier spike, if the broader growth trends continue, in the long run there should be less personal traffic on the roads. We'll see.

Online ordering in the digital realm is driving a stunning boom in the physical world of delivery. City streets and neighborhoods are full of trucks (7 percent of traffic in US cities), motorcycles, bicycles, and even ride-hailing services dropping off high volumes of products purchased from web browsers and smartphone apps.

Many city arteries are choked daily with double- and triple-parked delivery trucks. Curbside areas once exclusive to residents are being blocked. Bus lanes are being congested by truck drop-offs. These delivery vehicles have created a city congestion nightmare as they deliver tens of billions of packages in cities per year. Some experimentation in off-hour delivery shows some promise of alleviating congestion, but it's not a panacea.

All these new vehicles are causing an increase in environmental damage as well, from carbon emissions, energy use, and infrastructure wear-and-tear. Vast volumes of packaging materials are being used, creating greater waste management needs. With deliveries incentivized for speed, more traffic accidents are occurring as drivers take greater risks. Online purchasing is also damaging local economies as fewer shoppers patronize local stores.

New forms of city delivery, in the shape of both ground and airborne drones, are in the late stages of experimentation. It's looking increasingly likely that autonomous drones will make routine deliveries by ground and by descending from the air. New city regulations will be required in order to manage this new type of traffic. Cities will need to be prepared for a backlash from the noise they create and the inevitable accidents that occur.

Conscious of the increase in package volume and the attendant congestion and complexity of delivery, companies are exploring the use of collection centers. In this model, the delivery is made to lockers in a central area in a neighborhood and consumers are notified when items are ready for collection. Physical stores are also being used as collection points. Malls that are turning into ghost towns may find a second life as delivery-and-collection centers.

Assuming that current trends continue, delivery services will constitute a larger amount of urban traffic. In the years ahead, smart cities will need to decide how to handle the environmental harm, the congestion, the noise and chaos, the impact to local business, and other problems caused by these trends. Sure, the consumer will benefit from convenience, but a consensus will be needed to arrive at the price the community is willing to pay.

Appendixes

Appendix A
Smart City Strategies

The following examples of smart city strategies are a collection of relatively random choices, selected to represent almost every area of the world. After all, the smart city movement is global. You'll see that I've grouped the cities by region for convenience. You may find the list and its content fascinating, but hopefully also quite valuable in understanding both the similarities and diversity of smart city focus areas for cities. These areas and approaches aren't comprehensive in my summaries, and I apologize to each city in advance for any glaring omissions or errors. The items chosen were those that jumped out in the research on each city and were worth sharing simply for the purpose of illustrating the type of work being done. I encourage you to scan the list, and also to follow the website links and explore some of the city's strategies more deeply. My hope is that this list serves as not just a learning exercise but also an opportunity to be inspired and driven to action.

Note: Not every city had a dedicated smart city microsite, so I've done my best to link to a relevant page.

AFRICA

Country	Kenya
City	Konza Technopolis
Website	www.konza.go.ke/smart-city
Strategic Focus Areas and Approach	• A new city under construction, aimed at being a sustainable, world-class technology hub and a major economic driver for the nation • Infrastructure services: transportation, utilities, public safety, environment • Citizen services: access and participation • City services: city information, planning, and development • Business services: supportive services for local commerce

Country	South Africa
City	Cape Town
Website	www.capetown.gov.za
Strategic Focus Areas and Approach	• Digital government • Digital inclusion • Digital economy • Digital infrastructure • Free public Wi-Fi • Sustainability focus with particular emphasis on water management • Use of open data

ASIA

Country	India
City	New Delhi
Website	http://smartcity.ndmc.gov.in/pages/home.aspx
Strategic Focus Areas and Approach	• Improved physical and social infrastructure • Governance • Education • Sustainability • Civic participation • Technology solutions that include smart parking, wastewater recycling, smart lighting, and expanded use of solar

Country	Japan
City	Tokyo
Website	www.seisakukikaku.metro.tokyo.lg.jp/en/ basic-plan/actionplan-for-2020
Strategic Focus Areas and Approach	• Become a global financial and economic center • Increase the city's desirability as a tourist destination • Make environmental improvements • Prioritize the safety of residents and visitors • Promote physical and mental health • Reduce energy consumption

Country	Singapore (City-State)
City	Singapore
Website	www.smartnation.sg
Strategic Focus Areas and Approach	• Government, economy, and services powered by digital innovation • Facilitating innovation in the private and public sectors • Focusing on health services • Sharing and collaborating on solutions in the region and with the world • Virtual Singapore (digital twin): www.nrf.gov.sg/programmes/virtual-singapore • Using open data

Country	South Korea
City	Seoul
Website	www.seoulsolution.kr/en
Strategic Focus Areas and Approach	• Smart use of technology to support the city • Culture of civic participation • Improved infrastructure • Promotion as a city of culture • Free Wi-Fi for residents and visitors • Test bed for new urban technologies

AUSTRALIA

Country	Australia
City	Canterbury Bankstown
Website	https://haveyoursay.cbcity.nsw.gov.au/smart-cbcity-roadmap
Strategic Focus Areas and Approach	• Utilize data for better services and decision-making • Develop self-service solutions • Deliver a public performance dashboard • Build a culture of innovation • Improve building planning and design

Country	Australia
City	Melbourne
Website	www.melbourne.vic.gov.au/about-melbourne/melbourne-profile/smart-city/Pages/smart-city.aspx
Strategic Focus Areas and Approach	• Responsiveness to the changing needs of community, environment, and economy • Reduction of litter • Free Wi-Fi for all residents and visitors • Test-and-learn areas for exploring new technologies such as 5G and IoT • Innovation challenges • CityLab as a space to prototype and test new ideas and city services with the community • Use of open data

Country	Australia
City	North Sydney
Website	www.northsydney.nsw.gov.au/Business_Projects/Business_Economic_Development/Economic_Development/Smart_City_Strategy_and_Action_Plan
Strategic Focus Areas and Approach	• Focus on a great place to work, study, and visit • Improved infrastructure • Increased economic activity • Sustainability • More inclusiveness and connectivity • Civic engagement in decision-making on technology use in the community

EUROPE

Country	Ireland
City	Dublin
Website	https://smartdublin.ie
Strategic Focus Areas and Approach	• Develop better services • Promote innovative urban solutions • Improve economic activity • Increase engagement and collaboration across all sectors of the economy • Develop smart districts • Use open data

Country	Netherlands
City	Amsterdam
Website	https://amsterdamsmartcity.com/
Strategic Focus Areas and Approach	• Adopt new technologies such as drones and IoT • Improve energy, water, and waste management • Reduce traffic congestion • Minimize waste • Increase decision-making tools • Engage community in idea generation

Country	Russia
City	Moscow
Website	www.mos.ru/en/city/projects/smartcity
Strategic Focus Areas and Approach	• Creation and operation of central traffic management center • Wide range of digital services • Development of unified online medical system for all resident health needs • Civic engagement solutions • Focus on public safety • Free Wi-Fi across the city • Use open data

Country	Spain
City	Barcelona
Website	`https://ajuntament.barcelona.cat/` `digital/en/about-us`
Strategic Focus Areas and Approach	• Increased quality of life through the use of advanced technology • Investment in infrastructure • Sustainability • Civic engagement and collaborative decision-making with citizens • Technology use in improving traffic congestion and for lowering energy costs • Use of open data

Country	Sweden
City	Stockholm

Website	`https://international.stockholm.se/governance/`
	`smart-and-connected-city/strategy-for-a-smart-`
	`and-connected-city`

Strategic Focus Areas and Approach	• Deliver a high quality of life • Provide best environment for business • Focus on economic, ecologic, democratic, and social sustainability • Deliver innovative solutions, transparency, and connectivity • Adopt the Internet of Things, big data, and analytics • Use open data • Deploy integrated platforms

Country	United Kingdom
City	London
Website	www.london.gov.uk/what-we-do/business-and-economy/supporting-londons-sectors/smart-london
Strategic Focus Areas and Approach	• Become the smartest city in the world • Create more user-designed services • Create world-class connectivity, including the adoption of 5G • Engage citizens in innovation • Improve transportation • Use open data

MIDDLE EAST

Country	Israel
City	Tel Aviv
Website	www.tel-aviv.gov.il/en/abouttheCity/Pages/SmartCity.aspx
Strategic Focus Areas and Approach	• Focus on civic engagement and public participation • Creation and support of DigiTel, a communication platform that provides residents with information and services • Sustainable neighborhoods • Focus on support for start-ups • Vision to be the smartest city in the world • Use open data

Country	United Arab Emirates
City	Dubai
Website	www.smartdubai.ae
Strategic Focus Areas and Approach	• Create the happiest city on the planet • Deliver seamless, safe, efficient, and impactful city experiences • Use leading technologies, such as artificial intelligence (AI) and blockchain • Eliminate paper in government • Develop principles and ethics in the use of AI • Support start-ups and entrepreneurs • Implement the Data First initiative to support the adoption of data as a valuable resource

Country	Saudi Arabia
City	NEOM
Website	www.neom.com/en-us
Strategic Focus Areas and Approach	• New city that is in the planning stages • Will operate independently from the existing governmental framework, with its own tax and labor laws and an autonomous judicial system • Powered entirely by wind and solar • Proposed use of robots for areas such as security, logistics, home delivery, and caregiving • Technology-intensive approaches that include education, transport, and entertainment services

NORTH AMERICA

Country	Canada
City	Toronto
Website	www.toronto.ca/city-government/accountability-operations-customer-service/long-term-vision-plans-and-strategies/smart-cityto
Strategic Focus Areas and Approach	• Connectivity and inclusiveness of people to city services • Increased civic participation • Improved digital infrastructure • Support for evidence-based decision-making • Working relationship with Sidewalk Labs, an Alphabet company, to convert a section of the city into the most innovative district in the world • Use of open data

Country	United States
City	Columbus, Ohio
Website	www.columbus.gov/smartcity
Strategic Focus Areas and Approach	• Improved quality of life • Economic growth • Sustainability • Use of technology to improve energy use, public safety, and public services • Particular focus on innovation in the transportation space • Use open data

Country	United States
City	Henderson, Nevada
Website	www.cityofhenderson.com/information-technology/ smart-city-strategy
Strategic Focus Areas and Approach	• Increased quality of life • Focus on education, including learning opportunities and digital literacy • Increased economic competitiveness • Use of technology to improve public safety and transportation • Use of smart water meters to promote improved water management

Country	United States
City	Las Vegas, Nevada
Website	https://innovate.vegas/Programs-Projects/ smart-city
Strategic Focus Areas and Approach	• Creation of an innovation district • Public safety • Increased economic growth • Improved transportation options • Education programs • Healthcare • Programs for underserved communities • Use of open data

SOUTH AMERICA

Country	Argentina
City	Buenos Aires
Website	www.buenosaires.gob.ar
Strategic Focus Areas and Approach	• Transform public administration • Make the focus citizen-centered in all projects • Digitize government paperwork • Improve public transit system • Make data-driven decisions • Use open data

Country	Brazil
City	Rio de Janeiro
Website	http://prefeitura.rio
Strategic Focus Areas and Approach	• Improve the smart infrastructure • Increase civic engagement • Integrate city services and utilities into one operations center • Improve education • Focus on public safety and emergency response • Use open data

Country	Chile
City	Santiago
Website	www.gobiernosantiago.cl
Strategic Focus Areas and Approach	• Transition to clean and renewable energy • Improve transportation infrastructure and options • Increase economic opportunities • Enhance the promotion of culture and inclusion • Use open data

Appendix B
Smart City Organizations

Though the smart city movement is relatively new, it's a good sign that an increasing number of national and international organizations have formed in support of smart cities and more are emerging. For any industry, this is typically a reflection of maturation. As diverse stakeholders begin to coalesce around common interests and agendas, they align and form under various entities. The way to move ideas forward on a broad regional or international basis requires the creation of advocacy organizations. In this appendix, I've created a list of some of the more active organizations in the smart city domain as a way of providing a sample for you of where people and organizations are focusing. I regret, and apologize in advance for, any obvious omissions. By the way, there's still plenty of opportunity to form your own organization. Consider it, particularly if you don't find one that reflects your interests.

Organization	Alliance for Innovation
Website	www.transformgov.org
Summary	The Alliance for Innovation works to inspire innovation in local government by connecting a network of leaders across North America. It seeks to advance communities by implementing new technologies and making use of innovative solutions. The alliance works diligently to educate local governments on building an innovative culture and also provides support and a wide variety of access to learning opportunities.

Organization	C40 Cities
Website	www.c40.org
Summary	C40 Cities connects 94 of the world's cities in order to take bold climate action, leading the way toward a healthier and more sustainable future. Representing more than 700 million citizens and one-quarter of the global economy, mayors of the C40 cities are committed to delivering on the most ambitious goals of the Paris Agreement at the local level, as well as to cleaning the air you breathe.

Organization	Center for City Solutions
Website	https://www.nlc.org/program-initiative/center-for-city-solutions
Summary	Center for City Solutions provides research, education and analysis on key topics and trends that impact the people in America's communities. They help local leaders build strong communities by expanding their capacity, elevating successful city practices, providing in-depth research and tools, and finding and implementing on-the-ground solutions.

Organization	Center for Smart Cities and Regions
Website	https://ifis.asu.edu/content/center-smart-cities-and-regions
Summary	The mission of the Center for Smart Cities and Regions (CSCR) is to advance urban and regional innovation to make more inclusive, vibrant, resilient, and sustainable communities. The center collaborates with researchers, policymakers, planners, entrepreneurs, industry, and the public to enhance the ability of cities and regions to responsibly use emerging technological infrastructures and improve quality of life.

Organization	Center for Urban Innovation
Website	www.aspeninstitute.org/programs/center-urban-innovation
Summary	The Aspen Institute Center for Urban Innovation is a network hub that advances the effort to develop, regulate, and evaluate urban technologies. The center works to connect people from various sectors — nonprofit organizations, emerging businesses, and city leaders, for example — in order to promote human flourishing and digital infrastructures. It offers a place where people can collaborate and ask next-generation questions to find solutions together in order to promote the development of smart cities.

Organization	Chilean Innovation Lab
Website	`http://lab.gob.cl`
Summary	The Chilean Innovation Lab seeks to promote practices that become sustainable in Chile and that will mobilize an ecosystem of partners to address priority issues in the country. The government laboratory's primary focus is on creating new and innovative relationships between the government and the people through various methods. This includes a network of public innovators that allows anyone to contribute and articulate ideas that could further the objective of improving services that Chile provides to people.

Organization	Cities Today Institute
Website	`https://cities-today.com/institute`
Summary	The mission of the Cities Today Institute (CTI) is to assist community leaders as they design and implement policies, strategies, and projects by providing training and leadership forums, peer-to-peer mentoring, a shared research library, and funding partnerships.

Organization	Cities Alliance
Website	`https://www.citiesalliance.org`
Summary	Cities Alliance is a global partnership fighting urban poverty and promoting the role of cities. Cities Alliance promotes long-term programmatic approaches that support national and local governments to develop appropriate policy frameworks, strengthen local skills and capacity, undertake strategic city planning, and facilitate investment.

Organization	City Possible
Website	`https://citypossible.com`
Summary	City Possible is a model for urban innovation in which a global network of cities, companies, and communities work together to promote inclusive and sustainable urban co-development focused on addressing pressing urban challenges

Organization	Code for America
Website	www.codeforamerica.org
Summary	Code for America uses the principles and practices of the digital age to improve how government serves the American public, and how the public improves government. The organization enlists technology and design professionals to work with city governments in the United States in order to build open-source applications and promote openness, participation, and efficiency in government. It has grown into a cross-sector network of public sector change agents as well as a platform for civic hacking. International versions exist within the Code for All network: https://codeforall.org.

Organization	Coalition for Urban Transitions
Website	https://urbantransitions.global
Summary	The Coalition for Urban Transitions aims to drive the shift away from business-as-usual by empowering national governments with the evidence-based rationale and policy tools they need in order to prioritize more compact, connected, clean urban development. In this way, the initiative helps catalyze and inform implementation of the Sustainable Development Goals (SDGs), the New Urban Agenda, and Nationally Determined Contributions (NDCs) to meet the goals of the Paris Agreement.

Organization	Data Smart City Solutions
Website	https://datasmart.ash.harvard.edu
Summary	Data Smart City Solutions is working to catalyze the adoption of data projects on the local government level by serving as a central resource for cities interested in this emerging field. The group highlights best practices, top innovators, and promising case studies while also connecting leading industry, academic, and government officials. Its research focus is the intersection of government and data, ranging from open data and predictive analytics to civic engagement technology.

Organization	Digi.City
Website	www.digi.city
Summary	Digi.City is a platform designed to inform, inspire, and connect leaders as cities advance in the digital age. It brings together the public, private, and academic sectors; shares tools; and advocates for policies and programs that create more connected, more equitable, and more accessible communities.

Organization	EUROCITIES
Website	www.eurocities.eu
Summary	EUROCITIES is the network of major European cities. Its members are the elected local and municipal governments of major European cities. Through thematic forums (including issues related to smart cities) as well as a wide range of working groups, projects, activities, and events, the network offers members a platform for sharing knowledge and exchanging ideas. EUROCITIES influences and works with EU institutions to respond to common issues that affect the day-to-day lives of Europeans.

Organization	Global Resilient Cities Network
Website	https://www.rockpa.org/project/global-resilient-cities-network/
Summary	The Global Resilient Cities Network is a city-led organization that drives urban resilience action to protect vulnerable communities from climate change and other physical, social and economic urban adversities and challenges.

Organization	Global Smart Cities Alliance
Website	https://globalsmartcitiesalliance.org
Summary	The Global Smart Cities Alliance unites municipal, regional, and national governments with private-sector partners and cities' residents around a shared set of principles for the responsible and ethical use of smart city technologies. The alliance establishes and advances global policy standards to help accelerate best practices, mitigate potential risks, and foster greater openness and public trust.

Organization	IEEE Smart Cities
Website	https://smartcities.ieee.org
Summary	IEEE Smart Cities brings together the Institute of Electrical and Electronics Engineers' broad array of technical societies and organizations to advance the state of the art for smart city technologies for the benefit of society and to set the global standard in this regard. It does this by serving as a neutral broker of information among industry, academic, and government stakeholders.

Organization	Leading Cities
Website	https://leadingcities.org
Summary	Leading Cities is a global nonprofit organization that improves the quality of life in cities by the development of smart ecosystems that are sustainable, responsible, and inclusive. Its approach combines theoretical thinking, applied science analysis, and the identification of disruptive technologies and social patterns.

Organization	MetroLab Network
Website	https://metrolabnetwork.org
Summary	MetroLab Network is a collaborative of 29 cities, five counties, and 35 universities focused on civic innovation. The network believes that partnerships between local governments and universities are critical when it comes to bringing about urban transformation and that national and international collaboration will streamline civic innovation.

Organization	Metropolis
Website	https://www.metropolis.org/
Summary	Metropolis serves as the hub and platform for metropolises to connect, share experiences, and mobilize on a wide range of local and global issues, in addition to being the focal point of worldwide experience and expertise on metropolitan governance.

Organization	NewCities
Website	`http://newcities.org`
Summary	NewCities is a global nonprofit organization committed to shaping a better urban future. The organization has extensive experience in the development of innovative content that is most important in emerging urban trends. It hosts major events, knowledge-sharing platforms, and ongoing research sessions in order to identify the most pressing topics related to cities and urban development.

Organization	Public Technology Institute
Website	`www.pti.org`
Summary	Public Technology Institute supports local government executives and elected officials through research, education, executive-level consulting services and national recognition programs. Their expertise is in fields including IT, citizen engagement, E-government, GIS, public safety technology, energy and sustainability.

Organization	SMART Africa
Website	`https://smartafrica.org/`
Summary	SMART Africa is a bold and innovative commitment from African Heads of State and Government to accelerate sustainable socioeconomic development on the continent, ushering Africa into a knowledge economy through affordable access to broadband and usage of information and communications technologies.

Organization	Smart Cities Association
Website	`www.smartcitiesassociation.org`
Summary	The Smart Cities Association is a nonprofit organization created by community and industry experts to promote smart city roadmaps and reference models. It also seeks to ensure sustainable development of the digital economy of cities. City residents engage with the association with the help of the Experience tool, which enables input on different urban needs such as transportation, health, safety, environment, and tourism.

Organization	Smart Cities Council
Website	https://smartcitiescouncil.com
Summary	The Smart Cities Council is a network of leading companies advised by top universities, laboratories, and standards bodies that seeks to promote a world in which cities make use of intelligent design, digital technology, and smart/sustainable resources. It provides an online collaborative platform in order to assess a city's needs, stakeholders, and project plans. The council enables cross-city connections, which provide information on what projects other cities are working on. It also hosts conferences and provides educational opportunities.

Organization	Smart Cities Global Network
Website	https://scgn.smartdubai.ae
Summary	The Smart Cities Global Network is an international network of smart city stakeholders that connects cities and offers a comprehensive global platform for exchanging views, insights, and ideas on the best mechanisms to create the smart cities of the future.

Organization	Smarter Together
Website	www.smarter-together.eu
Summary	Smarter Together is a project funded by the H2020 programme of the European Union that focuses on five concrete areas of co-created and integrated smart solutions in cities: citizen engagement, district heating and renewable energy, holistic refurbishment, smart data, and e-mobility.

Organization	SmartNations Foundation
Website	www.smartnations.com
Summary	The SmartNations Foundation is a nonprofit organization developed in order to accelerate the adoption of emerging digital technologies and systems around the world in order to create a better world. The foundation seeks to enable full participation in the global digital transformation economy and society. It works closely with both emerging and developed countries to ensure that they're well prepared for the fast-evolving global era.

Organization	United Cities and Local Governments (UCLG)
Website	`www.uclg.org/en`
Summary	UCLG is the largest organization of local and regional governments in the world and committed to representing, defending, and amplifying the voices of local and regional governments to leave no one and no place behind.

Organization	United Smart Cities
Website	`www.unitedsmartcities.org/global-programs/u4ssc-ip`
Summary	United Smart Cities is a United Nations initiative coordinated by the International Telecommunication Union (ITU), United Nations Economic Commission for Europe (UNECE), and United Nations Human Settlements Programme (UN-Habitat) to accelerate the transformation of cities globally to be smarter and more sustainable with better quality of life for its citizens.

Organization	World Smart City
Website	`www.worldsmartcity.org`
Summary	The World Smart City organization's main objective is to further the development of smart cities in a common approach founded on standards. By hosting an annual World Smart City Forum event each year, the organization brings together a wide variety of groups, from the public sector as well as the private sector, seeking to promote innovative solutions within their communities. The group emphasizes the need for cities to increase efficiency in terms of how they operate and make use of their resources.

Organization	What Works Cities
Website	`www.bloomberg.org/program/government-innovation/what-works-cities`
Summary	The What Works Cities initiative tackles the challenge that city leaders lack the tools to use data and evidence to improve how governing gets done. By providing robust technical support, access to expertise, and peer-to-peer learning to cities, Bloomberg Philanthropies is encouraging mayors and cities to better use data and evidence to engage the public, improve services, evaluate progress, and fund "what works."

Organization	World Resources Institute Ross Center
Website	https://wrirosscities.org/
Summary	WRI Ross Center helps create accessible, equitable, healthy, and resilient urban areas for people, businesses, and the environment to thrive. Together with partners, they enable more connected, compact and coordinated cities.

Appendix C
Open Data Portals

ncreasing numbers of governments across the world are making many of their datasets available online. The concept that government data should be accessible to everyone without limitation and be freely used, reused, and redistributed is called *open data*. In this appendix, I've assembled a relatively random list of open data links that represent almost every area of the planet. It includes open data for both countries and cities. I encourage you to explore many of them. It's a great way to understand different cultures and regions. You'll see what areas have in common and also where they differ. Depending on your interest, open data can provide a variety of value, ranging from satisfying simple curiously to leveraging data to build solutions.

AFRICA

Country	Africa
City/State/Region	n/a
Open Data Portal	https://open.africa

Country	Ghana
City/State/Region	n/a
Open Data Portal	https://data.gov.gh

Country	Kenya
City/State/Region	n/a
Open Data Portal	www.opendata.go.ke

Country	Morocco
City/State/Region	n/a
Open Data Portal	www.data.gov.ma/fr

Country	Nigeria
City/State/Region	n/a
Open Data Portal	http://nigeria.opendataforafrica.org

Country	South Africa
City/State/Region	Cape Town
Open Data Portal	https://web1.capetown.gov.za/web1/opendataportal/Default

ASIA

Country	Bangladesh
City/State/Region	n/a
Open Data Portal	http://data.gov.bd

Country	China
City/State/Region	Hong Kong
Open Data Portal	https://data.gov.hk

Country	India
City/State/Region	n/a
Open Data Portal	http://data.gov.in

Country	Indonesia
City/State/Region	n/a
Open Data Portal	http://data.go.id

Country	Philippines
City/State/Region	n/a
Open Data Portal	http://data.gov.ph

Country	Singapore
City/State/Region	n/a
Open Data Portal	http://data.gov.sg

Country	South Korea
City/State/Region	Seoul
Open Data Portal	http://data.seoul.go.kr

Country	Thailand
City/State/Region	n/a
Open Data Portal	http://catalog.opendata.in.th

AUSTRALIA AND NEW ZEALAND

Country	Australia
City/State/Region	New South Wales
Open Data Portal	http://data.nsw.gov.au

Country	Australia
City/State/Region	Sydney
Open Data Portal	https://data.cityofsydney.nsw.gov.au

Country	Australia
City/State/Region	Western Australia
Open Data Portal	https://data.wa.gov.au

Country	New Zealand
City/State/Region	n/a
Open Data Portal	http://cat.open.org.nz/category/dataset

Country	New Zealand
City/State/Region	Auckland
Open Data Portal	https://data-aucklandcouncil.opendata.arcgis.com

EASTERN EUROPE AND RUSSIA

Country	Russia
City/State/Region	n/a
Open Data Portal	http://opengovdata.ru

Country	Ukraine
City/State/Region	n/a
Open Data Portal	http://data.gov.ua

Country	Moldova
City/State/Region	n/a
Open Data Portal	http://data.gov.md

WESTERN EUROPE

Country	Austria
City/State/Region	Vienna
Open Data Portal	http://data.wien.gv.at

Country	Finland
City/State/Region	n/a
Open Data Portal	https://www.betaavoindata.fi/fi

Country	Finland
City/State/Region	Helsinki
Open Data Portal	https://hri.fi/fi

Country	France
City/State/Region	Paris
Open Data Portal	http://opendata.paris.fr

Country	Germany
City/State/Region	n/a
Open Data Portal	http://offenedaten.de

Country	Germany
City/State/Region	Berlin
Open Data Portal	http://daten.berlin.de

Country	Germany
City/State/Region	Hamburg
Open Data Portal	http://daten.hamburg.de

Country	Ireland
City/State/Region	Dublin
Open Data Portal	https://data.smartdublin.ie

Country	Italy
City/State/Region	Bari
Open Data Portal	http://opendata.comune.bari.it

Country	Italy
City/State/Region	Bologna
Open Data Portal	http://dati.comune.bologna.it

Country	Netherlands
City/State/Region	n/a
Open Data Portal	http://opendatanederland.org

Country	Sweden
City/State/Region	Stockholm
Open Data Portal	http://open.stockholm.se

Country	United Kingdom
City/State/Region	London
Open Data Portal	https://data.london.gov.uk

Country	United Kingdom
City/State/Region	Manchester
Open Data Portal	http://www.manchester.gov.uk/info/500215/open_data

MIDDLE EAST

Country	Bahrain
City/State/Region	n/a
Open Data Portal	https://www.data.gov.bh

Country	Iran
City/State/Region	n/a
Open Data Portal	https://iranopendata.org/en

Country	Israel
City/State/Region	Tel Aviv
Open Data Portal	https://opendata.tel-aviv.gov.il/he/Pages/home.aspx

Country	Kingdom of Saudi Arabia
City/State/Region	n/a
Open Data Portal	https://data.gov.sa/en/home

Country	United Arab Emirates
City/State/Region	n/a
Open Data Portal	https://bayanat.ae

Country	Qatar
City/State/Region	n/a
Open Data Portal	www.data.gov.qa/pages/home

Country	United Arab Emirates
City/State/Region	Dubai
Open Data Portal	www.dm.gov.ae/en/OpenData/Pages/Default.aspx

NORTH AMERICA

Country	Canada
City/State/Region	Alberta
Open Data Portal	http://data.alberta.ca

Country	Canada
City/State/Region	Toronto
Open Data Portal	www.toronto.ca/open

Country	Mexico
City/State/Region	n/a
Open Data Portal	https://datos.gob.mx

Country	United States
City/State/Region	Alabama
Open Data Portal	http://open.alabama.gov

Country	United States
City/State/Region	Ann Arbor, Michigan
Open Data Portal	www.a2gov.org/services/data/Pages/default.aspx

Country	United States
City/State/Region	Baltimore, Maryland
Open Data Portal	http://data.baltimorecity.gov

Country	United States
City/State/Region	Boston, Massachusetts
Open Data Portal	https://data.cityofboston.gov

Country	United States
City/State/Region	California
Open Data Portal	http://www.data.ca.gov

Country	United States
City/State/Region	Detroit, Michigan
Open Data Portal	https://data.detroitmi.gov

Country	United States
City/State/Region	Houston, Texas
Open Data Portal	http://data.codeforhouston.com

Country	United States
City/State/Region	Nashville, Tennessee
Open Data Portal	https://data.nashville.gov

Country	United States
City/State/Region	New Orleans
Open Data Portal	http://data.nola.gov

Country	United States
City/State/Region	New York, New York
Open Data Portal	http://nycopendata.socrata.com

Country	United States
City/State/Region	Philadelphia, Pennsylvania
Open Data Portal	www.opendataphilly.org

Country	United States
City/State/Region	Palo Alto, California
Open Data Portal	https://data.cityofpaloalto.org/home

SOUTH AMERICA

Country	Argentina
City/State/Region	Buenos Aires
Open Data Portal	http://data.buenosaires.gob.ar

Country	Brazil
City/State/Region	n/a
Open Data Portal	http://dados.gov.br

Country	Chile
City/State/Region	n/a
Open Data Portal	www.consejotransparencia.cl/consejo/site/edic/base/port/pcatalogo.html

Appendix D

Solutions Built on Open Data

Among the top characteristics of a smart city is the effective management and use of data. In a digital world, data is an input that is powering capabilities and an output that is created as a product of activities. The volume, velocity, and variety of data continues to grow. At this scale, it even has a name: It's called *big data*. Original, eh?

City governments are catching up with the private sector by recognizing the value of data and beginning to leverage it to their advantage. After all, cities create an abundance of data. It may be the only thing that every city has in abundance. (I discuss the value of city data in detail in Chapter 9.)

Data that is made freely available by governments to everyone to use as they want, with no restrictions, is called *open data*. One of the most valuable ways in which open data is being used is for the creation of useful applications. Individuals and organizations of all kinds are leveraging the variety and volume of data to create all manner of utilities for city staff and community members. Rather than wait for a government to build a particular solution, open data empowers anyone to step up and generate value. It's a win-win. It produces important capabilities for a community typically without cost to the government, and these new applications can result in the creation of new businesses and employment.

The creation of solutions through open data is a global trend, and it can be a defining quality of your smart city efforts. I've selected just a few examples to help you become educated and inspired by what is possible. You'll see that I provide a link to the solution and also identify the main sources of open data for each one. Though most examples are in a city context, I've included a few others to illustrate the scope of uses in other types of governments. If you want to explore even more applications of open data, at the end of this section you'll find a link to almost 600 solutions built on open data in the European Union.

Name	A Healthier Commute
Website	https://open.canada.ca/en/apps/healthier-commute
Description	Discover how your daily single-person car commute affects your health, your wallet's health, and your community's health.
Open Data Source(s)	Natural Resources Canada Statistics Canada

Name	AIRNOW
Website	https://developer.epa.gov/airnow-widget
Description	Find location-specific reports on current and forecasted air quality for both ozone and fine particle pollution. The software creates a widget that can be easily embedded in any website.
Open Data Source(s)	US Environmental Protection Agency (EPA)

Name	Citymapper
Website	https://citymapper.com
Description	This public transit app and mapping service integrates data for all urban modes of transport — from walking and cycling to driving — with an emphasis on public transportation.
Open Data Source(s)	Local transit authorities

Name	Civic Insight
Website	http://civicinsight.com
Description	City data is used to present easy-to-consume information for community members and other stakeholders so that they can understand what construction and other related activities are happening in their neighborhood.
Open Data Source(s)	City permitting and related systems

Name	Clear My Record
Website	www.clearmyrecord.org
Description	This criminal record clearance application moves from the unworkable petition-based process that was in place to an expedited and automatic process.
Open Data Source(s)	California Department of Justice (CADOJ)

Name	Food Security Portal
Website	www.foodsecurityportal.org
Description	This suite of tools supports policymakers' ability to respond to the risks presented by food crises and to increase resilience to these risks, particularly among poor and rural populations.
Open Data Source(s)	US Department of Agriculture Economic Research Service Foreign Agricultural Service

Name	InfoAmazonia Colombia
Website	https://colombia.infoamazonia.org
Description	This transparency tool is helping Colombian officials reduce forest clearing to zero net levels by 2030 as part of the country's Amazon Vision Program.
Open Data Source(s)	Satellite information Institute of Hydrology, Meteorology, and Environmental Studies (IDEAM) Data journalists

Name	Neighborhood Scout
Website	www.neighborhoodscout.com
Description	This comprehensive database of hyperlocal real estate information is available to help home buyers decide where to live.
Open Data Source(s)	Includes: • US Bureau of the Census • US Department of Justice • National Center for Education Statistics • US Geological Service

Name	OpenSpending
Website	https://openspending.org
Description	On this global platform, you can search, visualize, and analyze fiscal data in the public sphere.
Open Data Source(s)	Various public agencies

Name	Parkopedia
Website	https://en.parkopedia.co.uk
Description	Users are given real-time parking information about more than 60 million parking spaces worldwide.
Open Data Source(s)	Local authorities Parking facility operators

Name	Poverty in NYC
Website	www1.nyc.gov/site/opportunity/poverty-in-nyc/poverty-in-nyc.page
Description	This tool better targets antipoverty initiatives and designs more effective metrics in measuring success.
Open Data Source(s)	American Community Survey

Name	Shoothill Gaugemap
Website	www.gaugemap.co.uk
Description	Near real-time data is presented on river, flow, and groundwater levels in the British Isles.
Open Data Source(s)	UK Environmental Agency Scottish Environment Protection Agency Natural Resources Wales Irish Office of Public Works

Name	SpotCrime
Website	https://spotcrime.com
Description	This crime data aggregator maps crime incidents and plots them on Google Maps.
Open Data Source(s)	City police departments

Name	The National Address Website
Website	https://adresse.data.gouv.fr
Description	This database is intended to bring together all the geolocated addresses of France.
Open Data Source(s)	IGN La Poste Etalab OpenStreetMap

Name	Urban Waste Water Treatment Directive
Website	https://uwwtd.eu
Description	This dissemination platform provides detailed information about urban wastewater areas, collection systems, treatment plants, discharge points, and environmentally sensitive areas.
Open Data Source(s)	European Environment Information and Observation Network European Environment Agency

Name	European Open Data Use Cases
Website	www.europeandataportal.eu/en/impact-studies/use-cases
Description	This collection holds almost 600 examples of open data in practice.
Open Data Source(s)	Various

Appendix E

City Performance Dashboards

As cities increasingly focus on higher performance, they're doing a better job of being transparent about progress. By publishing the targets and goals of an agency, leaders and staff can be more accountable. Traditionally, many publish annual reports in the form of printed books, or PDFs posted online. This continues to be the most common approach. However, more cities are beginning to take advantage of dynamic online performance dashboards that are continuously updated. Some use interfaces directly from source systems; others, from open data; and many enter the data manually. A performance dashboard is a management system that communicates objectives, goals, metrics, initiatives, and tasks. It enables a wide range of stakeholders to measure, monitor, and manage city operations in order to meet desired goals. The following is a list of city and country examples of government performance dashboards. Pay attention to the different styles and options. Perhaps some of the ideas here will inspire you to create your own dashboard.

ASIA

Country	China
City/State/Region	Hong Kong
Dashboard Link	https://data.gov.hk/en/city-dashboard

Country	India
City/State/Region	Hyderabad
Dashboard Link	https://tabsoft.co/2I7fdv0

Country	Indonesia
City/State/Region	Bandung
Dashboard Link	http://data.bandung.go.id/dashboard

Country	Japan
City/State/Region	n/a
Dashboard Link	https://dashboard.e-stat.go.jp/en/

AUSTRALIA AND NEW ZEALAND

Country	Australia
City/State/Region	Gold Coast
Dashboard Link	http://dashboard.cityofgoldcoast.com.au

Country	Australia
City/State/Region	Melbourne
Dashboard Link	https://www.melbourne.vic.gov.au/about-council/our-performance/Pages/performance-dashboard.aspx

Country	Australia
City/State/Region	Sydney
Dashboard Link	www.greater.sydney/dashboard

Country	New Zealand
City/State/Region	Auckland
Dashboard Link	www.aucklandcouncil.govt.nz/about-auckland-council/performance-transparency/Pages/default.aspx

EUROPE

Country	Ireland
City/State/Region	Dublin
Dashboard Link	www.dublindashboard.ie/pages/index

Country	Netherlands
City/State/Region	Amsterdam
Dashboard Link	http://citydashboard.waag.org

Country	United Kingdom
City/State/Region	n/a
Dashboard Link	www.gov.uk/performance

Country	United Kingdom
City/State/Region	Bristol
Dashboard Link	www.bristolonecity.com/dashboard

Country	United Kingdom
City/State/Region	Manchester
Dashboard Link	https://tabsoft.co/2I50nE9

MIDDLE EAST

Country	Bahrain
City/State/Region	n/a
Dashboard Link	www.data.gov.bh/en/Indices

Country	United Arab Emirates
City/State/Region	n/a
Dashboard Link	https://kpis.moccae.gov.ae/ — /page/home

NORTH AMERICA

Country	Canada
City/State/Region	Edmonton
Dashboard Link	https://dashboard.edmonton.ca

Country	Canada
City/State/Region	Vancouver
Dashboard Link	www.metrovancouver.org/dashboards/services/Pages/default.aspx

Country	United States
City/State/Region	Austin, Texas
Dashboard Link	https://cityofaustin.github.io/PerformanceATX/

Country	United States
City/State/Region	Honolulu, Hawaii
Dashboard Link	www.honolulu.gov/dashboard

Country	United States
City/State/Region	Los Angeles, California
Dashboard Link	https://sites.google.com/a/lacity.org/ mayors-dashboard/

Country	United States
City/State/Region	San Diego, California
Dashboard Link	https://performance.sandiego.gov/

Country	United States
City/State/Region	Seattle, Washington
Dashboard Link	https://performance.seattle.gov/stories/s/ Performance-Seattle/596j-asv2/

Country	United States
City/State/Region	Syracuse, New York
Dashboard Link	http://dashboards.syrgov.net/

SOUTH AMERICA

Country	Colombia
City/State/Region	Bogota
Dashboard Link	http://tablerocontrolciudadano.veeduriadistrital.gov.co:3838/TCC/

Index

Numbers

3D-printed homes, 61–62

5G technology, 73, 160, 164–165, 181

9/11 Commission Report, 237

A

academia, 120, 136, 145

acute shock, 229

advanced metering infrastructure (AMI), 190–191

affordable housing, 59–61, 109, 255

Africa. *See also* Konza Technopolis (Kenya)

  air-based drone delivery in, 69–70

  median age in, 51

  open data portals in, 333–334

  smart cities in, 42–43, 311–312

  urbanization of, 21–22, 50

agents-of-change, 140

agile project management, 122, 144

air quality

  AIRNOW open data reporting on, 346

  challenges related to, 30

  discussion, 17, 57, 253, 277, 297

air-based drones, 68–70, 308

Alliance for Healthy Cities, 254, 305

Alliance for Innovation, 323

American Cities Initiative, 138

Amsterdam (Netherlands), 42–43, 315

analog, 157–158, 160

annual budgeting, 114–116

anonymization, 243

application programming interfaces (APIs)

  for accessing data, 217

  discussion, 198–199, 201

  FIWARE, 199–201, 203

  GIS and, 202–203

  open data and, 202–203

  standardization of, 112

appointed leaders, 81–82, 148

aqueducts, 134–135

Arab Spring, 168–169

architectural review board (ARB), 270

architecture, 28

Argentina, 321, 343

artificial intelligence (AI)

  challenges related to, 171

  discussion, 19, 48, 160, 162, 169

  machine learning and, 170

  robotics and, 171

Arup Group, 231

Asia

  blockchain technology in, 175

  economic shifts in, 47

  open data portals in, 334–335

  smart cities in, 312–313

  urbanization of, 21, 50

Aspen Institute Center for Urban Innovation, 324

Association of Southeast Asian Nations, 195

Atlas of Innovation Districts, 147

Australia

  open data portals in, 335–336

  performance dashboard, 352

  smart cities in, 313–314

urbanization of, 21

automated license plate recognition (ALPR), 242

autonomous vehicles (AVs)

  automation levels in, 177

  challenges related to, 178

  data exhaust, 205–206

  on-demand, 266

  discussion, 19, 67, 160, 175–176

  future of, 303–304

  supply chain management and, 67–68

  wireless communication and, 177–178

B

back-end databases, 112

Bahrain, 339, 354

Ban Ki-moon, 39

Bangladesh, 334

Bannister, Luke, 178

Bell, Alexander Graham, 73

Ben & Jerry's, 84

Berlin (Germany), 69–70, 146

bicycles, 68–69, 187

big data, 169, 171, 206, 345

Bill & Melinda Gates Foundation, 59

biomass power, 71

biotechnology, 160

birthrates, 19–20, 51

Bitcoin, 171–172

"Bitcoin: A Peer-to-Peer Electronic Cash System," 171

blockchain technology

  applications for, 173

  discussion, 160, 171–172

blockchain technology
  (continued)
  government use of, 173–175
  implementation and regulation
    of, 175
Bloomberg, Michael, 138
Bloomberg Philanthropies
    I-Teams, 138
Bluetooth, 164–165, 183
bonds, 117
Brazil, 343
British Standards Institute, 29
buildings. *See also* green
    buildings
  AMI in, 190–191
  discussion, 71–72
  KPIs, 102
  regulations governing, 113
  system interdependency
    and, 49
built environment, 48
bureaucracy, 60, 107, 118
Burj Khalifa, 71
business activities, 12
business analysis, 121–122,
    124–125
business intelligence, 212
business licensing, 112–113
business-to-business (B2B)
    interactions, 163
business-to-consumer (B2C)
    interactions, 163

C

C40 Cities, 323
California Consumer Privacy Act
    (CCPA), 291
California Urban Forest
    Council, 250
Cambridge (England), 146
Canada, 71, 146, 319, 340, 354
Canterbury Bankstown
    (Australia), 313–314
carbon emissions

discussion, 55–56, 259,
    269, 297
green cities and, 248
light rail systems and, 68
Carney, John C., Jr., 173
Caterpillar, 84
Center for City Solutions, 324
Center for Smart Cities and
    Regions (CSCR), 324
challenge-based
    procurement, 120
Chan, Benson, 185–186
charities, 116
cheat sheet, 6
chief data officer (CDO), 209,
    223–224
chief information security
    officer, 240
chief resiliency officer (CRO), 230
chief sustainability officer
    (CO), 248
Chile, 325, 343
China
  carbon emissions in, 55
  discussion, 21, 134, 155, 189
  electric-powered vehicles
    in, 67
  migration and, 50
  open data portals in, 334
  performance dashboard, 351
  urbanization of, 21–22, 50
chronic stress, 229
circular economy, 258
cities
  building of, 14–15, 48, 268
  central role of, 1–2
  changing needs of, 45–46
  complex requirements of,
    47–48
  constitutions of, 81
  defined by people, 28–30
  factors shaping, 27
  future of, 2, 30, 295–296
  GDP generated by, 22,
    268, 297

growth patterns of, 24, 50
historical context of, 12–14, 21
interconnectedness of,
    72–73, 157
land use by, 12, 268
legal constitution of, 81
optimism regarding, 245–246
origins of, 11–14
percentage of planet in, 1,
    22, 40
population growth of, 21, 268,
    296–297
revenue and taxes in, 115
unsolved challenges to, 30–31
Cities Alliance, 325
Cities Coalition for Digital
    Rights, 160
Cities Today Institute, 325
citizen scientists, 273
city administrator, 81–82, 85–86
city leadership. *See also* smart
    city team
  characteristics of, 81
  essential for smart cities, 81
  main parts of, 81–82
  management versus, 80–81
  vision statement
    creation, 83–84
    examples, 84–85
    massive transformative
      purpose (MTP), 80
    overview, 79–82
city manager, 81–82, 85–86
City Possible, 325
city resiliency framework
    (CRF), 231
CityBridge, 118–119
CITYkeys, 103
Citymapper solution, 346
civic engagement
  apps for, 65
  challenges related to, 30
  discussion, 62–64, 267, 270
  forms of

Neolithic Revolution, 14

NEOM (Saudi Arabia), 318

Netherlands, 338, 353. *See also*
Amsterdam (Netherlands)

neurotechnology, 160

New York City (US)

9/11 attacks on, 237

Cities Coalition for Digital
Rights initiative and, 160

free Wi-Fi in, 118–119

grid design system in, 56

skyline, 71

before urbanization, 23

New Zealand, 336, 352–353

NewCities, 174, 329

Nexledger, 174

nexus points, 49

Nigeria, 334

noise, 69, 253, 277

nomadic lifestyle, 11, 14

nonagricultural activities, 12

nongovernmental organizations
(NGOs), 120, 269–270

nonprofit housing, 61

North America

economic shifts after WWII
in, 47

innovation districts in, 146

open data portals in, 340

performance dashboard, 354

smart cities in, 319–320

urbanization of, 21

North Sydney (Australia), 314

Norway, 67

not-in-my-backyard (NIMBY), 59

nuclear power, 70

O

Obama, Barack, 168

oceans, 39–40

oil, 13

on-demand transportation, 68

online payments, 162

Open & Agile Smart Cities
(OASC), 203

open data

APIs and, 202–203

disaster warning systems
and, 232

discussion, 215–216, 333, 345

FIWARE, 199–201, 203

future of, 299

hackathons and, 148

policies regarding, 112

principles of, 216

public safety and, 236

solutions, 346–350

Open Data Charter, 217–218

open data portals

in Africa, 333–334

APIs for accessing, 217

in Asia, 334–335

discussion, 65

in Europe, 336–339

in Middle East, 339–340

in North America, 340–342

open government, 216

open innovation, 151

open source software, 121

OpenSpending, 348

operations/program
management, 87–88, 103

Orbital Insight, 222–223

O'Reilly, Tim, 155

organizations. See specific
organizations

Our World in Data, 218

P

pandemics, 228, 232–233

Parag, Khanna, 268

Paramel, Renil, 185–186

Paris, 187–188

parking, 164–165, 170

Parkopedia, 348

parks, 136, 248–249, 256, 348

partial home rental, 61

participatory design, 65–66

partnership, 39

Patient Protection and
Affordable Care Act, 159

peace, 39–40

people, 32, 39

per-hour rental cars, 68

person-to-person (P2P)
interactions, 163, 181

Petronas Towers, 71

Philippines, 195, 222–223, 335

pilots, 143

Plato, 227

Pokémon Go, 161

police, 17, 234. *See also* public
safety

policies

cybersecurity, 240

discussion, 107–111

governing data, 211–212

smart city, 111–112

as urban innovation
trigger, 141

politics, 14, 63

Pont du Gard, 135

Ponte Morandi bridge, 52

population growth, 19–21

poverty

discussion, 15, 30, 109,
269, 348

extreme, 62, 278

in SDG, 39–40

Poverty in NYC, 348

Predator XP drone, 179

privacy

AI and, 171

dangers of ignoring, 291–292

discussion, 32–33, 241–
242, 277

drones and, 180

sanitation. *See* waste management

Santayana, George, 11

Santiago (Chile), 321

Saudi Arabia, 42, 339

Schmidt, Eric, 241

Schwab, Klaus, 160

self-driving vehicles. *See* autonomous vehicles (AV)

self-sufficiency, 256–257

semiconductors, 18

sensors
  AI and, 170
  discussion, 33
  IoT solutions and, 164–165
  low-data-rate networks and, 181–182
  privacy and data from, 111, 235, 242–243

Seoul (South Korea), 313

September 11, 2001 attacks, 237

service fees, 115–116

service worker class, 60

Shakespeare, William, 1, 28

Shanghai (China), 22

sharing economy, 68–69

shipping container homes, 61

Shoothill Gaugemap, 349

Sicinius, 28

Sidewalk Labs, 241–242

Sigfox, 186–187

signage, 196

Silicon Valley, 146

Singapore, 38, 189, 195, 313, 335

Singularity University, 80

sky cities, 61

skyscrapers, 71, 135

small cities, 33, 36–37

SMART acronym, 95, 210

SMART Africa, 329

smart airports, 39

smart campuses, 39

smart cities. See also specific smart cities
  core values of, 31
  defined by people, 29–30, 107
  definitions, 27–28, 31–33
  discussion, 1, 4, 27, 246
  future of, 296–297
  optimism regarding, 245–246, 278–279
  in SDG, 41

Smart Cities Association, 329

Smart Cities Council, 31, 330

Smart Cities for Dummies (Reichental)
  cheat sheet, 6
  icons used in, 3–4
  information beyond, 6
  structure of, 4–6
  updates to, 6
  written for, 2–3

Smart Cities Global Network, 330

Smart Cities Mission, 35

Smart Cities–Digital Solutions for a More Livable Future, 278

smart city team
  meetings, 86, 89–90
  members, 85–88
  RACI chart, 88–89

smart community. *See* smart cities

Smart Connections Consulting LLC, 165

smart contracts, 173

smart devices, 37

Smart Dubai vision statement, 84

smart factories, 38

smart grids, 189–191

smart homes, 37

smart hospitals, 39

smart islands, 37–38

smart nations, 37–38

smart regions, 39

smart shrinkage, 51

smart stadiums, 38

smart street lighting, 184, 187–189

smart trash cans, 165

smart villages, 39

smart water, 192–193

Smarter Together, 330

SmartNations Foundation, 330

smartphones, 37, 162

Smith, Frederick, 307

social media
  Arab Spring and, 168–169
  civic engagement via, 65, 166, 168–169
  disaster warning systems and, 232
  sharing strategic plan via, 104

social sustainability, 75

social systems, 17, 30

Society of Automotive Engineers, 177

solar power, 70

solar-powered vehicles, 67

South Africa, 58, 334

South America
  innovation districts in, 146
  open data portals in, 343
  performance dashboard, 356–357
  smart cities in, 42, 146, 321

South Korea, 42, 55, 175, 335

SpotCrime, 349

standard of living, 275–276

Stanton, Daniel, 54

Starship Technologies, 180

Startup-in-Residence (STiR) program, 120

start-ups, 120

Stockholm (Sweden), 146

storms, 229

strategic governance, 125–126, 128–130

About the Author

Dr. Jonathan Reichental is a multiple-award-winning technology and business leader whose 30-year career so far has spanned both the private and public sectors. He has occupied almost every role in the field of technology, including pulling Ethernet cables through ceilings, manning help desks, and overseeing system administration. He's been a senior software engineering manager and a director of technology innovation, and he has served as chief information officer at both O'Reilly Media and the city of Palo Alto, California.

Dr. Reichental runs his own business in Silicon Valley, called Human Future, and is a global keynote speaker and educator on topics that range from smart cities to the fourth industrial revolution and from quantum computing to blockchain technology.

Additionally, he is a professor and instructor at several universities, including the University of San Francisco, the University of California, Berkeley, and the Escola Superior d'Administració i Direcció d'Empreses (ESADE), part of Barcelona's Ramon Llull University. His video-based business and technology courses can be found online at LinkedIn Learning.

Dr. Reichental has been recognized as one of the 25 doers, dreamers, and drivers in government in America, and his innovative work in cities has been acknowledged by the White House.

Follow him on Twitter: @Reichental.

Dedication

This book is dedicated to my parents, Evanne and Tomi, and my brothers, David and Gideon. I love you all.

Author's Acknowledgments

I'd like to express my gratitude to everyone who has helped me write and produce this book. It really takes a team. I'm confident I couldn't have done it without so much valuable insight, input, and support from many remarkable people.

First, I want to thank James Keene, the former city manager of Palo Alto, California, who took a chance on a private industry technology leader with no government experience. Without him, it's likely I would never have entered local government or been exposed to the world of city management. Through my experience in Palo Alto, I fell in love with cities and it changed my life. Thanks, Jim.

A really big thanks to my two interns, Connor Chase and Meredith Lemann, who helped research and review material for this book. Connor produced high-quality input for the book's appendixes. His contributions always exceeded my expectations. Meredith was helpful in doing research and reviewing some of my written work. Her feedback was excellent, and much of it has been incorporated. Thank you both!

I want to thank Pete Peterson, dean of the School of Public Policy at Pepperdine University. He has also inspired my passion for cities. Pete was responsible for identifying his two students, Connor and Meredith, as my interns for the book. Thank you, sir.

Huge thanks to Zoe Eather, my friend and colleague, who, despite living on the other side of the world in Australia, is someone who continues to inspire me on this smart city journey. Zoe is a technical reviewer of this book, and as I expected, her input has been priceless. Thank you, Zoe!

There are a group of talented people who developed content specifically for this book. They are all friends and people I admire. I want to thank Bill Pugh, CEO of Smart Connections Consulting, who, in my view, is the king of connectivity knowledge. Thanks to Benson Chan and Renil Paramel, cofounders of Strategy of Things, who both helped develop the material related to the Internet of Things section of this book.

I want to thank Andres Assmus, founder of CityZeen, for his ideas and our discussions in preparation for writing this book.

I'm grateful to Michael Jansen, CEO and chairman of CityZenith, and his team, for providing digital twin content.

Thank you, Jeremy Prince, president of SigFox USA, and your team, for providing input and content on your wireless technology.

Thank you to the team at the FIWARE Foundation — in particular, Cristina Brandtstetter, chief marketing officer — for assisting with the FIWARE section.

I'm thankful to Orbital Insight and, specifically, Eric Lewandowski, Impact Initiative Lead, for assisting with a case study on geospatial analytics.

There's another group of people I'd like to thank who were supportive and inspiring in various ways. They include Mônica Guedes (thanks for all of your wonderful encouragement), Bas Boorsma (may the force be with you), Gil Friend, Jung Kim, Darren Bates, Ciaran Gilsenan, Arik Bronshtein, Erez Druk, Nate Levine, Rob Lloyd, Lalo Perez, Jeanny Weatherford, Chris Caravalho, Lisa Bolger, Sheila Tucker, Peter Pirnejad, Renato de Castro, Krishna Vaibhav, Chami Akmeemana, Chetan Choudhury, PK Gulati, Joyce Weinrib, Marina Rihani, Jim Duhovny, Melina Kaye Ortega (you made me a better man), Alison Williams, Steve Weiss, Cynthia Phillips, Frans-Anton Vermast, Frits Bussemaker, and Charlene Yu Vaughn.

Finally, I want to thank the entire team at Wiley for believing in me and for supporting this book. Thanks to Ashley Coffey, who reached out to me to ask if I'd write it; Katie Mohr, for helping to guide the process; and in particular, Paul Levesque, the senior project editor of the book.

If I left anyone out, I'm deeply sorry. I'll call you.

Publisher's Acknowledgments

Acquisitions Editor: Steve Hayes

Senior Project Editor: Paul Levesque

Copy Editor: Becky Whitney

Editorial Assistant: Matthew Lowe

Sr. Editorial Assistant: Cherie Case

Proofreader: Debbye Butler

Production Editor: Umar Saleem

Cover Image: © Busakorn Pongparnit / Getty Images